spiti

the forbidden valley

Patrick Sutherland

piti

the forbidden valley

Introduction by Tenzing Sonam

In the summer of 1990, I found myself on a crowded bus heading for Spiti, a little-known region tucked away in the folds of the North Indian Himalaya. I was deep inside the Inner Line, that invisible boundary that parallels India's long border with Tibet beyond which no outsider – ordinary Indians included – can travel without a special permit. I had been on the road for a week, making my way slowly up the gravity-defying Hindustan-Tibet Road, which follows the vertiginous gorge of the Sutlej River. The bus finally forked off at the thunderous confluence of the Sutlej and Spiti Rivers, deep within the confines of the mountains, boxed in on all sides by grim, looming ridges. I felt my excitement mounting. In a sense, this was a homecoming for me; as a Tibetan refugee, born and brought up in India, Spiti was as close to Tibet as I had ever been.

The Spiti Valley soon opened up, a sliver of flat land lined on either side by an endless concatenation of serrated peaks, their summits streaked by veins of lingering ice. Occasionally, the triangular heads of snow-covered mountains reared above these ramparts. The overwhelming colour was brown, in all its variations, broken only by the inky cobalt of the sky and the bottle green of the river. Whitewashed villages appeared periodically along the margins of the river – clusters of adobe houses in the traditional Tibetan style – surrounded by patchworks of fragile fields. The passengers on the bus, almost all locals, chattered away in a dialect of Tibetan that I could understand if I concentrated hard enough and their good-natured, rough-hewn faces were not unlike those of my parents who had fled their villages in Tibet soon after the Communist Chinese invasion of 1949. The turbulent upheavals and depredations that followed transformed Tibet's way of life forever. But in Spiti, which had come under the control of British India in the mid-nineteenth century and subsequently become a part of independent

India, the age-old customs and traditions of Tibet continued intact, preserved by its hermetic and forgotten existence within the Inner Line. I had the feeling that I was stepping back in time, of literally visiting the land of my forefathers.

Spiti is home to around 10,000 inhabitants who share with their Tibetan neighbours a common ethnicity, language and culture. Prior to China's takeover of Tibet, these ties were kept alive through marriage, trade and religious exchange. Spiti's close association with Tibet goes back at least to the 10th Century when it was a part of the Guge Kingdom of Upper Western Tibet. The pre-eminent Tibetan scholar and saint of that period, Lochen Rinchen Zangpo, passed through this region and left a lasting legacy, the miraculous 1,000-year-old temple of Tabo with its perfectly preserved murals and statues. From such auspicious beginnings, Tibetan Buddhism flourished in the valley and several monasteries were established over the centuries. Monks from Spiti regularly went to study at the great monasteries of Central Tibet.

During that first, brief visit to Spiti, I spent most of my time between Tabo and Kaza, the district capital and the largest town in the valley. There were no hotels in all of Spiti and accommodation could only be found at the government rest houses maintained by the Public Works Department. Taxis were nonexistent and the local buses that plied the dusty track along the valley floor were few and far between. Making a long distance phone call was next to impossible. Yet, I was delighted just to be there, struck simply by the fact of being in a completely Tibetan environment. For me, as for countless other Tibetans who grew up in exile, our homeland was an abstract entity, a mythical place that we could only reconstruct in our minds from pictures and stories. We had never seen a yak, could not imagine what a real Tibetan house might look like, had never been to really high altitudes.

But, enchanted as I was by my discovery of a place that mirrored old Tibet, I could nonetheless sense that change was in the air, that Spiti's long years of solitude were coming to an end. Everyone I met, especially the younger people, spoke excitedly of impending plans to deregulate the area and to allow in tourists. They conveyed a feeling of restlessness, of wanting to break out from their long and enforced isolation and become a part of the larger, modern world. I knew I was witnessing a place on the threshold of a major transformation, a medieval world coming face to face with the late 20th Century.

I went back to Spiti in 1995. The valley had undergone dramatic changes; the Inner Line restriction had finally been lifted and for the past three summers small but increasing groups of intrepid tourists – mostly Westerners – had made their way into the area. The immediate difference was the proliferation of hotels and restaurants in Kaza. A small fleet of four-wheel-drive taxis, although expensive, now made travelling between the villages more convenient. Satellite dishes sprouted from the roofs of the old town opening a window into the distant world outside the valley and allowing in the first whiffs of strange new cultures. In Tabo, preparations were underway for the millennium celebrations of Rinchen Zangpo's temple, which were to be held the following year; the Dalai Lama and a host of Indian dignitaries were expected along with thousands of Buddhist pilgrims and tourists. The sleepy village of my first acquaintance was being transformed beyond belief; the temple complex had been spruced up, its interiors restored and all around it, feverish construction was taking place, like in some latter-day boomtown.

On this occasion, I explored the length and breadth of Spiti, often staying at the homes of villagers whose warmth and hospitality never ceased to amaze me. They were mostly farmers who worked hard during the brief summer months to raise their crops of barley and peas. Their homes were generally without running water or electricity. A hole in the ground served as the toilet. Sitting around the family hearth – a wood burning stove in the middle of the kitchen – and sharing a simple meal with them, the outside world seemed unimaginably remote. I wondered what life might be like during the long winter months of forced inactivity when temperatures plunged to -30 degrees Celsius. Yet, this was the very period when the people of Spiti celebrated most of their festivals and ceremonies, a time of communal eating, drinking, singing and dancing.

The everyday life of these villages still revolved around the pivotal influences of the lama, the oracle, the astrologer and the traditional doctor, to whom the people turned for advice and guidance on all matters – from births, illnesses and deaths to marriages and harvests. Hundreds of local spirits, some malevolent and others benign, were believed to live in close proximity to the people and were regularly propitiated. Buddhism was the paramount guiding force and permeated every aspect of the people's lives.

An unusual feature of Spiti life was the system of khangchen (big house) and khangchung (small house). When the eldest son of a family got married, he inherited all its wealth and property and his parents and younger siblings moved out of the khangchen into the khangchung, which were normally adjacent to each other. The family jewellery was given to the eldest sister on her marriage and she moved to her husband's house. The younger brothers were made monks and younger sisters nuns thereby neutralising any discontent over inheritance. This meant that the population of Spiti stayed more or less constant for centuries and the ownership of land remained unchanged. But now, with the spread of education and the opening up of the economy, this ancient system was beginning to unravel.

For a period after 1959, when Tibet disappeared under Communist Chinese rule and its spiritual influence suddenly ceased, the monastic tradition of Spiti went into a slow decline. In 1969, a Tibetan high lama who had come to India as a refugee, Tsenshap Serkong Rinpoche, made the first of several trips to Spiti. The local inhabitants requested that he send them a qualified spiritual teacher on a more permanent basis and in 1976, he sent a Tibetan geshe (a learned monk), Sonam Wangdu, to Tabo. When Sonam Wangdu arrived, he found only two monks looking after the main temple, which was in a state of disrepair. By the time I visited in 1990, a new monastery had been built adjacent to the temple and, under the guidance of the geshe, a community of 35 monks, all from Spiti, were once again engaged in the traditional study and practice of Buddhism.

This was the beginning of a religious renewal in Spiti, both within the monasteries and in the day-to-day practices of the ordinary people. Where previously monks from the region had gone to study in the monasteries of Central Tibet, they now went to the monasteries established in India by the exile Tibetan community. The Dalai Lama made the first of three visits in 1983 when he conferred the Kalachakra Initiation at Tabo, a religious event of great significance that had a major impact on the region. Over the years, various Tibetan high lamas spent time in Spiti and ensured the continuing development of its spiritual traditions. In the past, it would have been a rare occasion for any of Tibet's religious elite, let alone the Dalai Lama, to have made the long and arduous journey to Spiti. Ironically, exile made this possible.

In the remote Pin Valley of Spiti, I came upon the Buchen, the last of Tibet's wandering religious actors. Once, Buchen troupes performed their open-air religious plays – impromptu dramatisations of religious and mythical events interspersed with songs, dances, breathtaking acrobatics and magic rituals – throughout Western Tibet. Now, the

Buchen of Spiti represented the last of this dying tradition. At a country fair in Kaza, I watched a Buchen group perform a truncated version of the stone-breaking ritual, for which they are famed. In this dramatic ceremony all the evil forces affecting a village were focused into a large boulder, which was then placed upon the belly of one of the performers lying flat on his back. The Buchen Master struck the boulder with a small stone and magically split it into two thereby dispelling the negative energies trapped inside.

In 1995, there were only five Buchen masters living in the Pin Valley. The youngest, who had only recently attained the status of a full master, was 25-year-old Ghatuk Tsering. He told me that he might be the last of the lineage as fewer and fewer younger people were willing to undergo the rigorous physical and spiritual training necessary to become a Buchen. Ghatuk Tsering himself, before becoming a Buchen, had gained some local renown as a disco-dancing champion!

Among the many people I met on this trip was a dynamic young monk, Tashi Namgyal, who had studied at the Buddhist School of Dialectics in Dharamsala, the exiled home of the Dalai Lama. He had returned to Spiti with the aim of starting a modern school that would teach the Tibetan language and Buddhism along with more contemporary subjects. This was an inspired and much-needed project. Although the opening up of Spiti was the immediate instigator of development and change, a greater threat to its cultural identity was the spread of Hindi as the preferred language of communication, especially among the younger people. This was not surprising for traditionally, the monasteries had been the only places where education of any sort was available and there, the emphasis was on Buddhist studies. When the Indian Government established schools in Spiti in the sixties and seventies, the medium of instruction was Hindi. A knowledge of Hindi became a prerequisite for government jobs and essential for any commercial dealings outside the valley.

Later, television brought with it the all-pervasive influence of Bollywood-inspired pop culture, which further promoted the use of Hindi. Spiti's traditional language was fast becoming obsolete and it was in this context that Tashi Namgyal's efforts took on a special significance.

It was another five years – in the early summer of 2000 – before I returned to Spiti. A greatly expanded Kaza announced itself from the distance with the ugly, green tin roofs and concrete buildings of its government quarter. I was dreading the worst but was relieved to find, despite the inevitable signs of progress – piles of empty mineral water bottles and other plastic rubbish – that the old town still retained some of its medieval charm, with its traditional mud houses and narrow alleys. The bazaar was packed with shops and stalls and there was even the ubiquitous STD telephone booth, which made long distance phone calls readily possible. A floating population of Indian traders had set up shop and remarkably, fresh vegetables and fruit were plentifully available. Many more restaurants and hotels had sprung up and the first gangs of Israeli bikers could be seen lounging about on their terraces. Groups of road-workers from Nepal and Bihar were everywhere, building new roads and repairing existing ones. Jeep trails now linked even the most remote of villages.

Yet, despite these changes, the much-anticipated tourist invasion had not materialised on the scale that people had expected – or hoped for. The vagaries of Spiti's climate and its hostile location meant that even its short tourist season was prone to disruption. While I was there, an unexpected burst of sustained rainfall caused severe landslides that cut off Spiti's southern entrance for several weeks. Travel, for the most part, was still limited to those willing to rough it out or to those with a genuine interest in the place and its culture. An unexpected benefit of this selective tourism seemed to be a new awareness among younger people about the importance of their own language and culture. From my own experience I knew that one of the indirect effects of the growing Western interest in Tibet and Tibetan Buddhism was to force younger Tibetans – who were otherwise enamoured of Western ways – to examine their own culture more closely. Tashi Namgyal's school was now up and running and Geshe Sonam Wangdu in Tabo had plans to start a similar school.

There was no doubt that Spiti was determinedly pushing ahead, embracing development and material progress. But the essential qualities that defined the place and its people for me when I first encountered it – their cultural heritage and spiritual landscape – seemed to me to have survived this first decade of change. As I left the valley, I realised how much Spiti meant to me, how much it still symbolised for me my lost homeland. I wondered what I would find the next time I came. Would the people of Spiti somehow achieve that elusive balance between the fullness of their traditional life and the inroads of the modern world? For their sake, and for ours as well, I hoped they would.

Dharamsala, December 2000

"There is nothing strong enough,
intense enough to say in defence of this culture,
this way of thinking and of living so far removed
from a world which ultimately reduces to a
mess of scrap metal."

Henri Cartier Bresson

On ne peut rien dire
d'assez fort, d'assez
intense pour défendre
cette culture, cette façon
de penser, et de vivre
si loin d'un monde
qui produit pour finir
une bouillie de
ferraille. —

Henri Cartier-Bresson

27.9.2000

spiti

the forbidden valley

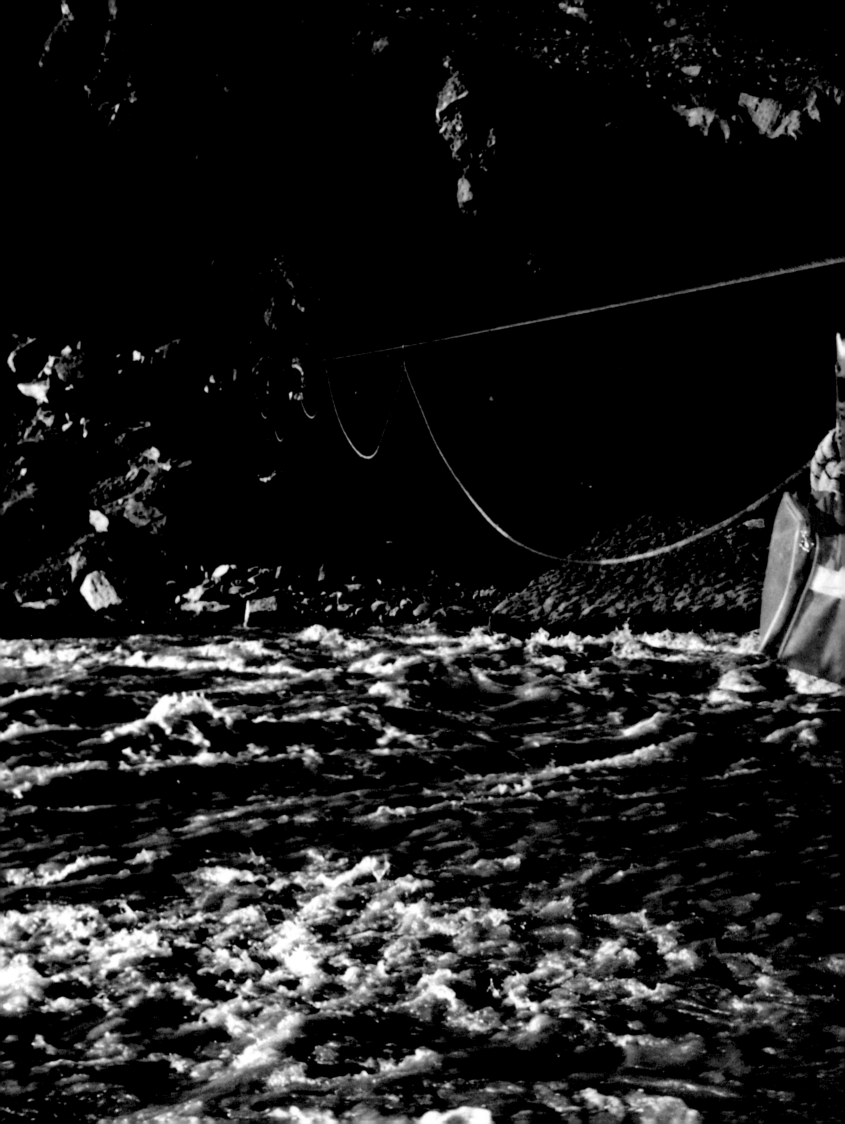

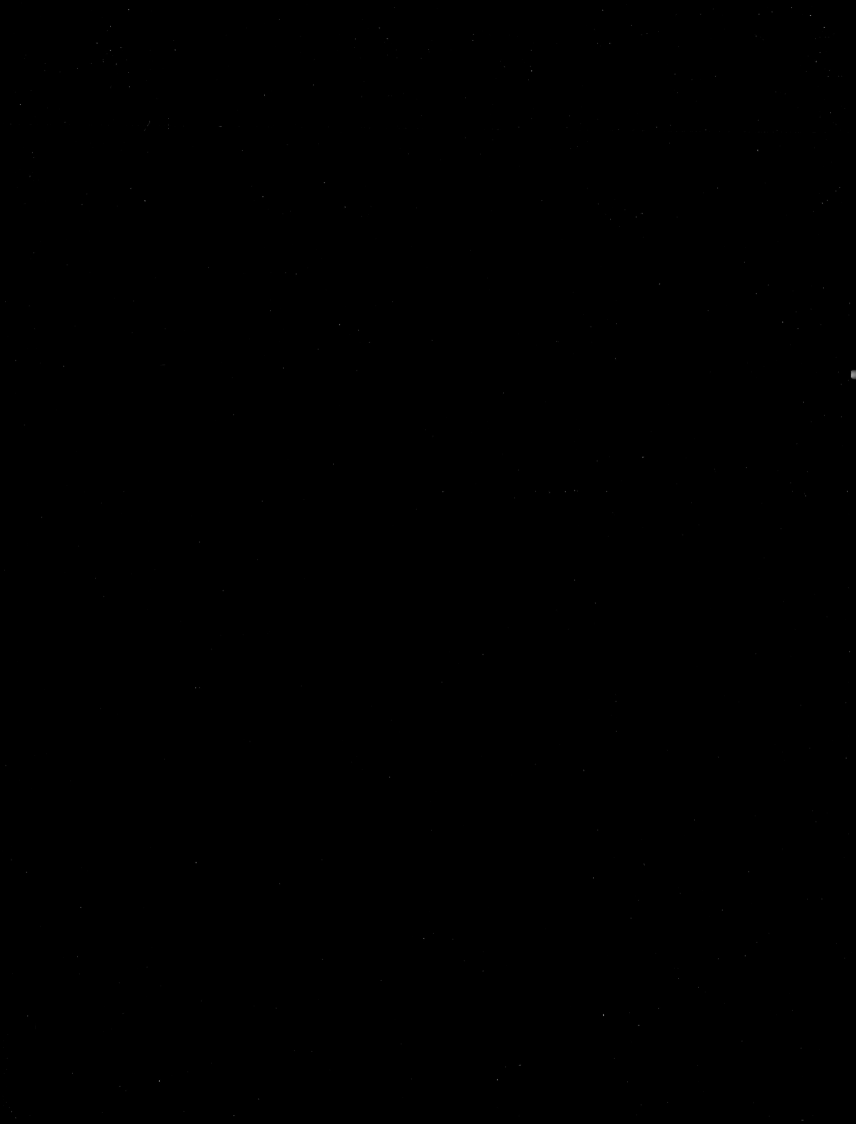

spiti
the forbidden valley

The late Khiu Tsering carrying paraffin and provisions home to Gede. He has spent the day turning the giant prayer wheel at Key monastery. The elderly often dedicate their last years to religious practice, collecting merit to improve their prospects of a favourable reincarnation.

Young monks wearing ancient wooden masks during the dance festival at Key Monastery. These young boys act as jokers during the performances, teasing the older monks by mimicking them and generally entertaining the audience by punctuating the long solemn dances with touches of humour.

Tsewang Rigzin, head Buchen lama of the village of Sagnam, performing traditional Spiti theatre in Pin Valley. Throughout the winter three or four parties of Buchen travel the valleys performing their theatre, a mixture of religious chants, traditional Buddhist stories, repartee and showmanship including sword dancing and body piercing.

A young monk on the roof of Key Monastery. Solar power is an ideal technology in this high altitude desert and is subsidised by the state government. Many houses now have solar powered lamps and some schools have solar powered cookers.

The Gelong Rinpoche and lamas at the Pin Valley monastic dance festival. The rinpoche is the reincarnation of the previous spiritual head of Gungri Monastery.

The late Gyadrupa painting a thanka in Key. The room is decorated both with religious icons and posters of Madonna and Samantha Fox. The latter brought home by his son, a soldier in the Indian army.

Monks at Key Monastery rehearsing for the annual cham or masked dance festival, an elaborate two-day rite of purification. Monks dressed in ancient brocade costumes and huge often grotesque wooden or papier mache masks enact events from the history of Tibetan Buddhism as well as the stages of the journey from death to reincarnation.

Young monks studying religious texts at Key Monastery. Traditionally monasteries were the only centre of formal education in Spiti. Now there are also nunneries and secular schools.

Ngawang Kelsang entering trance and skewering his cheek during a pingri, a boy's special birthday party in Kibbar. In trance this medium is possessed by a deity, who provides oracular hints about the child's future prospects, speaking through the medium in a language translatable only by his entourage.

The late Palden Ngodrup praying in the shrine room of his house in Hal. Such rooms are used daily for prayer and ritual. On special occasions, monks, an oracle, a healer or an exorcist may be invited. Offerings of water bowls and butter lamps are set out daily in front of thankas, painted Buddha sculptures and images of high lamas.

Young nuns studying religious texts at Pangmo Convent, built with funds raised by an American Buddhist nun. The plastic piping now brings water to the nunnery from a spring fed by snow melting on the mountains.

The late Kachen Lama, until recently the oldest and most venerable monk in Spiti. His arm is held in a sling suspended from the ceiling.

An old man in Pangmo.

A mika, a joker, staggers drunkenly through Kibber, confessing to the sins of a man who is dying of tuberculosis in a nearby house. Mikas are supposed to be able to trade lives, taking on board another man's sins in exchange for payment, bartering the risk of a lower reincarnation in the next life for cash in this one.

The interior of a typical Spiti house in Lossar. The ceilings of large rooms are supported with carved wooden pillars.

The cremation of an old woman outside Chichim. Traditionally bodies were dismembered and thrown into the river, but cremations are now common, using imported timber. Disposal of corpses is remarkably matter of fact, a reflection of the common Buddhist acceptance of reincarnation.

Monks in the kitchen of Key Monastery preparing food for the monastic community. A large cauldron of cricket ball-sized lumps of pak, a mixture of tsampa (roast barley flour), black tea and butter will be distributed along with a ration of Tibetan tea.

Masked monks circumambulating Key Monastery at the end of the cham, the annual monastic dance festival. The gods have come down to earth and villagers lie prostrate hoping to come under the protective power of the deities stepping over them.

Woman making chappatis in Bhur. The social centre of every house is a metal box stove which mainly burns dried dung.

A monk at the Kalachakra Initiation performed by the Dalai Lama at Tabo Monastery in 1996, marking its thousandth anniversary. Tabo is one of the oldest Mahayana Buddhist monasteries still in active use.

As the Dalai Lama descended from the Kunzam La a rainbow coloured halo appeared around the sun. Meteorological signs such as these are common when the Dalai Lama visits Spiti and are auspicious omens. After his departure, villagers wait in the rain for buses to take them down the valley to their homes.

A photographer and monks at the 1996 Kalachakra Initiation at Tabo Monastery. During the ten day festival the whole range of Buddhist teachings from the simplest and most down to earth to the most elaborate and transformative will be delivered.

Monks distributing offerings that have been blessed by the Dalai Lama at the 1996 Kalachakra Initiation at Tabo Monastery. The first monk is filling palms with sweets, raisins, nuts and broken biscuits, the second monk is playfully controlling the overzealous throng with thwacks from a stick.

Crossing Pin River after the annual dance festival held at Gungri Monastery. This 'jula' has now been replaced with a footbridge and a full roadbridge is under construction.

A public works department lorry ferries monks to the mountain pass at the head of Spiti where the Dalai Lama is presiding over an incense burning ceremony on his departure from the valley.

Roadworkers tarring a road. Metalled roads are being constructed all over the valley. The workers, mainly young women, shatter stones into small pieces which they mix with hot tar in trays and then spread to make the road surface. Increasingly the work is done by Nepalese and Bihari migrants.

A Tibetan refugee and child selling Chinese plimsolls at the Gungri Monastery Cham. This annual dance festival attracts large numbers of local devotees, peddlers and increasing numbers of tourists.

In Kibber a man treads moist earth to form the walls of his new house. In the background women return from the fields. The earth has been dug from the hillside and then sieved and mixed with water from a nearby stream. It seems less a process of building and more a reshaping of the landscape.

A mile above the shrine on the Kunzam La, the pass at the upper end of Spiti, the Dalai Lama and an entourage of monks perform an incense burning ceremony. Below the tent villagers tend bonfires of aromatic dwarf juniper gathered from the surrounding hillsides and wait to perform folk dances.

Women clearing snow from the roof of their house in Morang. Houses are constructed from dried mud which softens quickly when exposed to water. Many houses now have satellite television receiving Bollywood movies, game shows, advertising and international news.

A farmer loads his donkeys up with seed peas in Morang. Peas are the first cash crop in Spiti and fetch good prices in the markets in Delhi.

A pingri, a special birthday party for a boy in Kibber. This is a major social event in which the boy's family provides food for the whole village which in turn gives the child large amounts of money and kataks, (ceremonial white scarves). The money will be banked on his behalf. This gift giving is followed by an all night party.

A family ploughing their field with yaks in Kibber. Yaks are the classic Tibetan draught animal and thrive at high altitude. They are frequently crossed with cows because the female offspring, the dzomo, is both a good milker and hardy at high altitude.

Village elders in Kibber. These men carry with them the knowledge of traditional community rituals and often start the dancing at pingris and wedding parties. Their knowledge is passed on verbally from generation to generation.

Ploughed fields below Key. Most of the households in the village own land which is irrigated with meltwater from the snow and ice on the surrounding peaks. The staple crop is barley, which will ripen here at 14,000 feet, but the traditional Spiti pea, mustard and new crops like garden peas and potatoes are also grown.

The Chichim medium in a state of trance. The oracular deities that take possession of such mediums during trance are widely consulted for important decisions. Consultations often take place at major social events like marriages, birthdays and funerals.

The late Tsering Drolma outside the entrance to a house in Pangmo. Women shave their heads when they become nuns or are widowed and decide not to remarry. Like most nuns of her generation, Tsering has lived within the family home, dedicating her life to prayer and religious practice.

Geshe Sonam Ngodrup talks passionately about the genocide and destruction in Tibet and of the monastery in Tibet that he attended as a youth. Following the Chinese invasion he was imprisoned before escaping back to India. The long established trade and cultural links over the Tibetan border have ceased.

Urgyen Dhargye, a nagpa (tantric practitioner), widely respected as a healer and exorcist, is treating a young child who is suffering from fits. Spiti has high infant mortality rates and rampant tuberculosis. Villagers consult nagpas, oracles, lamas and astrologers for help with a variety of decisions and problems.

Women making deep fried breads for a wedding ceremony in Kibber. Every family in the village will be invited to the village hall to receive a handout of food and drink: bread, rice, beer, and tsalma (cooked barley dough).

Village elders from the bridegroom's party sing outside the bride's house during a traditional wedding in Kibber. Behind the closed door the brides family sings competing songs to repel the outsiders. From the rooftop they pelt the party below with barley flour and dried yak dung. Eventually the door will open to allow the visitors inside, to take the bride away.

The bridegroom's party dances in the middle of Kibber. The plastic bottles once contained brake fluid or motor oil but are now full of arak, a spirit made by distilling chang (local barley beer). The drink is consumed during the celebrations or distributed through the community.

The bride and her consort weeping before she leaves her family home. Her parents are both dead and as a song is sung about her life she breaks down. All of the older women and many men are crying too. Before she finally leaves on horseback she will ride in circles around her brother who is slumped dejectedly in the saddle.

Wedding celebrations in Kibber. All through the nights of the wedding, men and women drink and dance to the sound of drums, women singing and the wailing of a sunnah, a Himalayan clarinet. On the first night the bridegroom is not present and the bride sits in the middle of the room and weeps for hours amidst the drunken revelry.

The bridegroom garlanded with necklaces of rupees on the second night of his wedding. Traditionally, some time after the first son gets married, he is given all the land and the family house. His father and mother eventually retire to another house or to an annexe of the family house and devote themselves to religious practice.

A musician sleeping after the first night of a traditional wedding. The musicians have been playing for nearly twenty four hours, working and sleeping in relays, and are exhausted and drunk. The head of a yak that was butchered for the wedding, is part of the traditional payment to the musicians.

Villagers giving money and scarves to the bride, the groom and their relatives. The whole community is crammed into the village hall.

The upper Spiti Valley above Key Monastery. Spiti is situated in a remote high altitude desert on the border between India and Tibet. Over the last few centuries the valley has been occupied many times. The older monasteries were often built in the remotest and most defendable positions, in cliff faces or on hilltops.

The bridegroom's party waiting to escort the new bride around Kibber. She will be taken to the village temple and to the houses of her new relatives, given food and entertained. Kibber is known to have the best antique costumes in Spiti, fabulously embroidered brocade gowns and tasselled silk hats, owned communally by the village.

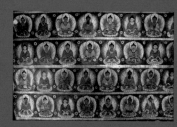

A thousand Buddha images cover a wall in Tabo Monastery. Some of these exquisite murals date back to 996 A.D. when the monastery was founded. Tabo is one of 108 religious sites spread from Mustang to Ladakh associated with Rinchen Zangpo, the great translator of many Buddhist sutras from Sanskrit into Tibetan.

For Clare, Catherine, Maddy and Jamie for their love and support despite my long absences and for the people of Spiti, without whose openness, generosity and hospitality this project would never have been possible.

These photographs were taken between 1993 and 1998, during four long journeys in Spiti. The project began as a collaboration with two Buddhist monks, Graham Woodhouse, an old friend of mine from Sheffield, and Tashi Namgyal a monk from Key Monastery in Spiti. On my first visit we travelled the length of the valley together, staying with families, witnessing all aspects of life from complex Buddhist rituals to daily domestic chores. Tashi introduced us to a network of his friends, relatives and contacts in Spiti. This took us deep inside the community and provided the foundation for the whole work. Graham travelled with me on many of the subsequent journeys, acting as both linguistic and cultural translator. What started as a short trip taking promotional pictures for the Rinchen Zangpo Society for Spiti Development, Tashi's fledgling educational project, became a personal obsession to document Spiti. In all I spent nearly six months living and photographing in the valley.

The people of Spiti welcomed me into their houses, took me into their lives and assisted me with my research. They invited me to weddings, birthday parties and funerals, into the houses of women who had just given birth and the houses of men who were dying. They nursed me and worried about me on the many occasions when I was ill or suffered altitude sickness. On each subsequent journey I was welcomed back like a close relative and urged to stay. Each time I arrived with photographs from the previous trip. These pictures have a dark side to them, revealing the passing of time, the speed of change and highlighting the many people I photographed who have since died. To be given such intimate access to this remarkable community has been a rare privilege. I hope I have done it justice.

It is impossible to mention everyone who has contributed to this work but central to it are Tashi Namgyal, for encouraging me to come to Spiti in the first place, Graham Woodhouse, for his companionship and patience, the Ven.Lochen Tulku, Rinpoche of Key monastery, for his support, Sher Singh and Usha from Kibber for their generosity and assistance with research, Dev Singh and Londen Dolma, Dorje Gyaltsen and Dorje Dolkar, all from Morang, Tsering Drolkar and Tsering Thondup from Pangmo, Thubten Chopel and Drolma Tsering from Chichim and Urgyen Dhargye from Kaza, all of whom provided unfailing warmth and hospitality.

In addition I would like to thank Neil Burgess at Network for his belief in the book and his commitment to quality, Jonathan Towell at Black Sun who has been a joy to work with, Roger Hutchings for his critical input at a crucial stage in the project, Henri Cartier Bresson and Martine Franck for their interest and expression of support, my friends at Network and my colleagues at the London College of Printing. Ilford, Sprayway, Wild Country and Snowsled assisted with materials and equipment in the early stages of the project. The London Institute, my employer, provided the essential financial support to bring this project to fruition.

The Rinchen Zangpo Society for Spiti Development, set up and run by people from Spiti, maintains its own school in Rangrik, Spiti, and a hostel for Spiti children in Yol, in the Kangra Valley. Donations to and information from Tashi Namgyal, General Secretary, Rinchen Zangpo Society for Spiti Development, Tika Lehsher, Yol Cantt – 176052, Teh. Dharamsala, Dist.Kangra, Himachal Pradesh, India.

Patrick Sutherland took a degree in anthropology at Durham University before studying documentary photography at Newport. His first long term project Wetland: Life in the Somerset Levels was published by Michael Joseph in 1986, went on to win a small literary award and was exhibited at the National Museum of Photography in Bradford. He has received numerous public documentary commissions and freelanced regularly for British newspapers and magazines. In 1990 he won a World Press Award for his pictures of intensive farming commissioned by the Impressions Gallery in York and published in the Independent Magazine. Patrick currently runs the postgraduate course in photojournalism at the London College of Printing. He is married with three children and lives in Norwich.

Tenzing Sonam was born in Darjeeling of Tibetan refugee parents in 1959. After graduating from Delhi University, he worked for a year in the Tibetan Government-in-exile in Dharamsala. He then specialized in documentary filmmaking at the University of California, Berkeley's Graduate School of Journalism. Along with his partner, Ritu Sarin, he set up White Crane Films in London in 1991. Tenzing and Ritu have produced and directed a number of documentaries on Tibetan subjects, including the award-winning "The Reincarnation of Khensur Rinpoche", which was broadcast throughout the world. "The Trials of Telo Rinpoche" and "Shadow Circus: The CIA in Tibet" were both commissioned by the BBC and subsequently broadcast in several countries. Tenzing has been living in Dharamsala for the past four years and is working on a Tibetan feature film.

A percentage of all profits from this book will go to the Rinchen Zangpo Society for Spiti Development which is working to preserve traditional Spiti culture and to provide the children of the valley with a decent standard of modern education.

Spiti, The Forbidden Valley
First Published by Network Photographers
December 2000

The right of Patrick Sutherland to be identified as the author of this work has been asserted by him in accordance with the Copyright, Design and Patents Act 1988

Origination by Osier Graphics, Croydon (part of the Fulmar plc Group)

Printed by Royle Corporate Print, Croydon (part of the Fulmar plc Group) on Clarity 170 gsm (Text), Naturalis 135 gsm (Endpapers) supplied by the Premier Paper Group, and 120 gsm Huntsman Chromo (Jacket) supplied by the Robert Horne Group

Bound by Grays Bookbinders Ltd, Mitcham

ISBN 095 367 56 3 7

THE LONDON INSTITUTE

Network Photographers

Book design by Black Sun plc
9 Burlington Lodge Studios
Rigault Road, Fulham
London SW6 4JJ

Tel: 0207 736 0011
Fax: 0207 736 1294
email: jtowell@blacksunplc.com
www.blacksunplc.co.uk

Kaplan Publishing are constantly ~~finding~~
ways to make a difference to you~~r~~
exciting online resources really ~~do make a~~
different to students looking for ~~more.~~

C000019033

This book comes with free EN-gage online resources so that you can study anytime, anywhere.

Having purchased this book, you have access to the following online study materials:

CONTENT	ACCA (including FFA,FAB,FMA)		AAT		FIA (excluding FFA,FAB,FMA)	
	Text	Kit	Text	Kit	Text	Kit
iPaper version of the book	✓	✓	✓	✓	✓	✓
Interactive electronic version of the book	✓					
Fixed tests / progress tests with instant answers	✓		✓			
Mock assessments online			✓	✓		
Material updates	✓	✓	✓	✓	✓	✓
Latest official ACCA exam questions		✓				
Extra question assistance using the signpost icon*		✓				
Timed questions with an online tutor debrief using the clock icon*		✓				
Interim assessment including questions and answers		✓			✓	
Technical articles	✓	✓			✓	✓

* Excludes F1, F2, F3, FFA, FAB, FMA

How to access your online resources

Kaplan Financial students will already have a Kaplan EN-gage account and these extra resources will be available to you online. You do not need to register again, as this process was completed when you enrolled. If you are having problems accessing online materials, please ask your course administrator.

If you are already a registered Kaplan EN-gage user go to www.EN-gage.co.uk and log in. Select the 'add a book' feature and enter the ISBN number of this book and the unique pass key at the bottom of this card. Then click 'finished' or 'add another book'. You may add as many books as you have purchased from this screen.

If you purchased through Kaplan Flexible Learning or via the Kaplan Publishing website you will automatically receive an e-mail invitation to Kaplan EN·gage online. Please register your details using this email to gain access to your content. If you do not receive the e-mail or book content, please contact Kaplan Flexible Learning.

If you are a new Kaplan EN-gage user register at www.EN-gage.co.uk and click on the link contained in the email we sent you to activate your account. Then select the 'add a book' feature, enter the ISBN number of this book and the unique pass key at the bottom of this card. Then click 'finished' or 'add another book'.

Your Code and Information

This code can only be used once for the registration of one book online. This registration and your online content will expire when the final sittings for the examinations covered by this book have taken place. Please allow one hour from the time you submit your book details for us to process your request.

Please scratch the film to access your EN-gage code.

Please be aware that this code is case-sensitive and you will need to include the dashes within the passcode, but not when entering the ISBN. For further technical support, please visit www.EN-gage.co.uk

ACCA
Paper F3 (INT/UK)

and

FIA

Diploma in Accounting and Business

Financial Accounting (FA/FFA)

Complete Text

British library cataloguing-in-publication data

A catalogue record for this book is available from the British Library.

Published by:
Kaplan Publishing UK
Unit 2 The Business Centre
Molly Millars Lane
Wokingham
Berkshire
RG41 2QZ

ISBN 978-0-85732-278-4

Acknowledgements

We are grateful to the Association of Chartered Certified Accountants and the Chartered Institute of Management Accountants for permission to reproduce past examination questions. The answers have been prepared by Kaplan Publishing.

Contents

Paper Introduction

How to Use the Materials

These Kaplan Publishing learning materials have been carefully designed to make your learning experience as easy as possible and to give you the best chances of success in your examinations.

The product range contains a number of features to help you in the study process. They include:

(1) Detailed study guide and syllabus objectives

(2) Description of the examination

(3) Study skills and revision guidance

(4) Complete text or essential text

(5) Question practice

The sections on the study guide, the syllabus objectives, the examination and study skills should all be read before you commence your studies. They are designed to familiarise you with the nature and content of the examination and give you tips on how to best to approach your learning.

The **complete text or essential text** comprises the main learning materials and gives guidance as to the importance of topics and where other related resources can be found. Each chapter includes:

- The **learning objectives** contained in each chapter, which have been carefully mapped to the examining body's own syllabus learning objectives or outcomes. You should use these to check you have a clear understanding of all the topics on which you might be assessed in the examination.

- The **chapter diagram** provides a visual reference for the content in the chapter, giving an overview of the topics and how they link together.

- The **content** for each topic area commences with a brief explanation or definition to put the topic into context before covering the topic in detail. You should follow your studying of the content with a review of the illustration/s. These are worked examples which will help you to understand better how to apply the content for the topic.

- **Test your understanding** sections provide an opportunity to assess your understanding of the key topics by applying what you have learned to short questions. Answers can be found at the back of each chapter.

- **Summary diagrams** complete each chapter to show the important links between topics and the overall content of the paper. These diagrams should be used to check that you have covered and understood the core topics before moving on.

- **Question practice** is provided at the back of each text.

Icon Explanations

Definition – these sections explain important areas of Knowledge which must be understood and reproduced in an exam environment.

Key Point – identifies topics which are key to success and are often examined.

New – identifies topics that are brand new in papers that build on, and therefore also contain, learning covered in earlier papers.

Expandable Text – within the online version of the work book is a more detailed explanation of key terms, these sections will help to provide a deeper understanding of core areas. Reference to this text is vital when self studying.

Test Your Understanding – following key points and definitions are exercises which give the opportunity to assess the understanding of these core areas. Within the work book the answers to these sections are left blank, explanations to the questions can be found within the online version which can be hidden or shown on screen to enable repetition of activities.

Illustration – to help develop an understanding of topics and the test your understanding exercises the illustrative examples can be used.

Exclamation Mark – this symbol signifies a topic which can be more difficult to understand, when reviewing these areas care should be taken.

Tutorial note – included to explain some of the technical points in more detail.

Footsteps – helpful tutor tips.

On-line subscribers

Our on-line resources are designed to increase the flexibility of your learning materials and provide you with immediate feedback on how your studies are progressing. Ask your local customer services staff if you are not already a subscriber and wish to join.

If you are subscribed to our on-line resources you will find:

(1) On-line reference ware: reproduces your Complete or Essential Text on-line, giving you anytime, anywhere access.

(2) On-line testing: provides you with additional on-line objective testing so you can practice what you have learned further.

(3) On-line performance management: immediate access to your on-line testing results. Review your performance by key topics and chart your achievement through the course relative to your peer group.

Paper introduction

Paper background

The aim of ACCA Paper FFA (INT), Financial Accounting, is to develop knowledge and understanding of the underlying principles and concepts relating to financial accounting and technical proficiency in the use of double-entry accounting techniques including the preparation of basic financial statements.

Objectives of the syllabus

- Explain the context and purpose of financial reporting.
- Define the qualitative characteristics of financial information and the fundamental bases of accounting.
- Demonstrate the use of double entry and accounting systems.
- Record transactions and events.
- Prepare a trial balance (including identifying and correcting errors).
- Prepare basic financial statements for incorporated and unincorporated entities.
- Prepare simple consolidated financial statements
- Interpretation of financial statements

Core areas of the syllabus

- The context and purpose of financial reporting
- The qualitative characteristics of financial information
- The use of double entry and accounting systems
- Recording transactions and events

- Preparing a trial balance
- Preparing basic financial statements
- Preparing simple consolidated statements
- Interpretation of financial statements

Syllabus objectives

We have reproduced the ACCA's syllabus below, showing where the objectives are explored within this book. Within the chapters, we have broken down the extensive information found in the syllabus into easily digestible and relevant sections, called Content Objectives. These correspond to the objectives at the beginning of each chapter.

Syllabus learning objective	Chapter reference
A THE CONTEXT AND PURPOSE OF FINANCIAL REPORTING	
1 The scope and purpose of, financial statements for external reporting	
(a) Define financial reporting – recording, analysing and summarising financial data.[k]	1
(b) Identify and define types of business entity – sole trader, partnership, limited liability company.[k]	1
(c) Recognise the legal differences between a sole trader, partnership and a limited liability company. [k]	1
(d) Identify the advantages and disadvantages of operating as a limited liability company, sole trader or partnership.[k]	1
(e) Understand the nature, principles and scope of financial reporting.[k]	1
2 Users' and stakeholders' needs	
(a) Identify the users of financial statements and state and differentiate between their information needs.[k]	1
3 The main elements of financial reports	
(a) Understand and identify the purpose of each of the main financial statements.[k]	2
(b) Define and identify assets, liabilities, equity, revenue and expenses.[k]	2 & 21

KAPLAN PUBLISHING

(xiii) comparability

(xiv) understandability

(xv) Business entity concept.

(b) Understand the balance between qualitative characteristics.[k]   21

C THE USE OF DOUBLE ENTRY AND ACCOUNTING SYSTEMS

1 Double entry bookkeeping principles including the maintenance of accounting records

(a) Identify and explain the function of the main data sources in an accounting system.[k]   10

(b) Outline the contents and purpose of different types of business documentation, including: quotation, sales order, purchase order, goods received note, goods despatched note, invoice, statement, credit note, debit note, remittance advice, receipt.[k]   10

(c) Understand and apply the concept of double entry accounting and the duality concept.[k]   3

(d) Understand and apply the accounting equation.[s]   2

(e) Understand how the accounting system contributes to providing useful accounting information and complies with organisational policies and deadlines.[k]   1

(f) Identify the main types of business transactions, e.g. sales, purchases, payments, receipts.[k]   2, 3 & 10

2 Ledger accounts, books of prime entry and journals

(a) Identify the main types of ledger accounts and books of prime entry, and understand their nature and function.[k]   3 & 10

(b) Understand and illustrate the uses of journals and the posting of journal entries into ledger accounts. [s]   3

(c) Identify correct journals from given narrative.[s]   3

(d) Illustrate how to balance and close a ledger account.[s]   3

KAPLAN PUBLISHING

KAPLAN PUBLISHING

KAPLAN PUBLISHING

(c) Describe the components of and prepare a consolidated statement of financial position or extracts thereof including.[s]

    (i) Fair value adjustments at acquisition on land and buildings (excluding depreciation adjustments)

    (ii) Fair value of consideration transferred from cash and shares (excluding deferred and contingent consideration)

    (iii) Elimination of inter-company trading balances (excluding cash and goods in transit)

    (iv) Removal of unrealised profit arising on inter-company trading

    (v) acquisition of subsidiaries part way through the financial year

(d) Calculate goodwill (excluding impairment of goodwill) using the full goodwill method only as follows:[s]   18 & 19

Fair value of consideration	X
Fair value of non-controlling interest	X
Less fair value of net assets at acquisition	(X)
Goodwill at acquisition	X

(e) Describe the components of and prepare a consolidated statement of comprehensive income or extracts thereof including:[s]   18 & 19

    (i) Elimination of inter-company trading balances (excluding cash and goods in transit)

    (ii) Removal of unrealised profit arising on inter-company trading

    (iii) Acquisition of subsidiaries part way through the financial year

2 Associates

(a) Define and identify an associate and significant influence and identify the situations where significant influence or participating interest exists. [k]   18 & 19

(b) Describe the key features of a parent-associate relationship and be able to identify an associate within a group structure. [k]   18 & 19

(c) Describe the principle of equity accounting[k]   18 & 19

H INTERPRETATION OF FINANCIAL STATEMENTS

1 Importance and purpose of analysis of financial statements

(a)	Describe how the interpretation and analysis of financial statements is used in a business environment.[k]	20
(b)	Explain the purpose of interpretation of ratios.[k]	20

2 Ratios

(a)	Calculate key accounting ratios.[s]	20
	(i) Profitability	
	(ii) Liquidity	
	(iii) Efficiency	
	(iv) Position	
(b)	Explain the interrelationships between ratios.[k]	20

3 Analysis of financial statements

(a)	Calculate and interpret the relationship between the elements of the financial statements with regard to profitability, liquidity, efficient use of resources and financial position.[s]	20
(b)	Draw valid conclusions from the information contained within the financial statements and present these to the appropriate user of the financial statements. [s]	20

The superscript numbers in square brackets indicate the intellectual depth at which the subject area could be assessed within the examination. Level 1 (knowledge and comprehension) broadly equates with the Knowledge module, Level 2 (application and analysis) with the Skills module and Level 3 (synthesis and evaluation) to the Professional level. However, lower level skills can continue to be assessed as you progress through each module and level.

The examination

Examination format

The syllabus is assessed by a two-hour paper or computer-based examination. Questions will assess all parts of the syllabus and will contain both computational and non-computational elements:

	Number of marks
Fifty 2-mark questions	100

Total time allowed: 2 hours

Paper-based examination tips

Spend the first few minutes of the examination reading the paper.

Divide the time you spend on questions in proportion to the marks on offer. One suggestion **for this exam** is to allocate 2 minutes to each mark available.

Multiple-choice questions: Read the questions carefully and work through any calculations required. If you don't know the answer, eliminate those options you know are incorrect and see if the answer becomes more obvious. Guess your final answer rather than leave it blank if necessary.

Computer-based examination (CBE) – tips

Be sure you understand how to use the software before you start the exam. If in doubt, ask the assessment centre staff to explain it to you.

Questions are **displayed on the screen** and answers are entered using keyboard and mouse. At the end of the exam, you are given a certificate showing the result you have achieved.

The CBE exam will not only examine multiple choice questions but could include questions that require a single number entry or a multiple response.

Do not attempt a CBE until you have **completed all study material** relating to it. **Do not skip any of the material** in the syllabus.

Read each question very carefully.

Double-check your answer before committing yourself to it.

Answer every question – if you do not know an answer, you don't lose anything by guessing. Think carefully before you **guess.**

With a multiple-choice question, eliminate first those answers that you know are wrong. Then choose the most appropriate answer from those that are left.

Remember that only **one answer to a multiple-choice question can be right.** After you have eliminated the ones that you know to be wrong, if you are still unsure, guess. But only do so after you have double-checked that you have only eliminated answers that are definitely wrong.

Don't panic if you realise you've answered a question incorrectly. Getting one question wrong will not mean the difference between passing and failing.

Study skills and revision guidance

This section aims to give guidance on how to study for your ACCA exams and to give ideas on how to improve your existing study techniques.

Preparing to study

Set your objectives

Before starting to study decide what you want to achieve – the type of pass you wish to obtain. This will decide the level of commitment and time you need to dedicate to your studies.

Devise a study plan

Determine which times of the week you will study.

Split these times into sessions of at least one hour for study of new material. Any shorter periods could be used for revision or practice.

Put the times you plan to study onto a study plan for the weeks from now until the exam and set yourself targets for each period of study – in your sessions make sure you cover the course, course assignments and revision.

If you are studying for more than one paper at a time, try to vary your subjects as this can help you to keep interested and see subjects as part of wider knowledge.

When working through your course, compare your progress with your plan and, if necessary, re-plan your work (perhaps including extra sessions) or, if you are ahead, do some extra revision/practice questions.

Effective studying

Active reading

You are not expected to learn the text by rote, rather, you must understand what you are reading and be able to use it to pass the exam and develop good practice. A good technique to use is SQ3Rs – Survey, Question, Read, Recall, Review:

(1) **Survey** the chapter – look at the headings and read the introduction, summary and objectives, so as to get an overview of what the chapter deals with.

(2) **Question** – whilst undertaking the survey, ask yourself the questions that you hope the chapter will answer for you.

(3) **Read** through the chapter thoroughly, answering the questions and making sure you can meet the objectives. Attempt the exercises and activities in the text, and work through all the examples.

(4) **Recall** – at the end of each section and at the end of the chapter, try to recall the main ideas of the section/chapter without referring to the text. This is best done after a short break of a couple of minutes after the reading stage.

(5) **Review** – check that your recall notes are correct.

You may also find it helpful to re-read the chapter to try to see the topic(s) it deals with as a whole.

Note-taking

Taking notes is a useful way of learning, but do not simply copy out the text. The notes must:

- be in your own words
- be concise
- cover the key points
- be well-organised
- be modified as you study further chapters in this text or in related ones.

Trying to summarise a chapter without referring to the text can be a useful way of determining which areas you know and which you don't.

KAPLAN PUBLISHING

Three ways of taking notes:

Summarise the key points of a chapter.

Make linear notes – a list of headings, divided up with subheadings listing the key points. If you use linear notes, you can use different colours to highlight key points and keep topic areas together. Use plenty of space to make your notes easy to use.

Try a diagrammatic form – the most common of which is a mind-map. To make a mind-map, put the main heading in the centre of the paper and put a circle around it. Then draw short lines radiating from this to the main sub-headings, which again have circles around them. Then continue the process from the sub-headings to sub-sub-headings, advantages, disadvantages, etc.

Highlighting and underlining

You may find it useful to underline or highlight key points in your study text – but do be selective. You may also wish to make notes in the margins.

Revision

The best approach to revision is to revise the course as you work through it. Also try to leave four to six weeks before the exam for final revision. Make sure you cover the whole syllabus and pay special attention to those areas where your knowledge is weak. Here are some recommendations:

Read through the text and your notes again and condense your notes into key phrases. It may help to put key revision points onto index cards to look at when you have a few minutes to spare.

Review any assignments you have completed and look at where you lost marks – put more work into those areas where you were weak.

Practise exam standard questions under timed conditions. If you are short of time, list the points that you would cover in your answer and then read the model answer, but do try to complete at least a few questions under exam conditions.

Also practise producing answer plans and comparing them to the model answer.

If you are stuck on a topic find somebody (a tutor) to explain it to you.

Read good newspapers and professional journals, especially ACCA's Student Accountant – this can give you an advantage in the exam.

Ensure you **know the structure of the exam** – how many questions and of what type you will be expected to answer. During your revision attempt all the different styles of questions you may be asked.

Further reading

You can find further reading and technical articles under the student section of ACCA's website.

A Students's Guide to IFRS by Clare Finch, Kaplan Publishing UK 2007.

For more details about the syllabus and the format of your exam please see your Complete Text or go online.

Paper introduction

Paper background

Objectives of the syllabus

Core areas of the syllabus

Syllabus objectives

Syllabus learning objective

The examination

Study skills and revision guidance

Preparing to study

Effective studying

You can find further reading and technical articles under the student section of ACCA's website.

Introduction to accounting

Chapter learning objectives

Upon completion of this chapter you will be able to:

- define accounting
- explain the different types of business entity:
  - sole trader
  - partnership
  - limited liability company
- explain who users of the financial statements are and their information needs
- explain the nature, principles and scope of accounting
- explain how the accounting system contributes to providing useful information and complies with organisational policies and deadlines.

1 Definition of accounting

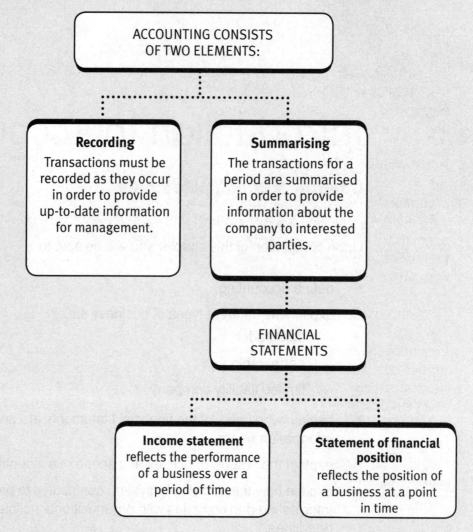

Analysing data is also an important feature of accounting. Financial statements are prepared so that we can examine and evaluate all information, in order to make key decisions.

2 Types of business entity

A business can be organised in one of several ways:

- Sole trader – a business owned and operated by one person.

- Partnership – a business owned and operated by two or more people.

- Company – a business owned by many people and operated by many (though not necessarily the same) people.

Differences between a sole trader, partnership and company

Sole trader

The simplest form of business is the sole trader. This is owned and managed by one person, although there might be any number of employees. A sole trader is fully and personally liable for any losses that the business might make.

Partnership

A partnership is a business owned jointly by a number of partners. The partners are jointly and severally liable for any losses that the business might make. Traditionally the big accounting firms have been partnerships, although some are converting their status to limited liability companies.

Companies

Companies are owned by shareholders. There can be one shareholder or many thousands of shareholders. Shareholders are also known as members. Each shareholder owns part of the company. As a group, they elect the directors who run the business. Directors often own shares in their companies, but not all shareholders are directors.

Companies are almost always limited companies. This means that the shareholders will not be personally liable for any losses the company incurs. Their liability is limited to the nominal value of the shares that they own. Their shares may become worthless, but they will not be forced to make good the losses.

This limited liability is achieved by treating the company as a completely separate legal entity.

For all three types of entity, the money put up by the individual, the partners or the shareholders, is referred to as the business capital. In the case of a company, this capital is divided into shares.

Advantages and disadvantages of operating as a limited company, sole trader or partnership

Sole trader

As the name suggests, this is an organisation owned by one person.

Accounting conventions recognise the business as a separate entity from its owner. However, legally, the business and personal affairs of a sole trader are not distinguished in any way. The most important consequences of this is that a sole trader has complete personal *unlimited liability*. Business debts which cannot be paid from business assets must be met from sale of personal assets, such as a house or a car.

Sole trading organisations are normally small because they have to rely on the financial resources of their owner.

The advantages of operating as a sole trader include flexibility and autonomy. A sole trader can manage the business as he or she likes and can introduce or withdraw capital at any time.

Partnership

A partnership is two or more persons associated for the purpose of a business or a profession. Like a sole trader, a partnership is not legally distinguished from its members. Personal assets of the partners may have to be used to pay the debts of the partnership business.

The advantages of trading as a partnership stem mainly from there being many owners rather than one. This means that:

- more resources may be available, including capital, specialist knowledge, skills and ideas;

- administrative expenses may be lower for a partnership than for the equivalent number of sole traders, due to economies of scale; and

- partners can substitute for each other.

Partners can introduce or withdraw capital at any time, provided that all the partners agree.

Limited company

A limited company is a distinct, artificial 'person' created in order to separate legal responsibility for the affairs of a business (or any other activity) from the personal affairs of the individuals who own and/or operate the business.

The owners are known as shareholders (or members) and the people who run the business are known as directors. In a small corporation, owners and directors are often the same people.

Limited Liability

The concept of limited liability is based on the premise that the company's debts and liabilities are those of the company and not those of the members.

Limited liability refers to the liability of each shareholder being limited to any unpaid amount on their shares. Usually, all the shares are fully paid so the members have no liability.

Comparison of limited companies to sole traders and partnerships

The fact that a company is a separate legal entity means that it is very different from a sole trader or partnership in a number of ways.

- Property holding

  The property of a limited company belongs to the company. A change in the ownership of shares in the company will have no effect on the ownership of the company's property. (In a partnership the firm's property belongs directly to the partners who can take it with them if they leave the partnership.)

- Transferable shares

  Shares in a limited company can usually be transferred without the consent of the other shareholders. In the absence of agreement to the contrary, a new partner cannot be introduced into a firm without the consent of all existing partners.

- Suing and being sued

  As a separate legal person, a limited company can sue and be sued in its own name. Judgements relating to companies do not affect the members personally.

- Number of members

  There is no upper limit on the number of members in a company. In a partnership, except in certain restricted categories, such as accountants and stockbrokers, the maximum number of partners is 20. This limitation on numbers makes it difficult for a partnership to raise large amounts of capital.

- Security for loans

  A company has greater scope for raising loans by, for example, borrowing on debentures (long-term borrowings) and may secure them with floating charges. A floating charge is a mortgage over the constantly fluctuating assets of a company providing security for the lender of money to a company. It does not prevent the company dealing with the assets in the ordinary course of business. Such a charge is useful when a company has no non-current assets such as land, but does have a large and valuable inventories.

  The law does not permit partnerships or individuals to secure loans with a floating charge.

- Taxation

  Because a company is legally separated from its members, it is taxed separately from its members. Tax payable by companies is known as corporation tax. Partners and sole traders are personally liable for income tax on the profits made by their business.

- Disadvantages of incorporation

  The disadvantages of being a limited company arise principally from restrictions imposed by the Companies Act 2006.

Formalities, publicity and expenses

When they are being formed, companies have to register and to file a Memorandum and Articles of Association (formal constitution documents) with the Registrar. Registration fees and legal costs have to be paid.

The accounts of larger limited companies are subject to an annual audit inspection (this requirement has been lifted for small companies). The costs associated with this can be high. Partnerships and sole traders are not subject to this requirement unless as members of professional bodies whose own rules apply.

A registered company's accounts and certain other documents are open to public inspection. The accounts of sole traders and partnerships are not open to public inspection.

Capital maintenance

Limited companies are subject to strict rules in connection with the introduction and withdrawal of capital and profits.

Management powers

Members of a company may not take part in its management unless they are directors, whereas all partners are entitled to share in management, unless the partnership agreement provides otherwise.

3 Users of the financial statements

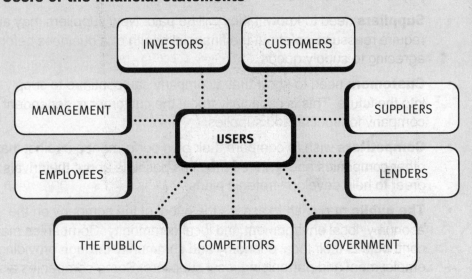

Different user groups are interested in a company's financial statements for different reasons:

* **Management** need detailed information in order to control their business and plan for the future. Budgets will be based upon past performance and future plans. These budgets will then be compared with actual results. Information will also be needed about the profitability of individual departments and products. Management information must be very up to date and is normally produced on a monthly basis.

- **Investors** and potential investors are interested in their potential profits and the security of their investment. Future profits may be estimated from the target company's past performance as shown in the income statement. The security of their investment will be revealed by the financial strength and solvency of the company as shown in the statement of financial position. The largest and most sophisticated groups of investors are the institutional investors, such as pension funds and unit trusts.

- **Employees** and trade union representatives need to know if an employer can offer secure employment and possible pay rises. They will also have a keen interest in the salaries and benefits enjoyed by senior management. Information about divisional profitability will also be useful if a part of the business is threatened with closure.

- **Lenders** need to know if they will be repaid. This will depend on the solvency of the company, which should be revealed by the statement of financial position. Long-term loans may also be backed by 'security' given by the business over specific assets. The value of these assets will be indicated in the statement of financial position.

- **Government** agencies need to know how the economy is performing in order to plan financial and industrial policies. The tax authorities also use financial statements as a basis for assessing the amount of tax payable by a business.

- **Suppliers** need to know if they will be paid. New suppliers may also require reassurance about the financial health of a business before agreeing to supply goods.

- **Customers** need to know that a company can continue to supply them into the future. This is especially true if the customer is dependent on a company for specialised supplies.

- **Competitors** wish to compare their own performance against that of other companies and learn as much as possible about their rivals in order to help develop strategic plans.

- **The public** may wish to assess the effect of the company on the economy, local environment and local community. Companies may contribute to their local economy and community through providing employment and patronising local suppliers. Some companies also run corporate responsibility programmes through which they support the environment, economy and community by, for example supporting recycling schemes.

Test your understanding 1

Which of the following users do you think require the most detailed financial information to be made available to them?

A   Competitors

B   Management of the business

C   Trade unions

D   Investors

4 Types of accounting

ACCOUNTING

Financial accounting

- Production of summary financial statements for external users.

- Prepared annually (six-monthly or quarterly in some countries).
- Generally required by law.
- Reflects past performance and current position.

- Information calculated and presented in accordance with international accounting standards.

Management accounting

- Production of detailed accounts, used by management to control the business and plan for the future.
- Normally prepared monthly, often on a rolling basis.
- Not mandatory.

- Includes budgets and forecasts of future activities, as well as reflecting past performance.
- Information computed and presented in order to be relevant to managers.

Financial accounting and management accounting

Financial accounting

Financial accounting is concerned with the production of financial statements for external users. These are a report on the directors' stewardship of the funds entrusted to them by the shareholders.

Investors need to be able to choose which companies to invest in and compare their investments. In order to facilitate comparison, financial accounts are prepared using accepted accounting conventions and standards. International Accounting Standards (IASs) and International Financial Reporting Standards (IFRSs) help to reduce the differences in the way that companies draw up their financial statements in different countries.

The financial statements are public documents, and therefore they will not reveal details about, for example, individual products' profitability.

Management accounting

Management require much more detailed and up-to-date information in order to control the business and plan for the future. They need to be able to cost-out products and production methods, assess profitability and so on. In order to facilitate this, management accounts present information in any way which may be useful to management, for example by operating unit or product line.

Management accounting is an integral part of management activity concerned with identifying, presenting and interpreting information used for:

- formulating strategy
- planning and controlling activities
- decision making
- optimising the use of resources.

KAPLAN PUBLISHING

5 How an accounting system contributes to providing useful information

The main features of an accounting system and how it helps in providing information to the business are as follows:

- In a computerised system all information about the business transactions can be quickly accessed. This will help in decision making.

- It provides details of transactions of the business in the relevant accounts.

- When the accounts are closed off the balances for each outstanding account are determined. This will give the value of assets and liabilities in the business.

- It gives a summary of outstanding balances.

- This summary can then be used for the preparation of financial statements.

- Normally the financial statements are prepared at regular intervals. The accounting system will allow the business to obtain the data and also prepare the financial statements to determine the profitability, liquidity, risks, etc. applicable to the business for a particular period. For internal reporting purposes this could be monthly, whilst for external reporting purposes this is usually yearly.

6 The regulatory system

Structure of the international regulatory system

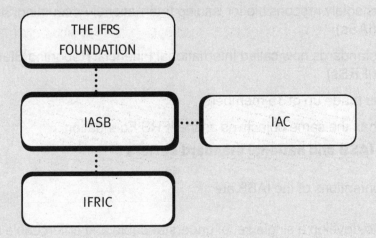

International Financial Reporting Standards (IFRS) Foundation

The IFRS Foundation (formerly known as the International Accounting Standards Committee Foundation (IASC)):

- is the supervisory body for the IASB
- has 22 trustees
- is responsible for governance issues and ensuring each body is properly funded.

The objectives of the IFRS Foundation are to:

- develop a set of global accounting standards which are of high quality, are understandable and are enforceable
- which require high quality, transparent and comparable information in financial statements to help those in the world's capital markets and other users make economic decisions
- promote using and applying these standards
- bring about the convergence of national and international accounting standards.

International Accounting Standards Board (IASB)

The IASB:

- is solely responsible for issuing International Accounting Standards (IASs)
- standards now called International Financial Reporting Standards (IFRSs)
- is made up of 15 members
- has the same objectives as the IFRS Foundation.

The IASB and national standard setters

The intentions of the IASB are:

- to develop a single set of understandable and enforceable high quality worldwide accounting standards, however
- the IASB cannot enforce compliance with its standards, therefore
- it needs the co-operation of national standard setters.

In order to achieve this the IASB works in partnership with the major national standard-setting bodies:

- All the most important national standard setters are represented on the IASB and their views are taken into account so that a consensus can be reached.

- All national standard setters can issue IASB discussion papers and exposure drafts for comment in their own countries, so that the views of all preparers and users of financial statements can be represented.

- Each major national standard setter 'leads' certain international standard-setting projects.

The IASB intends to develop a single set of understandable and enforceable high quality worldwide accounting standards.

As far as possible, future international standards will be more rigorous than previously and will no longer allow alternative treatments. The Chairman of the IASB, Sir David Tweedie has already stated that there will not be 'convergence for the sake of convergence by the issue of a set of 'lowest common denominator' accounting standards'.

Because the IASB on its own cannot enforce compliance with its standards, it needs the co-operation of national standard setters. Without their support, rigorous new international standards are unlikely to be adopted by everybody. Therefore, the IASB works in partnership with the major national standard setting bodies, including the UK Accounting Standards Board (ASB) and the US Financial Accounting Standards Board (FASB).

Each major national standard setter 'leads' certain international standard-setting projects, e.g. the UK ASB is carrying out much of the work to develop a new international standard on leasing.

All the major national standard-setters are now committed to international convergence.

The regulatory framework of accounting in each country which uses IFRS is affected by a number of legislative and quasi-legislative influences as well as IFRS:

- national company law

- EU directives

- security exchange rules.

Why a regulatory framework is necessary

A regulatory framework for the preparation of financial statements is necessary for the following reasons:

- Financial statements are used by a wide range of users – investors, lenders, customers, etc.

- They need to be useful to these users.

- They need to be comparable.

- They need to provide at the least some basic information.

- They increase users' understanding of, and confidence in, financial statements.

- They regulate the behaviour of companies towards their investors.

Accounting standards on their own would not be a complete regulatory framework. In order to fully regulate the preparation of financial statements and the obligations of companies and directors, legal and market regulations are also required.

Principles-based and rules-based framework

Principles-based framework:

- based upon a conceptual framework such as the IASB's Framework
- accounting standards are set on the basis of the conceptual framework.

Rules-based framework:

- 'Cookbook' approach
- accounting standards are a set of rules which companies must follow.

In the UK there is a principles-based framework in terms of the Statement of Principles and accounting standards and a rules-based framework in terms of the Companies Acts, EU directives and stock exchange rulings.

IFRIC

International Financial Reporting Interpretations Committee (IFRIC)

- issues rapid guidance on accounting matters where divergent interpretations of IFRSs have arisen

- issues interpretations called IFRIC 1, IFRIC 2, etc.

The IFRIC addresses issues of reasonably widespread importance, not issues that are of concern to only a small minority of entities. The interpretations cover both:

- newly identified financial reporting issues not specifically dealt with in IFRSs; or

- issues where unsatisfactory or conflicting interpretations have developed, or seem likely to develop in the absence of authoritative guidance, with a view to reaching a consensus on the appropriate treatment.

In 1997 the IASC formed the Standing Interpretations Committee (SIC) to ensure proper compliance with IFRSs by considering points of contention where divergent interpretations have emerged and issuing an authoritative view; 33 interpretations (entitled SIC 1, SIC 2, etc) were issued by the SIC before its change of name (see below).

SICs are important because IAS 1 (revised) states that financial statements cannot be described as complying with IFRSs unless they comply with each IAS/IFRS and each interpretation from the SIC/IFRIC.

In 2002 the SIC changed its name to the International Financial Reporting Interpretations Committee (IFRIC). Interpretations are now designated IFRIC 1, IFRIC 2, etc.

IFRS Advisory Council (IAC)

The Advisory Council (formerly known as the Standards Advisory Council – SAC) provides a forum for the IASB to consult a wide range of interested parties affected by the IASB's work, with the objective of:

- advising the Board on agenda decisions and priorities in the Board's work,
- informing the Board of the views of the organisations and individuals on the Council on major standard-setting projects, and
- giving other advice to the Board or to the Trustees.

Development of an IFRS

The procedure for the development of an IFRS is as follows:

- The IASB identifies a subject and appoints an advisory committee to advise on the issues.
- The IASB publishes an exposure draft for public comment, being a draft version of the intended standard.
- Following the consideration of comments received on the draft, the IASB publishes the final text of the IFRS.
- At any stage the IASB may issue a discussion paper to encourage comment.
- The publication of an IFRS, exposure draft or IFRIC interpretation requires the votes of at least eight of the 15 IASB members.

Status of IFRS's

Neither the IFRS Foundation, the IASB nor the accountancy profession has the power to enforce compliance with IFRSs. Nevertheless, some countries adopt IFRSs as their local standards, and others ensure that there is minimum difference between their standards and IFRSs. In recent years, the status of the IASB and its standards has increased, so IFRSs carry considerable persuasive force worldwide.

7 Company ownership and control

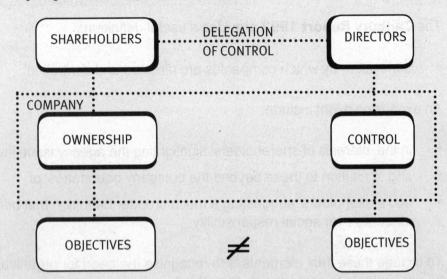

- A 'joint stock company' is a company which has issued shares.

- Since the formation of joint stock companies in the 19th century, they have become the dominant form of business organisation within the UK

- Companies that are quoted on a stock market such as the London Stock Exchange are often extremely complex and require a substantial investment in equity to fund them, i.e. they often have large numbers of shareholders.

- Shareholders delegate control to professional managers (the board of directors) to run the company on their behalf. The board act as agents (see later).

- Shareholders normally play a passive role in the day-to-day management of the company.

- Directors own less than 1% of the shares of most of the UK's 100 largest quoted companies and only four out of ten directors of listed companies own any shares in their business.

- Separation of ownership and control leads to a potential conflict of interests between directors and shareholders.

8 What is 'corporate governance'?

The **Cadbury Report 1992** provides a useful definition:

* 'the system by which companies are directed and controlled'.

An expansion might include:

* 'in the interests of shareholders' highlighting the agency issue involved
* 'and in relation to those beyond the company boundaries' or
* 'and stakeholders' suggesting a much broader definition that brings in concerns over social responsibility.

To include these final elements is to recognise the need for organisations to be accountable to someone or something.

Governance could therefore be described as:

* **'the system by which companies are directed and controlled in the interests of shareholders and other stakeholders'.**

Coverage of governance

Companies are directed and controlled from inside and outside the company. Good governance requires the following to be considered:

Direction from within:

* the nature and structure of those who set direction, the board of directors
* the need to monitor major forces through risk analysis
* the need to control operations: internal control.

Control from outside:

* the need to be knowledgeable about the regulatory framework that defines codes of best practice, compliance and legal statute
* the wider view of corporate position in the world through social responsibility and ethical decisions.

9 Purpose and objectives of corporate governance

Corporate governance has both purposes and objectives.

- The basic purpose of corporate governance is to monitor those parties within a company which control the resources owned by investors.

- The primary objective of sound corporate governance is to contribute to improved corporate performance and accountability in creating long-term shareholder value.

CORPORATE GOVERNANCE

PURPOSES

Primary:
Monitor those parties within a company who control the resources owned by investors.

Supporting:
- Ensure there is a suitable balance of power on the board of directors.
- Ensure executive directors are remunerated fairly.
- Make the board of directors responsible for monitoring and managing risk.
- Ensure the external auditors remain independent and free from the influence of the company.
- Address other issues, e.g. business ethics, corporate social responsibility (CSR), and protection of 'whistleblowers'.

OBJECTIVES

Primary:
Contribute to improved corporate performance and accountability in creating long-term shareholder value.

Supporting:
- Control the controllers by increasing the amount of reporting and disclosure to all stakeholders.
- Increase level of confidence and transparency in company activities for all investors (existing and potential) and thus promote growth .
- Ensure that the company is run in a legal and ethical manner.
- Build in control at the top that will 'cascade' down the organisation.

Test your understanding 2

Briefly describe the role of corporate governance.

Is governance relevant to all companies?

Issues in corporate governance relate to companies, and in particular listed companies whose shares are traded on major stock markets. However, similar issues might apply to smaller companies, and certainly to many large not-for-profit organisations.

	Large listed company	Private company	Not-for-profit organisation
Primary accountability	Shareholders and regulators	Shareholders	Fund providers, regulators, general public, members (where applicable).
Principal stakeholders	Shareholders	Shareholders	Donors, grant providers, regulators, general public, service users, members (if applicable).
Main methods of monitoring performance	Financial statements	Financial statements	Financial statements, other financial and non-financial measures.
Governance/ board structure	Executive and NEDs. Appointment through formal process in line with governance requirements.	Executive directors. Appointment may be the result of shareholding or other recruitment processes.	Volunteer trustees, paid and unpaid management team. Appointments through recruitment, recommendation or word of mouth, or election process.
Openness and transparency	In line with corporate governance requirements.	Limited disclosure requirements	Limited requirements but large demand due to methods of funding.

- Corporate governance is a matter of great importance for large public companies, where the separation of ownership from management is much wider than for small private companies.

- Public companies raise capital on the stock markets, and institutional investors hold vast portfolios of shares and other investments. Investors need to know that their money is reasonably safe.

- Should there be any doubts about the integrity or intentions of the individuals in charge of a public company, the value of the company's shares will be affected and the company will have difficulty raising any new capital should it wish to do so.

- The scope of corporate governance for private and not-for-profit organisations will be much reduced when compared with a listed company, especially as there are no legal or regulatory requirements to comply with.

- The ownership and control, organisational objectives, risks and therefore focus may be different from a listed company. However, many of the governance principles will still be applicable to other entities.

- The public and not-for-profit sectors have voluntary best practice guidelines for governance which, while appreciating the differences in organisation and objective, cover many of the same topics (composition of governing bodies, accountability, risk management, transparency, etc.) included within the Combined Code.

- In not-for-profit organisations, a key governance focus will be to demonstrate to existing and potential fund providers that money is being spent in an appropriate manner, in line with the organisations' objectives.

10 Internal corporate governance stakeholders

Within an organisation there are a number of internal parties involved in corporate governance. These parties can be referred to as internal stakeholders.

Stakeholder theory will be covered again later in this chapter, and in more detail in chapter 7. A useful definition of a stakeholder, for use at this point, is **'any person or group that can affect or be affected by the policies or activities of an organisation'**.

Each internal stakeholder has:

- an operational role within the company
- a role in the corporate governance of the company
- a number of interests in the company (referred to as the **stakeholder 'claim'**).

Stakeholder	Operational role	Corporate governance role	Main interests in company
Directors	Responsible for the actions of the corporation.	Control company in best interest of stakeholders.	• pay • performance-linked bonuses • share options • status • reputation • power.
Company secretary	Ensure compliance with company legislation and regulations and keep board members informed of their legal responsibilities.	Advise board on corporate governance matters.	• pay • performance-linked bonuses • job stability • career progression • status • working conditions.
Sub-board management	Run business operations. Implement board policies.	Identify and evaluate risks faced by company Enforce controls Monitor success Report concerns	
Employees	Carry out orders of management.	• Comply with internal controls • Report breaches.	

Employee representatives, e.g. trade unions	Protect employee interests.	Highlight and take action against breaches in governance requirements, e.g. protection of whistle-blowers.	• power • status.

Internal stakeholders

The board of directors

- Has the responsibility for giving direction to the company.

- Delegates most executive powers to the executive management, but reserves some decision-making powers to itself, such as decisions about raising finance, paying dividends and making major investments.

- Executive directors are individuals who combine their role as director with their position within the executive management of the company.

- Non-executive directors (NEDs) perform the functions of director only, without any executive responsibilities.

- Executive directors combine their stake in the company as a director with their stake as fully paid employees, and their interests are, therefore, likely to differ from those of the NEDs.

- More detail on directors will be found in chapter 3.

The company secretary

- Often responsible for advising the board on corporate governance matters and ensuring board procedures are followed.

- Duties vary with the size of the company, but are likely to include:
  - arranging meetings of the board
  - drafting and circulating minutes of board meetings
  - ensuring that board decisions are communicated to staff and outsiders
  - completing and signing of various returns
  - filing accounts with statutory authorities
  - maintaining statutory documents and registers required by the authorities.

- Company secretary may act as the general administrator and head office manager. This role may include a responsibility for maintaining accounting records, corresponding with legal advisers, tax authorities and trade associations.

- Does not have the same legal responsibilities as directors.

- Should always act in the interests of the company in any event of conflict or dispute with directors.

- Is responsible to the board and accountable through the chairman and Chief Executive Officer (CEO) for duties carried out.

- Has the same interests and claims in the company as other employees.

- Remuneration package should be settled by the board or remuneration committee.

Management

- Responsible for running business operations.

- Accountable to the board of directors (and more particularly to the CEO).

- Will take an interest in corporate governance decisions which may impact their current position and potential future positions (as main board directors, possibly).

- Individual managers, like executive directors, may want power, status and a high remuneration.

- As employees, they may see their stake in the company in terms of the need for a career and an income.

Employees

- Have a stake in their company because it provides them with a job and an income.

- Have expectations about what their company should do for them, e.g. security of employment, good pay and suitable working conditions.

- Some employee rights are protected by employment law, but the powers of employees are generally limited.

Trade unions

- Primary interest will be in the pay and working conditions of their members.

- Will be concerned by poor corporate governance, for example lack of protection for whistleblowers or poor management of health and safety risks, and hence assist in the checks and balances of power within a company.

- Can 'deliver' the compliance of a workforce, particularly in a situation of business reorganisation.

- Can optimise industrial relations, easing workforce negotiations, and hence ensure an efficient and supportive relationship.

- Can be used by management of the company to distribute information to employees or to ascertain their views, hence can play a helpful role in business.

- Power of trade unions will vary between countries, with it being much stronger in countries such as France where union rights are extended to all employees.

11 External corporate governance stakeholders

A company has many external stakeholders involved in corporate governance.

Each stakeholder has:

- a role to play in influencing the operation of the company
- its own interests and claims in the company.

External party	Main role	Interests and claims in company
Auditors	Independent review of company's reported financial position.	<ul><li>fees</li><li>reputation</li><li>quality of relationship</li><li>compliance with audit requirements.</li></ul>
Regulators	Implementing and monitoring regulations	<ul><li>compliance with regulations</li><li>effectiveness of regulations.</li></ul>

Government	Implementing and maintaining laws with which all companies must comply.	• compliance with laws • payment of taxes • level of employment • levels of imports/exports
Stock exchange	Implementing and maintaining rules and regulations for companies listed on the exchange.	• compliance with rules and regulations • fees.
Small investors	Limited power with use of vote.	• maximisation of shareholder value
Institutional investors	Through considered use of their votes can (and should) beneficially influence corporate policy.	• value of shares and dividend payments • security of funds invested • timeliness of information received from company • shareholder rights are observed.

Chapter summary

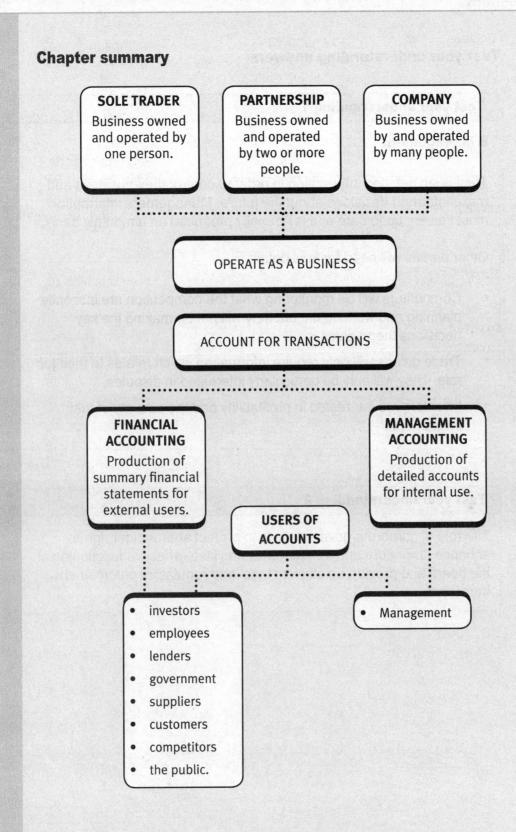

Test your understanding answers

Test your understanding 1

B Management

They need detailed information in order to control their business and make informed decisions about the future. Management information must be very up to date and is normally produced on a monthly basis.

Other parties will need far less detail:

- Competitors will be monitoring what the competition are currently planning and working on, but they will not be making the key decisions themselves.

- Trade unions will only require information which relates to their job role. They will only be particularly interested in disputes.

- Investors are interested in profitability and the security of their investment.

Test your understanding 2

The role of corporate governance is to protect shareholder rights, enhance disclosure and transparency, facilitate effective functioning of the board and provide an efficient legal and regulatory enforcement framework.

Statement of financial position and income statement

Chapter learning objectives

Upon completion of this chapter you will be able to:

- explain the main elements of financial statements:
  - statement of financial position
  - income statement

- explain the purpose of each of the main statements

- list the main types of business transactions

- explain how the accounting equation and business entity convention underpin the statement of financial position

- define assets and liabilities

- identify examples of receivables and payables

- explain how and why assets and liabilities are disclosed in the statement of financial position.

- draft a simple statement of financial position in vertical format

- explain the matching convention and how it applies to revenue and expenses

- explain how and why revenue and expenses are disclosed in the income statement

- illustrate how the statement of financial position and income statement are interrelated
- draft a simple income statement in vertical format
- identify the two sides of each transaction (duality concept)
- determine the accounting equation after each transaction.

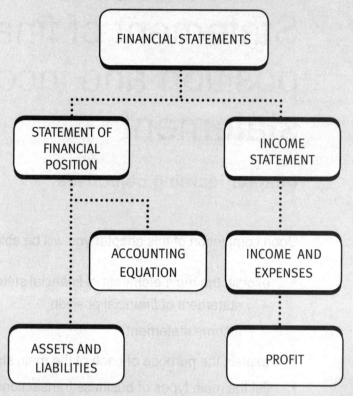

1 Financial statements

There are **two** key elements to the financial statements of a sole trader business:

- **Statement of financial position**, showing the financial position of a business at a point in time, and
- **Income statement**, showing the financial performance of a business over a period of time.

The financial statements show the effects of business transactions. The main types are:

- sales of goods (either for cash or on credit)

  If a sale is made for cash, then cash in the business will increase and a sales transaction will have also been created. The cash will be recorded in the statement of financial position and the sale will be recorded in the income statement.

If a sale is made on credit, then the payment for the goods has not been made immediately. Therefore we are still owed for these items. The sale will still be recorded in the income statement, however a receivable will be recorded in the statement of financial position.

- purchase of inventory for resale (either for cash or on credit)

  If we buy inventory for cash, then we are spending money. This decrease in cash will be recorded in the statement of financial position. The increase in inventory that we now own will also be recorded as an asset in the statement of financial position.

  If we buy inventory on credit, then we will owe the supplier for these goods. This is called a payable. Therefore inventory will increase and also a payable will be created. Both of these are entered onto the statement of financial position.

- purchase of non-current assets

  If we buy a non-current asset (e.g. a motor vehicle) then we are spending cash, so this will decrease. However, we have now gained a new asset, and both of these entries are recorded in the statement of financial position.

- payment of expenses such as utilities

  Making this payment will reduce our cash balance and this will affect our statement of financial position. We will have created an expense which we have made the payment for, utilities. This expense belongs on the income statement.

- introduction of new capital to the business

  If the owner of the business introduces funds into the business, this is called capital. We have increased the capital within the business and also increased our cash or bank balances. Both of these entries are recorded on the statement of financial position.

- withdrawal of funds from the business by the owner.

  If the owner then withdraws some of these funds back out of the business again, this is known as drawings. The capital will reduce and also the amount of funds within the bank account will too. Both of these are recorded on the statement of financial position.

The business entity concept

- The business entity concept states that financial accounting information relates only to the activities of the business entity and not to the activities of its owner.

- The business entity is treated as **separate** from its owners.

Entity concept

A company is both legally and for accounting purposes a separate entity distinct from its owners, the shareholders. On the other hand, the business of a sole trader is not a legal entity distinct from its proprietor; however, for accounting purposes, the business is regarded as being a separate entity and accounts are drawn up for the business separately from the sole trader's own personal financial dealings.

The entity concept is essential in order to be able to account for the business as a separate economic unit. Flows of money between the business and the proprietors are also separately identified from other money flows.

The correct terms for these cash movements are:

Cash movement from/to proprietors	Sole trader, partnership	Company
In	Either 'loans from proprietors' or 'increase in capital'	Share issue proceeds
Out	Either 'drawings' or 'reduction in capital'	

The key link between the owner and the business is the amount stated as capital which is the amount the business owes to the proprietor.

KAPLAN PUBLISHING

2 Statement of financial position

The vertical format of the statement of financial position is shown below:

Note: this format relates to a sole trader only. The company format is looked at later within chapter 15.

W Xang Statement of financial position as at 31 December 20X6

	$	$
Non-current assets		
Motor van/Land & buildings etc		X
Current assets		
Inventory	X	
Receivables	X	
Cash at bank	X	
Cash in hand	X	
	───	
		X
		───
		X
		───
Capital account		
Balance at 1 January 20X6	X	
Add: Net profit for year	X	
Increase in capital	X	
	───	
	X	
Less: Drawings for year	X	
	───	
		X
Non-current liabilities		X
Current liabilities		
Payables		X
		───
		X
		───

- The top half of the statement of financial position shows the assets of the business.

- The bottom half of the statement of financial position shows the capital and liabilities of the business.

3 Income statement

The format of the income statement is shown below:

Mr W Xang Income statement for the year ended 31 December 20X6

	$	$
Sales revenue		33,700
Cost of sales:		
Opening inventory	3,200	
Purchases	24,490	
	27,690	
Less: Closing inventory	(2,390)	
		(25,300)
Gross profit		8,400
Wages	3,385	
Rent	1,200	
Sundry expenses	365	
		(4,950)
Net profit		3,450

- **Income** is increases in economic benefits during the period in the form of inflows or enhancements of assets or decreases of liabilities that result in increases in equity, other than those relating to contributions from equity participants.

- **Expenses** are decreases in economic benefits during the period in the form of outflows or depletions of assets or increases of liabilities that result in decreases in equity, other than those relating to distributions to equity participants.

- The income statement shows the performance of the business over a period of time, in this case for a full year.

- The income statement is prepared following the accruals concept. This means that income and expenses are recorded in the income statement as they are earned/incurred regardless of whether cash has been received/paid.

- The sales revenue shows the income from goods sold in the year, regardless of whether those goods have been paid for.

KAPLAN PUBLISHING

- The cost of buying the goods sold must be deducted from the revenue. It is important that the cost of any goods remaining unsold is not included here.

- The current year's sales will include goods bought in the previous year, so this **opening inventory** must be added to the current year's purchases.

- Some of this year's purchases will be unsold at 31 December 20X6 and this **closing inventory** must be deducted from purchases to be set off against next year's sales.

- The income statement is split into two parts, the first part gives gross profit and the second part, net profit.

- Gross profit divided by sales revenue gives the **gross profit margin** which illustrates the profitability of the business at a trading level.

- We must distinguish between wages and drawings. Wages relate to payments to third parties (employees) and represent a deduction or charge in arriving at net profit. Amounts paid to the proprietor (even if he calls them 'salary'!) must be treated as drawings.

4 Relationship between the statement of financial position and income statement

The link between the statement of financial position and income statement is shown below:

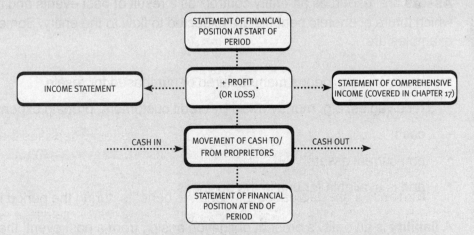

- The statement of financial position are not isolated statements; they are linked over time with the income statement.

- As the business records a profit in the income statement, that profit is added to the capital section of the statement of financial position, along with any capital introduced. Cash taken out of the business by the proprietor, called drawings, is deducted.

5 The accounting equation

ASSETS = PROPRIETOR'S CAPITAL + LIABILITIES

ASSETS − LIABILITIES = PROPRIETOR'S CAPITAL

The accounting equation

The statement of financial position shows the position of a business at one point in time. A statement of financial position will always satisfy the accounting equation as shown above.

- Each and every transaction that the business makes or enters into has two aspects to it and has a double effect on the business and the accounting equation. This is known as the duality concept.

- The accounting equation is a simple expression of the fact that at any point in time the assets of the business will be equal to its liabilities plus the capital of the business.

- It follows that assets less liabilities equal the capital of the business. Assets less liabilities are known as net assets.

Assets and liabilities

Assets are resources an entity controls as a result of past events and from which future economic benefits are expected to flow to the entity. Some examples are:

- inventory, e.g. goods manufactured or purchased for resale

- receivables, e.g. money owed by credit customers, prepaid expenses

- cash

- non-current assets

- and is available for use in the business.

A **liability** is an entity's present obligation arising from a past event, the settlement of which will result in an outflow of economic benefits from the entity. This is something owed by the business to someone else, such as:

- payables, e.g. amounts owed to credit suppliers, accrued expenses

- loans.

Equity is defined as the residual interest in the entity's assets after deducting its liabilities. You will become more familiar with this term when you come to look at Company accounts in chapter 17.

Capital is a type of liability. This is the amount that is due to the owner(s) of the business. It will increase each year by any new capital injected into the business and by the profit made by the business. It will decrease by any amounts withdrawn from the business by the owner(s).

Disclosure of assets and liabilities in the statement of financial position

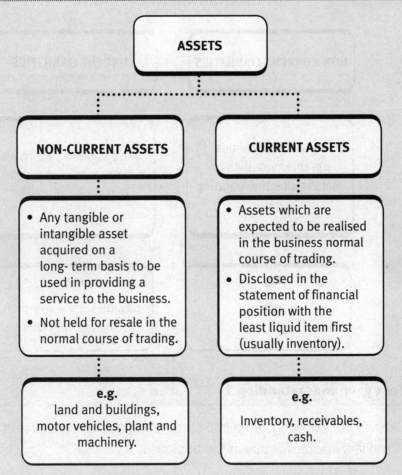

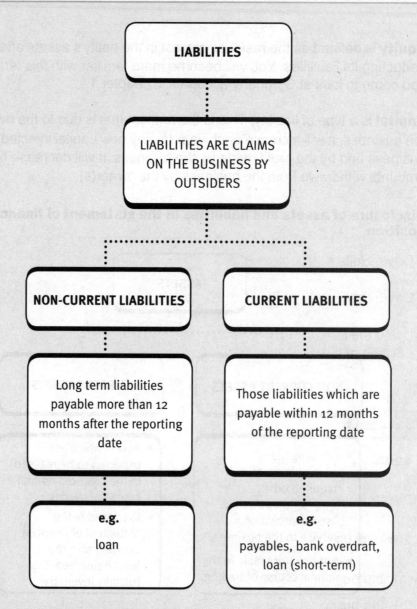

LIABILITIES

↓

LIABILITIES ARE CLAIMS ON THE BUSINESS BY OUTSIDERS

NON-CURRENT LIABILITIES

Long term liabilities payable more than 12 months after the reporting date

e.g.

loan

CURRENT LIABILITIES

Those liabilities which are payable within 12 months of the reporting date

e.g.

payables, bank overdraft, loan (short-term)

Test your understanding 1

Classify the following items into current and non-current assets and liabilities:

- land and buildings ~~Fixed Assets~~
- receivables ~~Current Assets~~
- cash ~~Current Assets~~
- loan repayable in two years' time ~~Long term Liability~~
- payables ~~Liability~~
- delivery van. ~~Fixed Assets~~

Illustration 1 – The accounting equation

This illustration involves a series of transactions using the dual effect of transactions and then the accounting equation to build up a set of financial statements. The transactions are as follows:

Day 1 Avon commences business introducing $1,000 cash.

Day 2 Buys a motor car for $400 cash.

Day 3 Buys inventory for $200 cash.

Day 4 Sells all the goods bought on Day 3 for $300 cash.

Day 5 Buys inventory for $400 on credit.

Using the accounting equation, we will draw up a statement of financial position at the end of each day's transactions.

Solution to the accounting equation

Solution

Day 1: Avon commences business introducing $1,000 cash

The dual effect of this transaction is:

(a) the business has $1,000 of cash

(b) the business owes the owner $1,000 – this is capital.

Statement of financial position Day 1

Assets	$	Capital and liabilities	$
Cash	1,000	Capital	1,000
	1,000		1,000

Day 2: Buys a motor car for $400 cash

The dual effect of this transaction is:

(a) the business has an asset of $400

(b) the business has spent $400 in cash

This transaction changes the form in which the assets are held.

Statement of financial position Day 2

	$		$
Assets		**Capital and liabilities**	
Cash	600	Capital	1,000
Car	400		
	1,000		1,000

Note that the acquiring of an asset must lead to one of the following:

- reducing another asset by a corresponding amount (as above)
- incurring a corresponding liability (Day 5)
- increasing the capital contributed by the proprietor (Day 1).

Day 3: Buys inventory for $200 cash

The dual effect of this transaction is:

(a) the business has $200 of inventory

(b) the business has spent $200 in cash.

Again this is merely a change in the form in which the assets are held. $200 is withdrawn from cash and invested in inventory.

KAPLAN PUBLISHING

Statement of financial position Day 3

	$		$
Assets		**Capital and liabilities**	
Motor car	400	Capital	1,000
Inventory	200		
Cash:			
($600 – $200)	400		
	1,000		1,000

Day 4: Sells all the goods bought on day 3 for $300 cash

This is an important new development. It is true that one asset (inventory) is being replaced by another (cash), but the amounts do not correspond.

	$
Cash acquired (sale proceeds)	300
Asset relinquished (inventory)	200
Difference (= profit)	100

Thus total assets have increased by $100. Since there are no liabilities involved, if the fundamental equation is to remain valid the capital must increase by $100.

Profit is the difference between purchase price and sale proceeds and it belongs to the proprietor(s) of the business. It is an increase in the capital of the business.

The dual effect of this transaction is:

(a) The business has received $300 of cash.

(b) The business has reduced inventory by $200 and made a profit of $100.

Statement of financial position Day 4

Assets		$	Capital and liabilities	$
Motor car		400	Capital	1,000
Cash:				
($400 + $300)		700	Add: Profit	100
		1,100		1,100

Day 5: Buys inventory for $400 on credit

The dual effect of this transaction is:

(a) The business has $400 of inventory.

(b) The business has a liability to the supplier of $400.

Assets can be increased by a corresponding increase in liabilities as follows:

Statement of financial position Day 5

Assets		$	Capital and liabilities	$
Motor car		400	Capital	1,000
Inventory		400	Add: Profit	100
Cash		700	Payables	400
		1,500		1,500

Note that the payables are acting in effect as a source of finance for the business.

Test your understanding 2

Continuing from the illustration above, prepare the statement of financial position at the end of each day after accounting for the transactions below:

Day 6 Sells half of the goods bought on Day 5 on credit for $250.

Day 7 Pays $200 to his supplier.

Day 8 Receives $100 from a customer.

Day 9 Proprietor draws $75 in cash.

Day 10 Pays rent of $40 in cash.

Day 11 Receives a loan of $600 repayable in two years.

Day 12 Pays cash of $30 for insurance.

Your starting point is the statement of financial position at the end of Day 5, from the illustration above.

Once you have dealt with each of the transactions, prepare a **statement of financial position** at the end of Day 12 and an **income statement** for the first 12 days of trading.

Statement of comprehensive income

Later on in this textbook you will be introduced to the Statement of comprehensive income. This relates to a company and not to a sole trader.

Test your understanding answers

Test your understanding 1

- Land and buildings – **non-current asset**.
- Receivables – **current asset**.
- Cash – **current asset**.
- Loan repayable in two years time – **non-current liability**.
- Payables – **current liability**.
- Delivery van – **non-current asset**.

Test your understanding 2

Day 6: Sells half of the goods bought on Day 5 on credit for $250

This transaction introduces two new concepts:

- **Sale on credit.** Essentially this is the same as a sale for cash, except that the asset increased is not cash, but receivables.
- Sale of **part** of the inventory. In practice this is the normal situation. The important accounting requirement is to separate:
  - inventory still held as an asset, from
  - cost of inventory sold.

Statement of financial position for Day 6

Assets	$	Capital and liabilities	$
Motor car	400	Capital introduced	1,000
Inventory	200	Add: Profit to date	
Receivables	250	($100 + $50)	150
Cash	700		
			1,150
		Payables	400
	1,550		1,550

Day 7: Pays $200 to his supplier

- The dual effect of this transaction is:

(a) The business has paid out $200 in cash.

(b) The business has reduced the payable (liability) by $200.

This is simply the reduction of one liability (payables) and one asset (cash) by a corresponding amount ($200).

Statement of financial position for Day 7

	$		$
Assets		**Capital and liabilities**	
Motor car	400	Capital	1,000
Inventory	200	Add: Profit to date	150
Receivables	250		
Cash ($700 – $200)	500		
			1,150
		Payables	
		($400 – $200)	200
	1,350		1,350

Day 8: Receives $100 from a customer

- The dual effect of this transaction is:

(a) The business has received $100 in cash.

(b) The receivables of the business have reduced by $100.

Statement of financial position for Day 8

Assets	$	Capital and liabilities	$
Motor car	400	Capital	1,000
Inventory	200	Add: Profit to date	150
Receivables			
($250 – $100)	150		1,150
Cash ($500 + $100)	600	Payables	200
	1,350		1,350

Day 9: Proprietor draws $75 in cash

This shows on the statement of financial position as a reduction of capital, and as a reduction of cash.

Cash or other assets taken out of the business by the owner are called 'amounts withdrawn', or 'drawings'.

- The dual effect of this transaction is:

(a) The business has reduced cash by $75.

(b) The business has a drawings balance of $75 which reduces capital.

Statement of financial position for Day 9

Assets	$	Capital and liabilities	$
Motor car	400	Capital	1,000
Inventory	200	Add: Profit to date	150
Receivables	150		
Cash ($600 – $75)	525		1,150
		Less: Drawings	(75)
			1,075
		Payables	200
	1,275		1,275

KAPLAN PUBLISHING

Day 10: Pays rent of $40

This is an example of a business expense.

The dual effect of this transaction is:

(a) The business pays out $40 in cash.

(b) The business has a rent expense of $40 which reduces profit.

Statement of financial position for Day 10

Assets	$	Capital and liabilities	$
Motor car	400	Capital	1,000
Inventory	200	Add: Profit to date	
Receivables	150	($150 – $40)	110
Cash ($525 – $40)	485		
			1,110
		Less: Drawings	(75)
			1,035
		Payables	200
	1,235		1,235

Day 11: Receives a loan of $600 repayable in two years' time

The dual effect of this transaction is:

(a) The business receives $600 in cash.

(b) The business has a liability of $600.

Statement of financial position for Day 11

Assets	$	Capital and liabilities	$
Motor car	400	Capital introduced	1,000
Inventory	200	Add: Profit to date	110
Receivables	150		
Cash ($485 + $600)	1,085		
			1,110
		Less: Drawings	(75)
			1,035
		Loan	600
		Payables	200
	1,835		1,835

Day 12: Pays cash of $30 for insurance

The dual effect of this transaction is:

(a) the business pays out $30 in cash

(b) the business has an insurance expense of $30 which reduces profit.

Statement of financial position for Day 12

Assets	$	Capital and liabilities	$
Motor car	400	Capital introduced	1,000
Inventory	200	Add: Profit to date	
Receivables	150	($110 – $30)	80
Cash ($1,085 – $30)	1,055		
	———		———
	1,805		
		Less: Drawings	(75)
			———
			1,005
		Loan	600
		Payables	200
	———		———
	1,805		1,805
	———		———

This marks the end of the transactions. The financial statements for the 12 day period can now be considered.

Avon, income statement for the 12 days				
			$	$
Sales revenue:	Cash			300
	Credit			250
				550
Cost of sales:	Purchases:	Cash	200	
		Credit	400	
			600	
Less: Closing inventory			(200)	
Cost of goods sold				(400)
Gross profit				150
Rent			40	
Insurance			30	
				(70)
Net profit				80

Avon, statement of financial position as at end of Day 12

		$	$
Non-current asset:	Motor car (at cost)		400
Current assets:	Inventory	200	
	Receivables	150	
	Cash	1,055	
		———	
			1,405
			———
			1,805
			———
Capital account:	Capital introduced	1,000	
	Net profit	80	
		———	
		1,080	
Less: Drawings		(75)	
		———	
			1,005
Non-current liability:	Loan		600
Current liabilities:	Payables		200
			———
			1,805
			———

3

Double entry bookkeeping

Chapter learning objectives

Upon completion of this chapter you will be able to:

- explain the concept of double entry and the duality concept

- explain the debit and credit principle

- explain the meaning of the balance on each type of account

- record cash transactions in ledger accounts

- record credit sale and purchase transactions in ledger accounts

- illustrate how to account for discounts

- explain sales and purchase returns and demonstrate their recording

- illustrate how to balance a ledger account

- extract the ledger balances into a trial balance

- identify the purpose of a trial balance

- prepare a simple income statement and statement of financial position from a trial balance

- explain and illustrate the process of closing the ledger accounts in the accounting records when the financial statements have been completed.

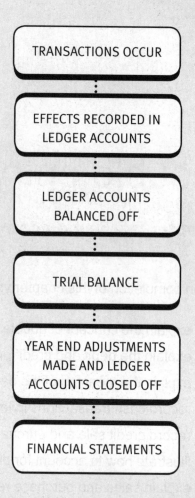

1 The duality concept and double entry bookkeeping

- Each transaction that a business enters into affects the financial statements in two ways, e.g.

  A business buys a non-current asset for cash.

  The two effects on the financial statements are:

  (1) There is an increase in non-current assets.

  (2) There is a decrease in cash.

- To follow the rules of double entry bookkeeping, each time a transaction is recorded, both effects must be taken into account.

- These two effects are equal and opposite such that the accounting equation will always prove correct:

> Assets – Liabilities = Capital

- Traditionally, one effect is referred to as the debit side (abbreviated to Dr) and the other as the credit side of the entry (abbreviated to Cr).

2 Ledger accounts, debits and credits

- Transactions are recorded in the relevant ledger accounts. There is a ledger account for each asset, liability, revenue and expense item.

- Each account has two sides – the debit and credit sides:

**Debit
(Dr)**   **Credit
(Cr)**

Name of account e.g. cash,
sales

Date Narrative $	Date Narrative $

- The duality concept means that each transaction will affect at least two ledger accounts.

- One account will be debited and the other credited.

- Whether an entry is to the debit or credit side of an account depends on the type of account and the transaction:

Debit	Credit
Increase in:	Increase in:
Expense (Income statement)	Liability (Statement of financial position)
Asset (Statement of financial position)	Income (Income statement)
Drawings (Statement of financial position)	Capital (Statement of financial position)

Summary of steps to record a transaction

(1) Identify the items that are affected.

(2) Consider whether they are being increased or decreased.

(3) Decide whether each account should be debited or credited.

(4) Check that a debit entry and a credit entry have been made and they are both for the same amount.

Recording cash transactions

Cash transactions are those where payment is made or received immediately.

Cheque payments or receipts are classed as cash transactions

Double entry involves the bank ledger:

- a debit entry is where funds are received
- a credit entry is where funds are paid out.

Test your understanding 1

Recording cash transactions

Show the following transactions in ledger accounts: (Tip: the ledger accounts you need are Bank, Rent, Drawings, and Sales)

(1) Kamran pays $80 for rent by cheque.

(2) Kamran sells goods for $230 cash which he banks.

(3) He then takes $70 out of the business for his personal living expenses.

(4) Kamran sells more goods for cash, receiving $3,400.

Test your understanding 2

Yusuf enters into the following transactions in his first month of trading:

(1) Buys goods for cash for $380.

(2) Pays $20 in sundry expenses.

(3) Makes $1,000 in sales.

(4) Receives a bank loan of $5,000.

(5) Pays $2,600 for fixtures and fittings.

KAPLAN PUBLISHING

What is the total entry to the credit side of the cash T account?

A $6,000

B $6,380

C $3,000

D $2,620

Recording credit sales and purchases

Credit sales and purchases are transactions where goods or services change hands immediately, but payment is not made or received until some time in the future.

Money that a business is owed is accounted for in the receivables ledger.

Money that a business owes is accounted for in the payables ledger.

Test your understanding 3

Norris notes down the following transactions that happened in June.

(1) Sell goods for cash for $60.

(2) Pay insurance premium by cheque – $400.

(3) Sell goods for $250 – the customer will pay in a month.

(4) Pay $50 petrol for the delivery van.

(5) Buy $170 goods for resale on credit.

(6) Take $57 out of the business for living expenses.

(7) Buy another $40 goods for resale, paying cash.

(8) Buy a new computer for the business for $800.

Record these transactions using ledger accounts

Test your understanding 4

For each of the following individual transactions state the two ledger accounts affected, and whether the ledger account should be debited or credited:

(1) Ole purchases goods for $5,000, and pays by cheque.

(2) Ole makes a sale to a customer for $500. The customer pays in 30 days' time.

(3) Ole pays a telephone bill amounting to $40, and pays by cheque.

(4) Ole receives bank interest income of $150.

(5) Ole purchases stationery for $12 and pays cash.

(6) Ole makes a sale to a customer for $400. The customer pays cash.

3 Recording sales and purchases returns

- It is normal for customers to return unwanted goods to a business; equally the business will occasionally have cause to return unwanted goods to their supplier.

- The double entries arising will depend upon whether the returned goods were initially purchased on credit:

	Originally a credit transaction	Originally a cash transaction
Sales returns (returns inwards)	Dr Sales returns Cr Receivables	Dr Sales returns Cr Cash
Purchases returns (returns outwards)	Dr Payables Cr Purchases returns	Dr Cash Cr Purchases returns

Test your understanding 5

For each of the following, state the double entry required to record the transaction in the accounts:

(1) Alfie invests $10,000 of his life savings into his business bank account.

(2) He then buys goods from Isabel, a supplier for $1,000 and pays by cheque.

(3) A sale is made for $400 – the customer pays by cheque.

(4) Alfie makes a sale for $600 and the customer promises to pay in the future.

(5) Alfie then buys goods from his supplier, Kamen, for $500 on credit.

(6) Alfie pays a telephone bill of $150 by cheque.

(7) The credit customer pays the balance on her account.

(8) Alfie pays Kamen $340.

(9) Bank interest of $30 is received.

(10) A cash customer returned $20 goods to Alfie for a refund.

(11) Alfie sent goods of $100 back to Kamen.

4 Discounts

Trade discounts

Trade discounts are given to try and increase the volume of sales being made by the supplier. By reducing the selling price, buying items in bulk then becomes more attractive. If you are able to source your products cheaper, you can then also sell them on to the consumer cheaper too. For example, if we were to buy over 1000 items, the supplier might be able to drop the price of those items by 5%.

Accounting for trade discounts

From an accounting perspective, trade discounts are deducted at the point of sale. When accounting for a sale that is subject to a trade discount - it is the net amount that should be recorded i.e. the trade discount does not get recorded separately.

Test your understanding 6

Oliver sells goods with a book value of $1,000 to Sam on a cash basis and allows her a trade discount of 10%.

Required:

Show how the above should be recorded in both the books of Oliver and Sam.

Early settlement discounts

This type of discount encourages people to pay for items much quicker. If you pay for the goods within a set time limit, then you will receive a % discount. For example, a cash discount of 3% is offered to any customers who pay within 14 days.

Whilst offering this discount makes the cash flow in quicker, it is still a 'lost cost' to the business who offers such a discount.

Accounting for settlement discounts

Discounts may be given in the case of credit transactions for prompt payment:

- A business may give its customer a discount – known as **Discount allowed**.

- A business may receive a discount from a supplier – known as **Discount received**.

The correct double entries are:

Discount allowed

Dr Discount allowed (expense) X

Cr Receivables X

The expense is shown beneath gross profit in the income statement, alongside other expenses of the business.

Discount received

Dr Payables X

Cr Discount received (income) X

The income is shown beneath gross profit in the income statement.

Settlement discounts and sales tax

Settlement discounts are always assumed to be taken for sales tax purposes (even when not) as the sales tax needs to be calculated on the invoice immediately.

For example a company sold goods for $100 net of sales tax and allowed its customer a settlement discount of 10% if paid within 14 days. Sales tax is charged at 17.5%.

What is the sales tax required for this transaction?
$100 × 90% × 17.5% = $15.75

As settlement discounts have an effect on the calculation of sales tax, the following procedure should be followed when dealing with cash discounts and sales tax.

(1) Calculate the net amount (usually given in the question)

(2) Deduct the settlement discount

(3) Calculate the sales tax on the after settlement discount amount

(Note: the accounting for sales tax will be studied in chapter 5)

Test your understanding 7

George owes a supplier, Herbie, $2,000 and is owed $3,400 by a customer, Iris. George offers a cash discount to his customers of 2.5% if they pay within 14 days and Herbie has offered George a cash discount of 3% for payment within ten days.

George pays Herbie within ten days and Iris takes advantage of the cash discount offered to her.

What ledger entries are required to record these discounts?

A	Dr	Payables	60	Dr	Discount allowed	85
	Cr	Discount received	60	Cr	Receivables	85
B	Dr	Discount allowed	60	Dr	Payables	85
	Cr	Receivables	60	Cr	Discount received	85
C	Dr	Payables	50	Dr	Discount allowed	102
	Cr	Discount received	50	Cr	Receivables	102
D	Dr	Discount allowed	50	Dr	Payables	102
	Cr	Receivables	50	Cr	Discount received	102

5 Balancing off a statement of financial position ledger account

Once the transactions for a period have been recorded, it will be necessary to find the balance on the ledger account:

(1) Total both sides of the T account and find the larger total.

(2) Put the larger total in the total box on the debit and credit side.

(3) Insert a balancing figure to the side of the T account which does not currently add up to the amount in the total box. Call this balancing figure 'balance c/f' (carried forward) or 'balance c/d' (carried down).

(4) Carry the balance down diagonally and call it 'balance b/f' (brought forward) or 'balance b/d' (brought down).

Test your understanding 8

Balance off the following account:

Cash

	$		$
Capital	10,000	Purchases	200
Sales	250	Rent	150
		Electricity	75

Test your understanding 9

Balance off the following account:

Bank

	$		$
Capital	10,000	Purchases	1,000
Sales	300	Rent	2,500
		Electricity	750
		New van	15,000

6 Closing off the ledger accounts

At the year end, the ledger accounts must be closed off in preparation for the recording of transactions in the next accounting period.

Statement of financial position ledger accounts

- Assets/liabilities at the end of a period = Assets/liabilities at start of the next period, e.g. the cash at bank at the end of one day will be the cash at bank at the start of the following day.

- Balancing the account will result in:
  - a balance c/f (being the asset/liability at the end of the accounting period)
  - a balance b/f (being the asset/liability at the start of the next accounting period).

KAPLAN PUBLISHING

Income statement ledger accounts

- At the end of a period any amounts that relate to that period are transferred out of the income and expenditure accounts into another ledger account called the income statement.

- This is done by closing the account.

- Do not show a balance c/f or balance b/f but instead put the balancing figure on the smallest side and label it 'income statement'.

Capital account

- At the start of the next accounting period the capital account will have an opening balance, i.e. a balance b/f equal to the amount that is owed to the owner at the start of that period.

- This amount is equal to what was owed to the owner at the start of the previous period, plus any capital that the owner introduced in the period, plus any profits earned in the period less any drawings taken out in the period.

- Therefore we transfer the balance on the income statement and the balance on the drawings account to the capital account at the end of the period so that it will have the correct opening balance at the start of the next.

Capital

	$		$
		Balance b/f	X
Loss for year	X	Profit for year	X
Drawings	X	Cash injections	X
Balance c/f	X		
	X		X
		Balance b/f	X

Test your understanding 10

Oddjob had $7,800 capital invested in his business at the start of the year. During the course of the year he took $3,100 cash out of the business for himself and also paid his wife, who did some secretarial work for the business, $500. The business' overall profit for the year was $8,900. Oddjob also paid $350 for a new personal suit using the business cheque book during the year.

What is the balance on the capital account at the end of the year?

A $12,750

B $13,250

C $13,600

D $13,100

7 The trial balance

- Once all ledger accounts have been balanced off a trial balance is prepared.

- A trial balance is a list of the 'balance b/f' on the ledger accounts according to whether they are on the debit or credit side. Trial balance as at 31 December 2005

Trial balance as at 31 December 2005

Name of account	Dr $	Cr $
Sales		X
Purchases	X	
Receivables	X	
Payables		X
Capital		X
	X	X

What does the trial balance prove?

The trial balance will balance if for every debit entry made, an equal credit entry was made and the balances were correctly extracted and cast (added up!).

- The purpose of a trial balance is:

- to check that for every debit entry made, an equal credit entry has been made.

- as a first step in preparing the financial statements.

Note that a number of adjustments will be made after the trial balance is extracted. These adjustments do not therefore appear in the trial balance.

8 Opening balances in the ledger accounts

- If a business has been in operation in the previous year, then at the beginning of any accounting period it will have assets and liabilities such as cash and non-current assets.

- Any opening amounts are shown in statement of financial position ledger accounts as opening balances.

- The opening balance on an asset account is a debit entry.

- The opening balance on a liability account is a credit entry.

- Transactions during the year are then entered as normal in the ledger account, and at the year-end it is balanced off taking into account the opening balance.

Note: Income statement ledger accounts do not have an opening balance.

Test your understanding 11

Johnny had receivables of $4,500 at the start of 20X5. During the year to 31 December 20X5 he makes credit sales of $45,000 and receives cash of $46,500 from credit customers.

What is the balance on the receivables account at 31 December 20X5?

A $6,000Dr

B $6,000Cr

C $3,000Dr

D $3,000Cr

9 Preparation of financial statements

The process seen thus far is as follows:

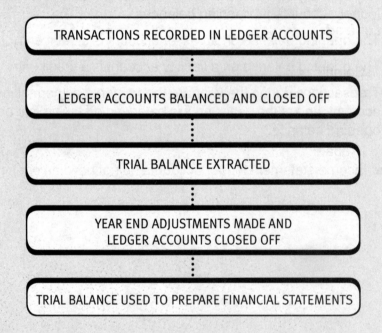

TRANSACTIONS RECORDED IN LEDGER ACCOUNTS

LEDGER ACCOUNTS BALANCED AND CLOSED OFF

TRIAL BALANCE EXTRACTED

YEAR END ADJUSTMENTS MADE AND LEDGER ACCOUNTS CLOSED OFF

TRIAL BALANCE USED TO PREPARE FINANCIAL STATEMENTS

Examination questions may draw on any particular stage of this process.

Test your understanding 12

Matthew set up a business and in the first nine days of trading the following transactions occurred:

1 January	Matthew introduces $10,000 capital by cheque.
2 January	Matthew buys supplies worth $4,000 and pays by cheque.
3 January	Matthew buys a delivery van for $2,000 and pays by cheque.
4 January	Matthew buys $1,000 of purchases on credit.
5 January	Matthew sells goods for $1,500 and receives a cheque of that amount.
6 January	Matthew sells all his remaining goods for $5,000 on credit.
7 January	Matthew pays $800 to his supplier by cheque.
8 January	Matthew pays rent of $200 by cheque.
9 January	Matthew draws $100 for living expenses from the business bank account.

Required:

(a) Complete the relevant ledger accounts.

(b) Extract a trial balance.

(c) Prepare the income statement for the first nine days.

(d) Prepare the Statement of financial position as at 9 January.

Chapter summary

> **TRANSACTIONS OCCUR**

> **TWO EFFECTS RECORDED IN LEDGER ACCOUNTS**
>
> Debit = credit
>
> | Dr = increase in | Cr = increase in |
> |---|---|
> | Expense | Liability |
> | Asset | Income |
> | Drawings | Capital |

> **LEDGER ACCOUNTS BALANCED OFF**
>
> 1 Total both sides and find the larger total.
> 2 Put the larger total in both total boxes.
> 3 Insert a balancing figure as required in statement of financial position accounts, call this balancing figure 'Balance c/f'. For income and expense accounts, take this balancing figure to the profit and loss account T account.
> 4 For statement of financial position accounts, carry the balance down diagonally and call it 'balance b/f'.

> **TRIAL BALANCE**
>
> Is extracted. Double entry has been correctly upheld as long as total debits = total credits.

> **YEAR END ADJUSTMENTS AND LEDGER ACCOUNTS CLOSED OFF**
>
> • statement of financial position accounts result in a balance c/f.
> • income statement accounts are closed off to the income statement ledger account.
> • the balance on the income statement and drawings ledger accounts are transferred to the capital account.

> **FINANCIAL STATEMENTS**

Test your understanding answers

Test your understanding 1

Bank

	$		$
Sales (2)	230	Rent (1)	80
Sales (4)	3,400	Drawings (3)	70

Sales

	$		$
		Bank (2)	230
		Bank (4)	3,400

Rent

	$		$
Bank (1)	80		

Drawings

	$		$
Bank (3)	70		

Test your understanding 2

The correct answer is C

Cash

	$		$
Sales	1,000	Purchases	380
Loan	5,000	Sundry expenses	20
		Fixtures and fittings	2,600

Test your understanding 3

Bank

	$		$
Sales (1)	60	Insurance (2)	400
		Motor expenses (4)	50
		Drawings (6)	57
		Purchases (7)	40
		Non-current assets (8)	800

Sales

	$		$
		Bank (1)	60
		Receivables (3)	250

Insurance (expense)

	$		$
Bank (2)	400		

Receivables

	$		$
Sales (3)	250		

Motor expenses

	$		$
Bank (4)	50		

Purchases

	$		$
Payables (5)	170		
Cash (7)	40		

Payables

	$		$
		Purchases (5)	170

Drawings

	$		$
Bank (6)	57		

Non-current asset (computer)

	$		$
Bank (8)	800		

Test your understanding 4

			$	$
1	Dr	Purchases	5,000	
	Cr	Bank		5,000
2	Dr	Receivables	500	
	Cr	Sales		500
3	Dr	Telephone expense	40	
	Cr	Bank		40
4	Dr	Bank	150	
	Cr	Interest income		150
5	Dr	Stationery expense	12	
	Cr	Cash		12
6	Dr	Cash	400	
	Cr	Sales		400

Test your understanding 5

			$	$
1	Dr	Bank	10,000	
	Cr	Capital		10,000
2	Dr	Purchases	1,000	
	Cr	Bank		1,000
3	Dr	Bank	400	
	Cr	Sales		400
4	Dr	Receivables	600	
	Cr	Sales		600
5	Dr	Purchases	500	
	Cr	Payables		500
6	Dr	Telephone expense	150	
	Cr	Bank		150
7	Dr	Bank	600	
	Cr	Receivables		600
8	Dr	Payables	340	
	Cr	Bank		340
9	Dr	Bank	30	
	Cr	Interest income		30
10	Dr	Sales returns	20	
	Cr	Bank		20
11	Dr	Payables	100	
	Cr	Purchases returns		100

Test your understanding 6

Oliver's books:

Dr	Cash	900
Cr	Sales	900

(Net sale = $1,000 – 10%)

Sam's books:

Dr	Purchases	900
Cr	Cash	900

(Net purchase = $1,000 – 10%)

Test your understanding 7

The correct answer is A

Payables

	$		$
Cash (97% x 2,000)	1,940	Balance b/f	2,000
Discount received	60		
	2,000		2,000

Receivables

	$		$
Balance b/f	3,400	Cash (97.5% x 3,400)	3,315
		Discount allowed	85
	3,400		3,400

Discount received

	$		$
		Payables	60

Discount allowed

	$		$
Receivables	85		

Test your understanding 8

Cash

	$		$
Capital	10,000	Purchases	200
Sales	250	Rent	150
		Electricity	75
		Balance c/f	9,825
	10,250		10,250
Balance b/f	9,825		

Test your understanding 9

Bank

	$		$
Capital	10,000	Purchases	1,000
Sales	300	Rent	2,500
		Electricity	750
Balance c/f	8,950	New van	15,000
	19,250		19,250
		Balance b/f	8,950

Test your understanding 10

The correct answer is B.

Capital

	$		$
Drawings	3,100	Balance b/f	7,800
Drawings (suit)	350	Profit for the year	8,900
Balance c/f	13,250		
	16,700		16,700
		Balance b/f	13,250

Test your understanding 11

The correct answer is C.

Receivables

	$		$
Balance b/f	4,500		
Sales	45,000	Cash received	46,500
		Balance c/f	3,000
	49,500		49,500
Balance b/f	3,000		

Test your understanding 12

Bank

		$			$
1 Jan	Capital	10,000	2 Jan	Purchases	4,000
5 Jan	Sales	1,500	3 Jan	Delivery van	2,000
			7 Jan	Payables	800
			8 Jan	Rent	200
			9 Jan	Drawings	100
				Balance c/f	4,400
		11,500			11,500
	Balance b/f	4,400			

Capital

		$			$
	Balance c/f	10,000	1 Jan	Bank	10,000
		10,000			10,000
				Bal b/f	10,000

Purchases

		$			$
2 Jan	Bank	4,000		To I/S	5,000
4 Jan	Payables	1,000			
		5,000			5,000

KAPLAN PUBLISHING

Delivery van

		$		$
3 Jan	Bank	2,000	Balance c/f	2,000
		2,000		2,000
	Balance b/f	2,000		

Payables

		$			$
7 Jan	Bank	800	4 Jan	Purchases	1,000
	Balance c/f	200			
		1,000			1,000
				Balance b/f	200

Sales

		$			$
To I/S		6,500	5 Jan	Bank	1,500
			6 Jan	Receivables	5,000
		6,500			6,500

Receivables

		$		$
7 Jan	Sales	5,000	Balance c/f	5,000
		5,000		5,000
	Balance b/f	5,000		

Rent

		$		$
8 Jan	Bank	200	To I/S	200
		200		200

Drawings

		$		$
9 Jan	Bank	100	Balance c/f	100
		100		100
	Balance b/f	100		

Trial balance as at 9 January

	Dr	Cr
	$	$
Bank	4,400	
Capital		10,000
Purchases	5,000	
Delivery van	2,000	
Payables		200
Sales		6,500
Receivables	5,000	
Rent	200	
Drawings	100	
	16,700	16,700

Income statement for the period ended 9 January

	$	$
Sales		6,500
Opening inventory	–	
Purchases	5000	
Closing inventory	–	
		5,000
Gross profit		1,500
Expenses		
Rent		200
Net profit		1,300

Statement of financial position as at 9 January

	$	$
Non current assets		
Delivery van		2,000
Current assets		
Inventory	–	
Receivables	5,000	
Bank	4,400	
	——	
		9,400
		——
		11,400
		——
Capital		10,000
Profit		1,300
Drawings		(100)
		——
		11,200
Current liabilities		
Payables		200
		——
		11,400
		——

Inventory

Chapter learning objectives

Upon completion of this chapter you will be able to:

- explain the need for adjustments for inventory in preparing financial statements

- illustrate income statements with opening and closing inventory

- explain and demonstrate how opening and closing inventory are recorded in the inventory account

- explain the IAS 2 requirements regarding the valuation of closing inventory

- define the cost and net realisable value of closing inventory

- discuss alternative methods of valuing inventory

- explain and demonstrate how to calculate the value of closing inventory from given movements in inventory levels, using FIFO (first in first out) and AVCO (average cost)

- assess the effect of using either FIFO or AVCO on both profit and asset value

- explain the IASB requirements for inventories

- explain the use of continuous and period-end inventory records.

1 Valuation of inventory

Inventory consists of:

- goods purchased for resale
- consumable stores (such as oil)
- raw materials and components (used in the production process)
- partly-finished goods (usually called **work in progress – WIP**)
- finished goods (which have been manufactured by the business).

IAS 2 Inventory

Inventory is included in the statement of financial position at:

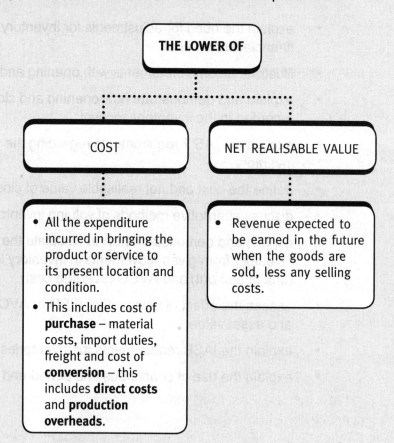

THE LOWER OF

COST

- All the expenditure incurred in bringing the product or service to its present location and condition.
- This includes cost of **purchase** – material costs, import duties, freight and cost of **conversion** – this includes **direct costs** and **production overheads**.

NET REALISABLE VALUE

- Revenue expected to be earned in the future when the goods are sold, less any selling costs.

Cost

Cost includes all the expenditure incurred in bringing the product or service to its present location and condition.

This includes:

- Cost of purchase – material costs, import duties, freight.

- Cost of conversion – this includes direct costs and production overheads.

Costs which must be **excluded** from the cost of inventory are:

- selling costs
- storage costs
- abnormal waste of materials, labour or other costs
- administrative overheads.

Cost vs NRV

Example

Gordano is a small furniture manufacturing company. All of its timber is imported from Scandinavia and there are only three basic products - bookcases, dining tables and cupboards. The company has 200 completed bookcases in inventory at the end of the year. For final accounts purposes, these will be stated at the lower of cost and net realisable value. How is 'cost' arrived at?

Solution

'Cost' will include several elements:

- Cost of purchase. First of all we must identify the timber used in the manufacture of bookcases (as opposed to dining tables and cupboards). The relevant costs will include the cost of the timber, the import duty and all the insurance and freight expenses associated with transporting the timber from Scandinavia to the factory.

- Cost of conversion. This will include costs which can be directly linked to the bookcases produced during the year. This includes labour costs 'booked' and sundry material costs (e.g. hinges and screws). Production overheads present particular problems. Costs such as factory heating and light, salaries of supervisors and depreciation of equipment are likely to relate to the three product ranges. These costs must be allocated to these product ranges on a reasonable basis. In particular, any percentage additions to cover overheads must be based on the normal level of production. If this provision was not made, the inventory could be overvalued at the end of a period of low production, because there would be a smaller number of items over which to spread the overhead cost.

These groups of cost must relate to either:

- bookcases sold during the year, or
- bookcases in inventory at the year-end (i.e. 200 bookcases).

NRV

The comparison between cost and NRV must be made item by item, not on the total inventory value. It may be acceptable to consider groups of items together if all are worth less than cost.

Test your understanding 1

Cole's business sells three products X, Y and Z. The following information was available at the year-end:

	X	Y	Z
	$	$	$
Cost	7	10	19
Net realisable value (NRV)	10	8	15
Units	100	200	300

What is the value of the closing inventory?

A $8,400

B $6,800

C $7,100

D $7,200

Test your understanding 2

In what circumstances might the NRV of inventories be lower than their cost?

Test your understanding 3

IAS 2 Inventories defines the items that may be included in computing the value of an inventory of finished goods manufactured by a business.

Which one of the following lists consists only of items which may be included in the statement of financial position value of such inventories according to IAS 2?

A Foreman's wages, carriage inwards, carriage outwards, raw materials

B Raw materials, carriage inwards, costs of storage of finished goods, plant depreciation

C Plant depreciation, carriage inwards, raw materials, foreman's wages

D Carriage outwards, raw materials, foreman's wages, plant depreciation

Inventory valuation

Inventory valuation

It can be a complicated procedure to arrive at the valuation placed on closing inventory, because:

- Initially the existence of the inventory, and the quantities thereof, have to be ascertained by means of an inventory count.

- Following on from this, a valuation has to be placed on the inventory which, as will be seen, may differ according to whatever accounting policy a company adopts.

The matching and prudence concept

*   The concept of matching justifies the carrying forward of purchases not sold by the end of the accounting period, to leave the remaining purchases to be 'matched' with sales.

    When it comes to placing a value on the inventory carried forward, we have a further concept to consider: the prudence concept.

    If it weren't for this concept, we would carry forward inventory at its cost to the business. The prudence concept, however, requires the application of a degree of caution in making estimates under conditions of uncertainty.

In the context of the value of inventory, this means that if goods are expected to be sold below cost after the statement of financial position date (for example, because they are damaged or obsolete), account must be taken of the loss in order to prepare the statement of financial position.

The amount at which inventory should be stated in the statement of financial position is the lower of cost and net realisable value.

Inventory records

Keeping inventory records

A business may choose to keep inventory records on a continuous basis throughout the year or only count inventory at the period end.

In preparing the financial statements, the calculation of what is in closing inventory can be a major exercise for a business. The business may need to count its inventory at the statement of financial position date. A formal title for the sheets recording the inventory count is 'period-end inventory records'.

An alternative would be to have records which show the amount of inventory at any date, i.e. continuous inventory records. These records may take a variety of forms but, in essence, a record of each item of inventory would be maintained showing all the receipts and issues for that item.

The merits of continuous inventory records are as follows:

- There is better information for inventory control.

- Excessive build up of certain lines of inventory whilst having insufficient inventory of other lines is avoided.

- Less work is needed to calculate inventory at the end of the accounting period.

The merits of period-end inventory records are as follows:

- They are cheaper in most situations than the costs of maintaining continuous inventory records.

- Even if there is a continuous inventory record, there will still be a need to check the accuracy of the information recorded by having a physical check of some of the inventory lines.

2 Adjustments for inventory in the financial statements

- In order to be able to prepare a set of financial statements, inventory must be accounted for at the end of the period.

- Opening inventory must be included in cost of sales as these goods are available for sale along with purchases during the year.

- Closing inventory must be deducted from cost of sales as these goods are held at the period end and have not been sold.

Profit

In order to be able to prepare a set of financial statements, it is first necessary to learn how to account for any items of goods held at the end of the year, i.e. closing inventory. (In some countries inventory is referred to as 'stock'.)

Example

A trader starts in business and by the end of his first year he has purchased goods costing $21,000 and has made sales totalling $25,000. Goods which cost him $3,000 have not been sold by the end of the year.

What profit has he made in the year?

Solution

The unsold goods are referred to as closing inventory. This inventory is deducted from purchases in the income statement.

Gross profit is thus:

	$	$
Sales revenue		25,000
Purchases	21,000	
Less: Closing inventory	(3,000)	
Cost of sales		(18,000)
Gross profit		7,000

Closing inventory of $3,000 will appear on the statement of financial position as an asset.

Illustration 1 – Adjustments for inventory

Peter buys and sells washing machines. He has been trading for many years. On 1 January 20X7, his opening inventory is 30 washing machines which cost $9,500. He purchased 65 machines in the year amounting to $150,000 and on 31 December 20X7 he has 25 washing machines left in inventory with a cost of $7,500. Peter has sold 70 machines with a sales value of $215,000 in the year.

Calculate the gross profit for the year ended 31 December 20X7.

Solution

Solution

- Gross profit is sales revenue less cost of sales.

- We must match the 70 machines sold with the cost of those machines and exclude from cost of sales the machines that are left in inventory.

- Opening inventory must be included in cost of sales as some of the goods sold during the year come from the goods the trader started off with at the beginning of the year.

KAPLAN PUBLISHING

- We can calculate the gross profit as follows:

	$	$
Sales revenue		215,000
Opening inventory (at cost)	9,500	
Purchases (at cost)	150,000	
	159,500	
Less: Closing inventory (at cost)	(7,500)	
Cost of sales		(152,000)
Gross profit		63,000

3 Recording inventory in the ledger accounts

- Inventory is only recorded in the ledger accounts at the end of the accounting period.

- In the inventory ledger account the opening inventory will be the brought forward balance from the previous period. This must be transferred to the income statement ledger account with the following entry:

  Dr Income statement (Ledger account)

  Cr Inventory (Ledger account).

- The closing inventory is entered into the ledger accounts with the following entry:

  Dr Inventory (Ledger account)

  Cr Income statement (Ledger account).

- Once these entries have been completed, the income statement ledger account contains both opening and closing inventory and the inventory ledger account shows the closing inventory for the period to be shown in the statement of financial position.

Illustration 2 – Recording inventory in the ledger accounts

Continuing from previous Illustration, we will now see how the ledger accounts for inventory are prepared.

We will look at the ledger accounts at the following times:

(a) Immediately before extracting a trial balance at 31 December 20X7.

(b) Immediately after the year-end adjustments and closing off of the ledger accounts.

(a) **Ledger accounts before extracting a trial balance**

Inventory

20X7	$		$
1 Jan Balance b/f	9,500		

The inventory is an asset and therefore is a debit entry in the inventory account.

Purchases

20X7	$		$
Various suppliers	150,000		

Sales revenue

	$	20X7	$
		Various customers	215,000

- The balance of $9,500 in inventory account originated from last year's statement of financial position when it appeared as closing inventory. This figure remains unchanged in the inventory account until the very end of the year when closing inventory at 31 December 20X7 is considered.

- The closing inventory figure is not usually provided to us until after we have extracted the trial balance at 31 December 20X7.

- The purchases and sales figures have been built up over the year and represent the year's accumulated transactions.

- The trial balance will include opening inventory, purchases and sales revenue in respect of the inventory transactions.

(b) Ledger accounts reflecting the closing inventory

- Closing inventory for accounting purposes has been valued at $7,500.

Step 1

The income statement forms part of the double entry. At the year end the accumulated totals from the sales and purchases accounts must be transferred to it using the following journal entries:

Dr Sales revenue	$215,000
Cr Income statement	$215,000
Dr Income statement	$150,000
Cr Purchases	$150,000

These transfers are shown in the ledger accounts below.

Step 2

The opening inventory figure ($9,500) must also be transferred to the income statement account in order to arrive at cost of sales.

Dr Income statement $9,500 Cr Inventory $9,500

Step 3

The income statement cannot be completed (and hence gross profit calculated) until the closing inventory is included.

Dr Inventory $7,500 Cr Income statement $7,500

After summarising and balancing off, the ledger then becomes:

Inventory

20X7	$	20X7	$
1 Jan Balance b/f	9,500	31 Dec Income statement	9,500
31 Dec Income statement	7,500	31 Dec Balance c/f	7,500
	17,000		17,000
20X8			
1 Jan Balance b/f	7,500		

Purchases

20X7	$	20X7	$
Various dates		31 Dec	
Payables	150,000	Income statement	150,000

Sales revenue

20X7	$	20X7	$
31 Dec		Various dates	
Income statement	215,000	Receivables	215,000

Income statement ('T' account form)

20X7	$	20X7	$
31 Dec		31 Dec	
Purchases	150,000	Sales revenue	215,000
Inventory	9,500	Inventory	7,500
Gross profit c/f	63,000		
	222,500		222,500
		Gross profit b/f	63,000

Key points

Key points:

- The sales revenue and the purchases accounts are cleared out to and summarised in the income statement.

- Opening inventory is cleared out to the income statement and closing inventory is entered into the inventory account and the income statement.

- The balance on the inventory account remains at the end of the period and is listed in the statement of financial position under current assets as inventory.

- The first part of the income statement can be balanced at this stage to show the gross profit figure carried down and brought down.

- The above layout of the income statement is not particularly useful, but it assists the appreciation of the actual double entry processes and the realisation that the income statement is part of the double entry.

KAPLAN PUBLISHING

The more common layout of the first part of the income statement is:

	$	$
Sales revenue		215,000
Opening inventory	9,500	
Add: Purchases	150,000	
	159,500	
Less: Closing inventory	(7,500)	
Cost of sales		(152,000)
Gross profit		63,000

Test your understanding 4

The trading position of a simple cash-based business for its first week of trading was as follows:

	$
Capital introduced by the owner	1,000
Purchases for cash	800
Sales for cash	900

At the end of the week there were goods which had cost $300 left in inventory.

Write up the ledger accounts for the first week, including the income statement, and then prepare a vertical income statement together with a statement of financial position at the end of the first week.

Test your understanding 5

The business described in Test your understanding 1 now continues into its second week. Its transactions are as follows:

	$
Sales for cash	1,000
Purchases for cash	1,100

The goods left in inventory at the end of this second week originally cost $500.

Write up the ledger accounts for the second week, including the income statement, and then prepare a vertical income statement together with a statement of financial position at the end of the second week.

4 Drawings of inventory

It is not unusual for a sole trader to take inventory from their business for their own use. This type of transaction is a form of drawings.

The correct double entry to account for such drawings is:

Dr Drawings	cost of inventory taken
Cr Cost of sales	cost of inventory taken

The credit entry ensures that the cost of inventory taken is not included as part of the cost of inventory sold in the income statement.

5 Methods of calculating cost of inventory

Method	Key points	
Unit cost	This is the actual cost of purchasing identifiable units of inventory.	Only used when items of inventory are individually distinguishable and of high value
FIFO – first in first out	For costing purposes, the first items of inventory received are assumed to be the first ones sold.	The cost of closing inventory is the cost of the younger inventory.
AVCO – Average cost	The cost of an item of inventory is calculated by taking the average of all inventory held.	The average cost can be calculated periodically or continuously.

Test your understanding 6

Sam started her business on 1 January and provides details of the following transactions:

Purchases

(1) January 5 units at $4/unit
(2) January 5 units at $5/unit
(3) January 5 units at $5.50/unit

She then sold 7 units for $10/unit on 5 January.

(a) Calculate the value of the closing inventory at the end of the first week of trading using the FIFO and the AVCO methods.

(b) Prepare the income statement for the first week of trading under both FIFO and AVCO.

Test your understanding 7

A business commenced on 1 January and purchases are made as follows:

Month	No of units	Unit price $	Value $
Jan	380	2.00	760
Feb	400	2.50	1,000
Mar	350	2.50	875
Apr	420	2.75	1,155
May	430	3.00	1,290
Jun	440	3.25	1,430
	2,420		6,510

In June, 1,420 articles were sold for $7,000.

What is the cost of closing inventory and gross profit for the period using the FIFO method:

	Closing inventory	Gross profit
	$	$
A	2,690	3,180
B	2,310	2,800
C	3,077	3,567

Profit and Statement of financial position

The impact of valuation methods on profit and the statement of financial position.

Different valuation methods will result in different closing inventory values.

This will in turn impact both profit and statement of financial position asset value.

Similarly any incorrect valuation of inventory will impact the financial statements.

If inventory is overvalued then:

- assets are overstated in the statement of financial position
- profit is overstated in the income statement (as cost of sales is too low)

If inventory is undervalued then:

- assets are understated in the statement of financial position
- profit is understated in the income statement (as cost of sales is too high).

6 Disclosure

Inventories

Inventories are valued at the lower of cost and net realisable value. They will be analysed as follows in the notes to the accounts:

	20XX £000
Raw materials and consumables	X
Work in progress	X
Finished goods and goods for resale	X
	‾‾‾
	X
	‾‾‾

Chapter summary

```
                    ┌─────────────────────────┐
                    │        INVENTORY        │
                    │   Valued at the lower   │
                    │     of cost and NVR     │
                    └─────────────────────────┘
```

ADJUSTMENTS FOR INVENTORY

Opening inventory must be transferred to the income statement, closing inventory must be entered into the accounts at the year end.

VALUATION OF INVENTORY

Methods used:
- Unit cost
- FIFO
- AVCO

IAS 2 INVENTORIES

Provides rules on valuation of inventory as well as disclosure requirements

RECORD INVENTORY IN THE LEDGER ACCOUNTS

Closing inventory:

Dr Inventory a/c
Cr Income statement ledger

Drawings of Inventory:

Dr Drawings
Cr Cost of Sales

Test your understanding answers

Test your understanding 1

The correct answer is B

X	$7	(cost) x 100	=	$700
Y	$8	(NRV) x 200	=	$1,600
Z	$15	(NRV) x 300	=	$4,500
				_____
Total				$6,800

Test your understanding 2

NRV may be relevant in special cases, such as where goods are slow-moving, damaged or obsolete. However, most items of inventory will be stated at cost.

Test your understanding 3

The correct answer is C

The other three answers contain items which cannot be included in inventory according to IAS 2.

Test your understanding 4

First, the transactions are entered into the ledger accounts, and the accounts are balanced. Revenue and purchases are then transferred to the income statement ledger account.

Capital

	$		$
		Cash	1,000

Cash

	$		$
Capital	1,000	Purchases	800
Sales revenue	900	Balance c/f	1,100
	─────		─────
	1,900		1,900
	─────		─────
Balance b/f	1,100		

Sales revenue

	$		$
Income statement	900	Cash	900
	────		────

Purchases

	$		$
Cash	800	Income statement	800
	────		────

Next, the closing inventory must be accounted for in the inventory account and the income statement account. There is no opening inventory as this is the first week of trading for the business.

Inventory

	$		$
Income statement	300		

Income statement

	$		$
Purchases	800	Sales revenue	900
Gross profit c/f	400	Closing inventory	300
	1,200		1,200
		Gross profit b/f	400

The income statement is prepared in the vertical format by rearranging the income statement ledger account

Income Statement for Week 1

	$	$
Sales Revenue		900
Cost of goods sold:		
Purchases	800	
Less: Closing inventory	(300)	
		(500)
Gross Profit		400

The statement of financial position is prepared by listing the balances brought down from the ledger accounts.

Statement of financial position as at Week 1

Inventory	300
Cash	1,100
	1,400
Capital	1,000
Profit for the week	400
	1,400

Test your understanding 5

First, the ledger accounts must be written up. You must remember that there are opening balances on the statement of financial position accounts (cash and capital) but the income statement accounts have no opening balances as they were transferred to the income statement in Week 1.

Cash

	$		$
Balance b/f	1,100	Purchases	1,100
Sales Revenue	1,000	Balance c/f	1,000
	2,100		2,100
Balance b/f	1,000		

Sales revenue

	$		$
Income statement	1,000	Cash	1,000

Purchases

	$		$
Cash	1,100	Income statement	1,100

Income statement

	$		$
Purchases	1,100	Sales revenue	1,000

The opening inventory must be transferred to the income statement, and the closing inventory entered into the ledger accounts (inventory and income statement) leaving the balance carried forward which will be included in the statement of financial position.

Inventory

	$		$
Balance b/f	300	Income statement	300
Income statement	500		

Income statement

	$		$
Purchases	1,100	Sales revenue	1,000
Opening inventory	300	Closing inventory	500
Gross profit c/f	100		
	1,500		1,500
		Gross profit b/f	100

Income statement for week 2

	$	$
Sales revenue		1,000
Cost of goods sold:		
Opening inventory	300	
Purchases	1,100	
	1,400	
Less: Closing inventory	(500)	
		(900)
Gross profit		100

Statement of financial position as at week 2

	$
Inventory	500
Cash	1,000
	1,500
Capital at start of Week 2	1,400
Profit for Week 2	100
	1,500

Test your understanding 6

Units purchased (5 x 3) = 15

Units sold = 7
_____

Closing inventory = 8

(a) **FIFO**

3 units @ $5 =	$15.00
5 units @ $5.50 =	$27.50
	$42.50

AVCO Average cost per unit: ((5 x $4) + (5 x $5) + (5 x $5.50))/15 = $4.83

Closing inventory = 8 x $4.83 = $38.64

(b) FIFO

	$	$
Sales (7 x $10)		70
Cost of sales		
Purchases (5 x $4) + (5 x $5) + (5 x $5.50)	72.50	
Less: Closing inventory	(42.50)	
		(30)
Profit		40

	$	$
Sales (7 x $10)		70
Cost of sales		
Purchases (5 x $4) + (5 x $5) + (5 x $5.50)	72.50	
Less: Closing inventory	(38.64)	
		(33.86)
Profit		36.14

Test your understanding 7

- The correct answer is C
- Inventory valuation (inventory in hand 2,420 – 1,420 = 1,000 units)
- FIFO – inventory valued at latest purchase prices

		$
440	articles at $3.25	1,430
430	articles at $3.00	1,290
130	articles at $2.75	357
1,000		3,077

Calculation of gross profit:

	$	$
Sales revenue		7,000
Purchases	6,510	
Less:		
Closing inventory	(3,077)	
Cost of goods sold		(3,433)
Gross profit		3,567

Test your understanding 7

KAPLAN PUBLISHING

5

Sales tax

Chapter learning objectives

Upon completion of this chapter you will be able to:

- explain the general principles of the operation of a sales tax
- calculate sales tax on transactions correctly
- enter sales tax on sales and purchases into the ledger accounts.

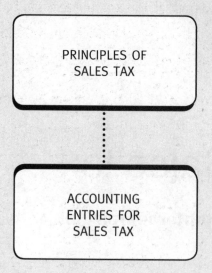

1 Principles of sales tax

- A business that is registered for sales tax is essentially a collection agent for the government.

- Sales tax is charged on purchases (input tax) and sales (output tax).

- Sales tax is excluded from the reported sales and purchases of the business.

- Periodically the business pays the sales tax to the tax authorities.

- If output tax exceeds input tax, the business pays the excess to the tax authorities.

- If input tax exceeds output tax, the business is repaid the excess by the tax authorities.

- Sales tax is sometimes called value added tax (VAT) or goods and services tax.

- Sales tax is charged on most goods and services.

2 Calculation of sales tax

- It is common for a rate of 17.5% sales tax to be charged on the selling price.

- The following is therefore true:

Proforma

Net selling price (tax exclusive price)	100.0%
Sales tax	10.0%
Gross selling price (tax inclusive price)	110.0%

- The net selling price is the amount that the business wishes to achieve.
- The gross selling price is the price charged to customers.
- The difference is paid to the tax authorities.

Note: You should be prepared to apply any % to the proforma above.

Illustration 1 – Calculation of sales tax

Calculation of sales tax

Orlando sells the following goods:

(1) to Bruno at a tax inclusive price of $470.
(2) to Cosmo at a tax exclusive price of $700.

How much sales tax is Orlando collecting on behalf of the government if the rate of sales tax is 17.5%?

Solution

Solution

Sales tax can be calculated using the relevant percentage depending on whether the price is tax inclusive or exclusive.

Sales to Bruno (sales price tax inclusive) (17.5%/117.5%) x $470 = $70

Sales to Cosmo (sales price tax exclusive) (17.5%/100%) x $700 = $122.50

Total sales tax collected: $70 + $122.50 = $192.50

Test your understanding 1

Lorenzo purchases goods for $170,625 (including sales tax) and sells goods for $230,500 (including sales tax).

What amount of sales tax is ultimately payable to the tax authorities?

A $8,918

B $14,926

C $4,471

D $10,479

The sales tax rate is 17.5%.

3 Accounting entries for sales tax

The usual bookkeeping entries for purchases and sales are only slightly amended by sales tax, the main addition being the introduction of a sales tax account, which is a receivable or payable account with the tax authorities.

Sales tax paid on purchases (input tax)

Dr Purchases – excluding sales tax (net cost)

Dr Sales tax (sales tax)

Cr Payables/cash – including sales tax (gross cost)

- The purchases account does not include sales tax because it is not an expense – it will be recovered.

- The payables account does include sales tax, as the supplier must be paid the full amount due.

Sales tax charged on sales (output tax)

Dr Receivables/cash – sales price including sales tax (gross selling price)

Cr Sales – sales price excluding sales tax (net selling price)

Cr Sales tax (sales tax)

- The sales account does not include sales tax because it is not income – it will have to be paid to the tax authorities.

- The receivables account does include sales tax, as the customer must pay the full amount due.

Payment of sales (output) tax

Dr Sales tax (amount paid)

Cr Cash (amount paid)

- If output tax exceeds input tax, a payment must be made to the tax authorities.

Receipt of sales (output) tax

Dr Cash (amount received)

Cr Sales tax (amount received)

- If input tax exceeds output tax, there will be a receipt from the tax authorities.

Test your understanding 2

		Net	Sales tax	Total
		$	$	$
Purchases	(all on credit)	180,000	31,500	211,500
Sales	(all on credit)	260,000	45,500	305,500

Record these transactions in the ledger accounts.

Test your understanding 3

Valerie's business is registered for sales tax purposes. During the quarter ending 31 March 20X6, she made the following sales, all of which were subject to sales tax at 17.5%:

$10,000 excluding sales tax

$7,402 including sales tax

$6,745 excluding sales tax

$11,632 including sales tax.

She also made the following purchases all of which were subject to sales tax at 17.5%:

$15,000 excluding sales tax

$12,455 including sales tax

$11,338 including sales tax

$9,870 including sales tax.

What is the balance on the sales tax account on 31 March 20X6?

A $7,639 Dr

B $1,875 Dr

C $7,639 Cr

D $1,875 Cr

Chapter summary

Principles of sales tax

- It is charged on purchases and sales.
- It is excluded from the reported sales and purchases of the business.
- The business is a collection agent for the government.
- It is paid periodically to the tax authorities (or it is repaid to the business if taxable purchases exceed sales).

Accounting entries for sales tax

- Sales and purchases ledger accounts are net of sales tax.
- Receivables and payables ledger accounts are inclusive of sales tax as the business collects the sales tax from customers and pays it to suppliers.
- The sales tax account is a payable (or receivable) account in the statement of financial position.

Test your understanding answers

Test your understanding 1

The correct answer is A

	$
Output tax:	
Sales (including sales tax)	230,500
Sales tax (17.5/117.5)	34,330
Input tax:	
Purchases (including sales tax)	170,625
Sales tax (17.5/117.5)	25,412
Payable to tax authorities:	
Output tax – Input tax (34,330 – 25,412)	8,918

Test your understanding 2

Sales

	$		$
		Receivables	260,000
			260,000

Note that sales are recorded excluding sales tax, as this is not income for the business.

Purchases

	$		$
Payables	180,000		
	180,000		

Note that purchases are recorded net of sales tax, as this is not a cost to the business.

Receivables

	$		$
Sales/Sales tax	305,500		
	305,500		

Receivables are recorded including sales tax (the gross amount) as the customer must pay to the business the cost of the goods plus the sales tax.

Payables

	$		$
		Purchases/Sales tax	211,500
			211,500

As with receivables, the payables must be recorded inclusive of sales tax, as the business needs to pay its suppliers the gross amount.

Sales tax account (a personal account with tax authorities)

	$		$
Payables	31,500	Receivables	45,500
Balance c/f	14,000		————
	————		45,500
	45,500		————
	————	Balance b/f	14,000
			————

Note: As the balance on the sales tax account represents a normal trade liability it is included in accounts payable on the statement of financial position.

Test your understanding 3

The correct answer is B

Sales tax

Purchases:	$	Sales:	$
15,000 x 17.5%	2,625	10,000 x 17.5%	1,750
12,455 x 17.5/117.5	1,855	7,402 x 17.5/117.5	1,102
11,338 x 17.5/117.5	1,689	6,745 x 17.5%	1,180
9,870 x 17.5/117.5	1,470	11,632 x 17.5/117.5	1,732
		Balance b/f	1,875
	————		————
	7,639		7,639
	————		————
Balance b/f	1,875		

6

Accruals and prepayments

Chapter learning objectives

Upon completion of this chapter you will be able to:

- explain the need for adjustments for accruals and prepayments in preparing financial statements
- illustrate the process of adjusting for accruals and prepayments in preparing financial statements.

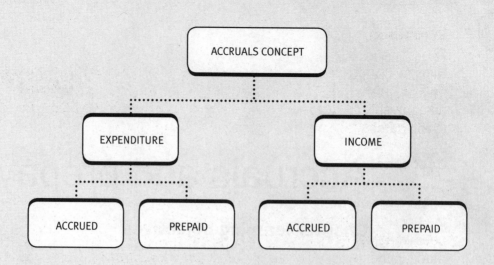

1 Accruals basis of accounting

The accruals basis of accounting means that to calculate the profit for the period, we must include all the income and expenditure relating to the period, whether or not the cash has been received or paid or an invoice received.

Profit is therefore:

Income earned	X
Expenditure incurred	(X)
	───
Profit	X

Accruals concept

The accruals concept is identified as an important accounting concept by IAS 1 Presentation of Financial Statements. The concept is that income and expenses should be matched together and dealt with in the income statement for the period to which they relate, regardless of the period in which the cash was actually received or paid. Therefore all of the expenses involved in making the sales for a period should be matched with the sales income and dealt with in the period in which the sales themselves are accounted for.

Sales revenue

The sales revenue for an accounting period is included in the income statement when the sales are made. This means that, when a sale is made on credit, it is recognised in the income statement when the agreement is made and the invoice is sent to the customer rather than waiting until the cash for the sale is received. This is done by setting up a receivable in the statement of financial position for the amount of cash that is due from the sale (debit receivables and credit sales revenue).

Purchases

Similarly purchases are matched to the period in which they were made by accounting for all credit purchases when they took place and setting up a payable in the statement of financial position for the amount due (debit purchases and credit payables).

Cost of sales

The major cost involved in making sales in a period is the actual cost of the goods that are being sold. As we saw in a previous chapter, we need to adjust for opening and closing inventory to ensure that the sales made in the period are matched with the actual costs of those goods. Any goods unsold are carried forward to the next period so that they are accounted for when they are actually sold.

Expenses

The expenses of the period that the business has incurred in making its sales, such as rent, electricity and telephone, must also be matched with the sales for the period. This means that the actual expense incurred in the period should be included in the income statement rather than simply the amount of the expense that has been paid in cash.

2 Accrued expenditure

An accrual arises where expenses of the business, relating to the year, have not been paid by the year end.

In this case, it is necessary to record the extra expense relevant to the year and create a corresponding statement of financial position liability (called an accrual):

Dr Expense account   X

Cr Accrual   X

An accrual will therefore reduce profit in the income statement.

Illustration 1 – Accrued expenditure

Accrued expenditure

A business' electricity charges amount to $12,000 pa. In the year to 31 December 20X5, $9,000 has been paid. The electricity for the final quarter is paid in January 20X6.

What year-end accrual is required and what is the electricity expense for the year?

Show the relevant entries in the ledger accounts.

Solution

Solution

- The total expense charged to the income statement in respect of electricity should be $12,000.

- The year-end accrual is the $3,000 expense that has not been paid in cash.

- The double entry required is:

- Dr Electricity expense $3,000

- Cr Accruals $3,000

Ledger accounts and accrued expenses

Method 1: know the accrual

Electricity expense

	$		$
Cash	9,000	Income statement (ß)	12,000
Accrual c/f	3,000		
	12,000		12,000
		Accrual b/f	3,000

Method 2: know the income statement charge

Electricity expense

	$		$
Cash	9,000	Income statement	12,000
Accrual c/f (ß)	3,000		
	———		———
	12,000		12,000
	———		———
		Accrual b/f	3,000

Test your understanding 1

John Simnel's business has an accounting year end of 31 December 20X1. He rents factory space at a rental cost of $5,000 per quarter, payable in arrears.

During the year to 31 December 20X1 his cash payments of rent have been as follows:

- 31 March (for the quarter to 31 March 20X1) $5,000
- 29 June (for the quarter to 30 June 20X1) $5,000
- 2 October (for the quarter to 30 September 20X1) $5,000

The final payment due on 31 December 20X1 for the quarter to that date was not paid until 4 January 20X2.

Show the ledger accounts required to record the above transactions.

Accrued expenditure will reduce profit in the Income statement and will also create a current liability on the Statement of financial position.

For example, if we were to put through an accrual of $500 for telephone expenses. The double entry would be:

Dr Telephone expenses $500

Cr Accruals $500

The additional telephone expense would reduce profits by $500. The additional accrual would increase our current liabilities by $500.

3 Prepaid expenditure

A prepayment arises where some of the following year's expenses have been paid in the current year.

In this case, it is necessary to remove that part of the expense which is not relevant to this year and create a corresponding statement of financial position asset (called a prepayment):

Dr Prepayment   X

Cr Expense account   X

A prepayment will therefore increase profit in the income statement.

Illustration 2 – Prepaid expenditure

The annual insurance charge for a business is $24,000 pa. $30,000 was paid on 1 January 20X5 in respect of future insurance charges.

What is the year-end prepayment and what is the insurance expense for the year?

Show the relevant entries in the ledger accounts.

Solution to recording accrued expenditure

Solution

- The total expense charged to the income statement in respect of insurance should be $24,000.

- The year-end prepayment is the $6,000 that has been paid in respect of 20X6.

The double entry required is:

Dr Prepayment $6,000

Cr Insurance expense $6,000

Insurance – expense

	$		$
Cash	30,000	Income statement	24,000
		Prepayments c/f	6,000
	_____		_____
	30,000		30,000
	_____		_____

Test your understanding 2

Tubby Wadlow pays the rental expense on his market stall in advance. He starts business on 1 January 20X5 and on that date pays $1,200 in respect of the first quarter's rent. During his first year of trade he also pays the following amounts:

- 3 March (in respect of the quarter ended 30 June) $1,200
- 14 June (in respect of the quarter ended 30 September) $1,200
- 25 September (in respect of the quarter $1,400 ended 31 December)
- 13 December (in respect of the first quarter of 20X6) $1,400

Show these transactions in the rental expense account.

Prepaid expenditure increases profit on the Income statement and also creates a current asset to be included on the Statement of financial position.

For example, if we were to put a prepayment of $1,000 in our financial statements for insurance, the double entry would be:

Dr Prepayments $1,000

Cr Insurance expense $1,000

The prepayments side would increase our current assets by the $1,000. The insurance expense would decrease by the $1,000, and hence increase our overall profits.

Proforma expense T account

Expense

	$		$
Balance b/f (opening prepaid expense)	X	Balance b/f (opening accrued expense)	X
Bank (total paid during the year)	X	Income statement (total expense for the year)	X
Balance c/f (closing accrued expense)	X	Balance c/f (closing prepaid expense)	X
	X		X
Balance b/f (opening prepaid expense)	X	Balance b/f (opening accrued expense)	X

Test your understanding 3

On 1 January 20X5, Willy Mossop owed $2,000 in respect of the previous year's electricity. Willy made the following payments during the year ended 31 December 20X5:

- 6 February $2,800
- 8 May $3,000
- 5 August $2,750
- 10 November $3,100

At 31 December 20X5, Willy calculated that he owed $1,800 in respect of electricity for the last part of the year.

What is the electricity charge to the income statement?

A $1,800

B $11,450

C $11,650

D $13,450

KAPLAN PUBLISHING

4 Accrued income

Accrued income arises where income has been earned in the accounting period but has not yet been received.

In this case, it is necessary to record the extra income in the income statement and create a corresponding asset in the statement of financial position (called accrued income):

Dr Accrued income (SFP) X

Cr Income (IS) X

Accrued income creates an additional current asset on our Statement of financial position. It also creates additional income on our Income statement, and hence this will increase overall profits.

Illustration 3 – Accrued income

Accrued income

A business earns bank interest income of $300 per month. $3,000 bank interest income has been received in the year to 31 December 20X5.

What is the year-end asset and what is the bank interest income for the year?

Show the relevant entries in the ledger accounts.

Solution to recording prepaid expenditure

Solution

- The total amount credited to the income statement in respect of interest should be $3,600 (12 x $300).

- The year-end accrued income asset is the $600 that has not yet been received.

The double entry required is:

Dr Accrued income (SFP) $600

Cr Bank interest income (IS) $600

Bank interest income			
	$		$
Income statement	3,600	Bank	3,000
		Accrued income c/f	600
	_____		_____
	3,600		3,600
	_____		_____
Accrued income b/f	600		

5 Prepaid income

Prepaid income arises where income has been received in the accounting period but which relates to the next accounting period.

In this case, it is necessary to remove the income not relating to the year from the income statement and create a corresponding liability in the statement of financial position (called prepaid income):

Dr Income (IS)   X

Cr Prepaid Income (SFP)   X

Illustration 4 – Prepaid income

Prepaid income

A business rents out a property at an income of $4,000 per month. $64,000 has been received in the year ended 31 December 20X5.

What is the year-end liability and what is the rental income for the year?

Show the relevant entries in the ledger accounts.

Solution

Solution

- The total amount credited to the income statement in respect of rent should be $48,000 (12 x $4,000).

- The year-end prepaid income liability is the $16,000 ($64,000 – $48,000) that has been received in respect of next year.

The double entry required is:

Dr Rental income $16,000

Cr Prepaid income (SFP) $16,000

Rental income

	$		$
Income statement	48,000	Cash	64,000
	———		———
Prepaid income c/f	16,000		64,000
	———		———
	64,000	Prepaid income b/f	16,000

Prepaid income reduces income on the Income statement and hence reduces overall profits too. It also creates a current liability on our Statement of financial position.

Proforma income T account

Income

	$		$
Balance b/f (opening accrued income)	X	Balance b/f (opening prepaid income)	X
Income statement (total revenue for the year)	X	Cash (total received during the year)	X
Balance c/f (closing prepaid income)	X	Balance c/f (closing accrued income)	X
	—		—
	X		X
	—		—
Balance b/f (opening accrued income)	X	Balance b/f (opening prepaid income)	X

Test your understanding 4

Accrued and prepaid income

Libby Farquar receives income from two rental units as follows:

	Unit 1		Unit 2	
Period	$	Received	$	Received
1.10.X4 – 31.12.X4	2,100	30.9.X4	1,300	2.1.X5
1.1.X5 – 31.3.X5	2,150	27.12.X4	1,300	4.4.X5
1.4.X5 – 30.6.X5	2,150	25.3.X5	1,300	1.7.X5
1.7.X5 – 30.9.X5	2,200	21.6.X5	1,400	6.10.X5
1.10.X5 – 31.12.X5	2,200	21.9.X5	1,400	2.1.X6
1.1.X6 – 31.3.X6	2,200	29.12.X5	1,400	4.4.X6

What is Libby's rental income in the income statement for the year ended 31 December 20X5?

A $5,400

B $8,700

C $14,000

D $14,100

Chapter summary

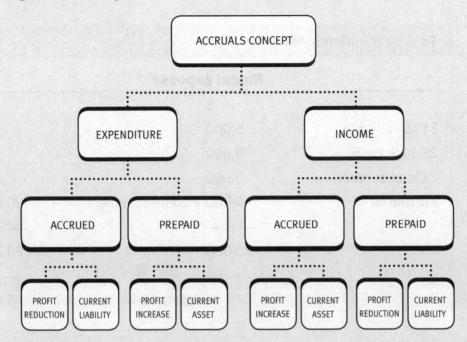

Test your understanding answers

Test your understanding 1

Rental expense

	$		$
31 March cash	5,000		
29 June cash	5,000		
2 October cash	5,000		
Accrual c/f	5,000	Income statement	20,000
	20,000		20,000
		Accrual b/f	5,000

Test your understanding 2

Rental expense

	$		$
1 January cash	1,200		
3 March cash	1,200		
14 June cash	1,200		
25 September cash	1,400	Income statement	5,000
13 December cash	1,400	Prepayment c/f	1,400
	6,400		6,400
Prepayment b/f	1,400		

Test your understanding 3

The correct answer is B

Electricity expense

	$		$
6 February cash	2,800	Accrual b/f	2,000
8 May cash	3,000		
5 August cash	2,750		
10 November cash	3,100	Income statement	11,450
Accrual c/f	1,800		
	———		———
	13,450		13,450
	———		———
		Accrual b/f	1,800

Test your understanding 4

The correct answer is D

Rental income (Unit 1)

	$		$
		Prepaid income b/f	2,150
		25.3.X5 cash	2,150
		21.6.X5 cash	2,200
Income statement	8,700	21.9.X5 cash	2,200
Prepaid income c/f	2,200	29.12.X5 cash	2,200
	———		———
	10,900		10,900
	———		———
		Prepaid income b/f	2,200

Rental income (Unit 2)

	$		$
Accrued income b/f	1,300	2.1.X5 cash	1,300
		4.4.X5 cash	1,300
		1.7.X5 cash	1,300
Income statement	5,400	6.10.X5 cash	1,400
		Accrued income c/f	1,400
	6,700		6,700
Accrued income b/f	1,400		

Total income: $8,700 + $5,400 = $14,100

Irrecoverable debts and allowances for receivables

Chapter learning objectives

Upon completion of this chapter you will be able to:

- identify the benefits and costs of offering credit facilities to customers
- explain the purpose of an aged receivables analysis
- explain the purpose of credit limits
- prepare the bookkeeping entries to write off an irrecoverable debt
- record an irrecoverable debt recovered
- identify the impact of irrecoverable debts on the income statement and statement of financial position
- prepare the bookkeeping entries to create and adjust an allowance for receivables
- illustrate how to include movements in the allowance for receivables in the income statement and how the closing balance of the allowance should appear in the statement of financial position.

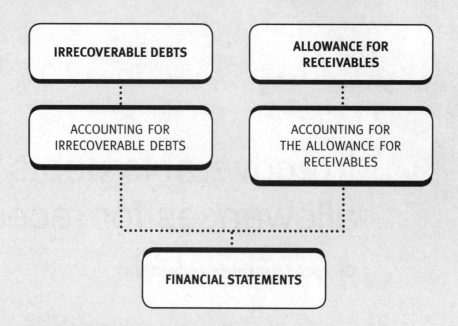

1 The provision of credit facilities

The majority of businesses will sell to their customers on credit and state a defined time within which they must pay (a credit period). The main benefits and costs of doing so are as follows:

Benefits/costs

Benefits

- The business may be able to enter new markets.
- There is a possibility of increased sales.
- Customer loyalty may be encouraged.

Costs

- Can be costly in terms of lost interest since the business is accepting payment later.
- Cash flow of the business may deteriorate.
- There is a potential risk of irrecoverable debts.

Aged receivables analysis

Where credit facilities are offered, it is normal for a business to maintain an aged receivables analysis.

- Analysis is usually a list, ordered by name, showing how much each customer owes and how old their debts are.

- The credit control function of a business uses the analysis to keep track of outstanding debts and follow up any that are overdue.

- Timely collection of debts improves cash flow and reduces the risk of them becoming irrecoverable.

Credit limits

It is also normal for a business to set a credit limit for each customer. This is the maximum amount of credit that the business is willing to provide.

The use of credit limits may:

- reduce risk to business of irrecoverable debts by limiting the amount sold on credit

- help build up the trust of a new customer

- be part of the credit control strategy of a business.

2 Irrecoverable debts

In this exam you must be prepared to see both the terms 'bad' and 'irrecoverable' debts being used frequently.

- The accruals concept dictates that when a sale is made, it is recognised in the accounts, regardless of whether or not the cash has been received.

- If sales are made on credit, there may be problems collecting the amounts owing from customers.

- Some customers may refuse to pay their debt or be declared bankrupt and unable to pay the amounts owing.

- Some customers may be in financial difficulties or may dispute the amount owed and there may be some doubt as to whether their debt will be paid.

- If it is highly unlikely that the amount owed by a customer will be received, then this debt is known as an irrecoverable debt. As it will probably never be received, it is written off by writing it out of the ledger accounts completely.

- If there is some doubt whether a customer can or will pay his debt, an allowance for receivables is created. These debts are not yet irrecoverable. However the creation of an **allowance for receivables** means that the possible loss is accounted for immediately, in line with the concept of prudence. The amount of the original debt will still remain in the ledger account just in case the customer does eventually pay.

Receivables and irrecoverable debts

Receivables and irrecoverable debts

If a sale is for cash, the customer pays for the goods immediately the sale is made. If the sale is on credit terms the customer will probably take the goods with him or arrange to have them delivered but he will not pay for the goods at that time. Instead, the customer will be given or sent an invoice detailing the goods and their price and the normal payment terms. This will tell the customer when he is expected to pay for those goods.

Under the accruals concept, a sale is included in the ledger accounts at the time that it is made.

For a cash sale, this will be when the cash or cheque is paid by the customer and the double entry will be:

　　Dr Cash

　　Cr Sales revenue

For a sale on credit, the sale is made at the time that the invoice is sent to the customer and therefore the accounting entries are made at that time as follows:

　　Dr Receivables

　　Cr Sales revenue

When the customer eventually settles the invoice the double entry will be:

　　Dr Cash account

　　Cr Receivables

This then clears out the balance on the customer's account.

3 Accounting for irrecoverable debts

An **irrecoverable debt** is a debt which is, or is considered to be, uncollectable.

With such debts it is prudent to remove them from the accounts and to charge the amount as an expense for irrecoverable debts to the income statement. The original sale remains in the accounts as this did actually take place.

The double entry required to achieve this is:

Dr Irrecoverable debts expense

Cr Receivables

Test your understanding 1

Araf & Co have total accounts receivable at the end of their accounting period of $45,000. Of these it is discovered that one, Mr Xiun who owes $790, has been declared bankrupt, and another who gave his name as Mr Jones has totally disappeared owing Araf & Co $1,240.

Calculate the effect in the financial statements of writing off these debts as irrecoverable.

4 Accounting for irrecoverable debts recovered

There is a possible situation where a debt is written off as irrecoverable in one accounting period, perhaps because the customer has been declared bankrupt, and the money, or part of the money, due is then unexpectedly received in a subsequent accounting period.

When a debt is written off the double entry is:

Dr Irrecoverable debts expense

Cr Receivables (removing the debt from the accounts)

When cash is received from a customer the normal double entry is:

Dr Cash

Cr Receivables

When an irrecoverable debt is recovered, the credit entry (above) cannot be taken to receivables as the debt has already been taken out of the receivables balance.

Instead the accounting entry is:

Dr Cash

Cr Irrecoverable debts expense

Some businesses may wish to keep a separate 'irrecoverable debts recovered' account to separate the actual cost of irrecoverable debts in the period.

Test your understanding 2

Celia Jones had receivables of $3,655 at 31 December 20X7. At that date she wrote off a debt from Lenny Smith of $699. During the year to 31 December 20X8 Celia made credit sales of $17,832 and received cash from her customers totalling $16,936. She also received the $699 from Lenny Smith that had already been written off in 20X7.

What is the final balance on the receivables account at 31 December 20X7 and 20X8?

	20X7	20X8
	$	$
A	2,956	3,852
B	2,956	3,153
C	3,655	4,551
D	3,655	3,852

---

5 Allowance for receivables

There may be some debts in the accounts where there is some cause for concern but they are not yet definitely irrecoverable.

It is prudent to recognise the possible expense of not collecting the debt in the income statement, but the receivable must remain in the accounts in case the customer does in fact pay up.

An allowance is set up which is a credit balance. This is netted off against trade receivables in the statement of financial position to give a net figure for receivables that are probably recoverable.

There are two types of allowance that may appear in the organisation's accounts:

- There will be some specific debts where the customer is known to be in financial difficulties, is disputing their invoice, or is refusing to pay for some other reason (bad service for example), and therefore the amount owing may not be recoverable. The allowance for such a debt is known as a **specific allowance**.

- The past experience and history of a business will indicate that not all of its trade receivables will be recoverable in full. It may not be possible to identify the amount that will not be paid but an estimate may be made that a certain percentage of customers are likely not to pay. An additional allowance will be made for these items, often known as a **general allowance**.

6 Accounting for the allowance for receivables

An allowance for receivables is set up with the following journal:

Dr Irrecoverable debts expense

Cr Allowance for receivables

If there is already an allowance for receivables in the accounts (opening allowance), only the movement in the allowance is charged to the income statement (closing allowance less opening allowance).

As the allowance can increase or decrease, there may be a debit or a credit in the irrecoverable debts account so the above journal may be reversed.

When calculating and accounting for a movement in the allowance for receivables, the following steps should be taken:

(1) Write off irrecoverable debts.

(2) Calculate the receivables balance as adjusted for the write-offs.

(3) Ascertain the specific allowance for receivables required.

(4) Deduct the debt specifically provided for from the receivables balance (be sure to deduct the full amount of debt rather than the amount of specific allowance).

(5) Multiply the remaining receivables balance by the general allowance percentage to give the general allowance required.

%(closing receivables – irrecoverable debts – debts specifically allowed for).

(6) Add the specific and general allowances required together.

(7) Compare to the brought forward allowance.

(8) Account for the change in allowance.

Illustration

On 31 December 20X1 Jake Williams had receivables of $10,000. From past experience Jake estimated that the equivalent of 3% of these customers were likely never to pay their debts and he therefore wished to make an allowance for this amount.

During 20X2 Jake made sales on credit totalling $100,000 and received cash from his customers of $94,000. He still considered that the equivalent of 3% of the closing receivables may never pay and should be allowed for.

During 20X3 Jake made sales of $95,000 and collected $96,000 from his receivables. At 31 December 20X3 Jake still considered that the equivalent of 3% of his receivables should be allowed for.

Calculate the allowance for receivables and the irrecoverable debt expense as well as the closing balance of receivables for each of the years 20X1, 20X2, 20X3.

Solution

20X1 Receivables

	$		$
At 31 December	10,000	Balance c/f	10,000
	10,000		10,000
Balance b/f	10,000		

Allowance required: $10,000 x 3%
= $300

Allowance for receivables

	$		$
Balance c/f	300	31 Dec	
		Irrecoverable debts	300
	300		300
		Balance b/f	300

Irrecoverable debts expense

	$		$
31 Dec		31 Dec	
Allowance for receivables	300	Income statement	300
	300		300

Statement of financial position presentation

	$	$
Current assets		
Receivables	10,000	
Less: Allowance for receivables	(300)	
		9,700

20X2 Receivables

	$		$
Balance b/f	10,000		
Sales	100,000	Cash	94,000
		Balance c/f	16,000
	110,000		110,000
Balance b/f	16,000		
Allowance required: $16,000 x 3% = $480			

Allowance for receivables

	$		$
		Balance b/f	300
Balance b/f	480	31 Dec	
		increase in allowance	180
	480		480
		Balance b/f	480

Irrecoverable debts expense

	$		$
31 Dec		31 Dec	
Allowance for receivables	180	Income statement	180
	180		180

Statement of financial position presentation

	$	$
Current assets		
Receivables	16,000	
Less: Allowance for receivables	(480)	
		15,520

20X3 Receivables

	$		$
Balance b/f	16,000		
Sales	95,000	Cash	96,000
		Balance	15,000
	111,000	c/f	
Balance b/f	15,000		111,000

Allowance required: $15,000 x 3%
= $450

Allowance for receivables

	$		$
31 Dec		Balance b/f	480
decrease in allowance	30		
Balance c/f	450		
	480		480
		Balance b/f	450

Irrecoverable debts expense

	$		$
31 Dec		31 Dec	
Income statement	30	Allowance for receivables	30
	30		30

Statement of financial position presentation

	$	$
Current assets		
Receivables	15,000	
Less: Allowance for receivables	(450)	
		14,550

Test your understanding 3

John Stamp has opening balances at 1 January 20X6 on his trade receivables account and allowance for receivables account of $68,000 and $3,400 respectively. During the year to 31 December 20X6 John Stamp makes credit sales of $354,000 and receives cash from his receivables of $340,000.

At 31 December 20X6 John Stamp reviews his receivables listing and acknowledges that he is unlikely ever to receive debts totalling $2,000. These are to be written off as irrecoverable. Past experience indicates that John should also make an allowance equivalent to 5% of his remaining receivables after writing off the irrecoverable debts.

What is the amount charged to John's income statement for irrecoverable debt expense in the year ended 31 December 20X6?

A $2,700

B $6,100

C $2,600

D $6,000

What will the effect be of Irrecoverable debts on both the Income Statement and the Statement of financial position?

Chapter summary

IRRECOVERABLE DEBTS
- Amounts that the business will not receive from its customers
- May be due to bankruptcy, fraud or disputes

ALLOWANCE FOR RECEIVABLES
- There may be some doubt as to the collectability of some of the business' receivables balances
- An allowance is made to recognise the possible expense of not receiving the cash

ACCOUNTING FOR IRRECOVERABLE DEBTS

To recognise the expense in the income statement:

Dr   Irrecoverable debts expense

Cr   Receivables

ACCOUNTING FOR THE ALLOWANCE FOR RECEIVABLES

To record an increase or setting up the allowance:

Dr   Irrecoverable debts expense

Cr   Allowance for receivables

The journal entry is reversed if the allowance is reduced

ACCOUNTING FOR IRRECOVERABLE DEBTS RECOVERED

The debt has been taken out of receivables, the journal is:

Dr Cash

Cr Debt

FINANCIAL STATEMENTS

STATEMENT OF FINANCIAL POSITION

Receivables	X
Allowance for receivables	(X)
Net receivables	X

INCOME STATEMENT

Charge for irrecoverable debts

=

Irrecoverable debts written off

+/−

Change in allowance for receivables

Test your understanding answers

Test your understanding 1

As the two debts are considered to be irrecoverable, they must be removed from receivables:

Receivables

	$		$
Balance at period end	45,000	Irrecoverable debts	
		– Mr Xiun	790
		Irrecoverable debts	
		– Mr Jones	1,240
		Balance c/f	42,970
	45,000		45,000
Balance b/f	42,970		

Irrecoverable debts expense

	$		$
Receivables			
– Mr Xiun	790		
Receivables			
– Mr Jones	1,240		
		Income statement	2,030
	2,030		2,030

Note that the sales revenue account has not been altered and the original sales to Mr Xiun and Mr Jones remain. This is because these sales actually took place and it is only after the sale that the expense of not being able to collect these debts has occurred.

Test your understanding 2

The correct answer is A

20X7 Receivables

	$		$
31 Dec	3,655	Irrecoverable debts	
		– Lenny Smith	699
		Balance c/f	2,956
	3,655		3,655
Balance b/f	2,956		

20X7 Irrecoverable debts expense

	$		$
Receivables			
– Lenny Smith	699	Income statement	699
	699		699

20X8 Receivables

	$		$
Balance b/f	2,956		
Sales	17,832	Cash received	16,936
		Balance c/f	3,852
	20,788		20,788
Balance b/f	3,852		

20X8 Irrecoverable debts expense

	$		$
Income statement	699	Cash	699
	699		699

Test your understanding 3

The correct answer is C

Receivables

20X6	$	20X6	$
1 Jan Balance b/f	68,000	31 Dec cash	340,000
31 Dec			
Sales revenue	354,000	31 Dec	
		Irrecoverable debts	2,000
		31 Dec	
		Balance c/f	80,000
	422,000		422,000
20X7			
1 Jan Balance b/f	80,000		

Irrecoverable debts expense

20X6	$	20X6	$
31 Dec Receivables	2,000		
31 Dec Allowance		31 Dec	
for receivables	600	Income statement	2,600
	2,600		2,600

KAPLAN PUBLISHING

Allowance for receivables

20X6	$	20X6	$
		1 Jan Balance b/f	3,400
31 Dec Balance c/f	4,000	31 Dec	
		Irrecoverable debts	600
	4,000		4,000
		20X7	
		1 Jan Balance b/f	4,000

Note that only the one irrecoverable debts expense account is used both to write off irrecoverable debts and to increase or decrease the allowance for receivables. There is no need to use separate accounts for each type of expense.

Working – Allowance for receivables

5% x $80,000 = $4,000

$4000 – b/f 3,400 = movement of 600

The **Statement of financial position** will show a receivables balance of 80,000. Underneath this separately the allowance for receivables c/f balance of 4,000 will be deducted to give a sub-total of $76,000.

The **Income statement** will show the $2,600 as an expense. This expense will cause a decrease in overall profits.

8

Non-current assets

Chapter learning objectives

Upon completion of this chapter you will be able to:

- define non-current assets

- distinguish between capital and revenue expenditure

- explain the function and purpose of an asset register

- explain and illustrate the ledger entries to record the acquisition of non-current assets

- define and explain the purpose of depreciation

- explain the straight-line and reducing balance methods of depreciation and make necessary calculations

- explain and illustrate how depreciation expense and accumulated depreciation are recorded in ledger accounts

- explain and illustrate how depreciation is presented in the income statement and statement of financial position

- explain the relevance of consistency and subjectivity in accounting for depreciation

- make the necessary adjustments if changes are made in the estimated useful life/residual value of a non-current asset

- explain and illustrate the ledger entries to record the disposal of non-current assets for cash

- explain and illustrate the ledger entries to record the disposal of non-current assets through part exchange

- explain and illustrate the inclusion of profits or losses on disposal in the income statement

- explain and record the revaluation of a non-current asset in ledger accounts and in the statement of financial position

- explain the impact of a revaluation on accounting for depreciation and disposal of a non-current asset

- explain and illustrate how non-current asset balances and movements are disclosed in company financial statements.

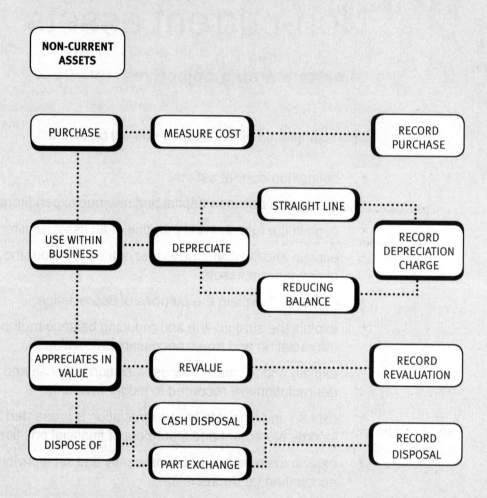

1 Non-current assets

Non-current assets are distinguished from current assets by the following characteristics: they:

- are long-term in nature

- are not normally acquired for resale

- are could be tangible or intangible

- are used to generate income directly or indirectly for a business

- are not normally liquid assets (i.e. not easily and quickly converted into cash without a significant loss in value).

2 Capital and revenue expenditure

It follows that a business' expenditure may be classified as one of two types:

CAPITAL EXPENDITURE	REVENUE EXPENDITURE
• Expenditure on the acquisition of non-current assets required for use in the business, not for resale. • Expenditure on existing non-current assets aimed at increasing their earning capacity.	• Expenditure on current assets. • Expenditure relating to running the business (such as administration costs). • Expenditure on maintaining the earning capacity of non-current assets e.g. repairs and renewals.
Capital expenditure is long-term in nature as the business intends to receive the benefits of the expenditure over a long period of time.	Revenue expenditure relates to the current accounting period and is used to generate revenue in the business.

3 Non-current asset registers

Non-current asset registers are, as the name suggests, a record of the non-current assets held by a business. These form part of the internal control system of an organisation.

Non-current asset register

Details held on such a register may include:

- cost
- date of purchase
- description of asset
- serial/reference number
- location of asset
- depreciation method
- expected useful life
- net book value.

4 Acquisition of a non-current asset

A non-current asset register is maintained in order to control non-current assets and keep track of what is owned and where it is kept.

It is periodically reconciled to the non-current asset accounts maintained in the general ledger.

- The cost of a non-current asset is any amount incurred to acquire the asset and bring it into working condition

Includes	Excludes
Capital expenditure such as	Revenue expenditure such as:
• purchase price	• repairs
• delivery costs	• renewals
• legal fees	• repainting
• subsequent expenditure which enhances the asset	

- The correct double entry to record the purchase is:

Dr Non-current asset X

Cr Bank/Cash/Payables X

- A separate cost account should be kept for each category of non-current asset, e.g. motor vehicles, fixtures and fittings.

Subsequent expenditure

Subsequent expenditure on the non-current asset can only be recorded as part of the cost (or capitalised), if it enhances the benefits of the asset, i.e. increases the revenues capable of being generated by the asset.

An example of subsequent expenditure which meets this criterion, and so can be capitalised, is an extension to a shop building which provides extra selling space.

An example of subsequent expenditure which does not meet this criterion is repair work. Any repair costs must be debited to the income statement, i.e. expensed.

Test your understanding 1

Acquisition of a non-current asset

Bilbo Baggins started a business providing limousine taxi services on 1 January 20X5. In the year to 31 December he incurred the following costs:

	$
Office premises	250,000
Legal fees associated with purchase of office	10,000
Cost of materials and labour to paint office in Bilbo's favourite colour, purple	300
Mercedes E series estate cars	116,000
Number plates for cars	210
Delivery charge for cars	180
Road licence fee for cars	480
Drivers' wages for first year of operation	60,000
Blank taxi receipts printed with Bilbo Baggins' business name and number	450

What amounts should be capitalised as 'Land and buildings' and 'Motor vehicles'?

	Land and buildings	Motor vehicles
A	260,000	116,390
B	250,000	116,870
C	250,300	116,390
D	260,300	116,870

5 Depreciation

- IAS 16 defines depreciation as 'the measure of the cost or revalued amount of the economic benefits of the tangible non-current asset that has been consumed during the period'.

- In simple terms, depreciation is a mechanism to reflect the cost of using a non-current asset.

- Depreciation matches the cost of using a non-current asset to the revenues generated by that asset over its useful life.

- Depreciation must also be matched to the pattern of use of the asset. This must be regularly reviewed and may be changed if the method no longer matches the usage of the asset.

- This is achieved by recording a depreciation charge each year, the effect of which is twofold ('the dual effect'):

  - Reduce the statement of financial position value of the non-current asset by cumulative depreciation to reflect the wearing out.

  - Record the depreciation charge as an expense in the income statement to match to the revenue generated by the non-current asset.

Depreciation

Depreciation may arise from:

- use

- physical wear and tear

- passing of time, e.g. a ten-year lease on a property

- obsolescence through technology and market changes, e.g. plant and machinery of a specialised nature

- depletion, e.g. the extraction of a mineral from a quarry.

The purpose of depreciation is not to show the asset at its current value in the statement of financial position, nor is it intended to provide a fund for the replacement of the asset. It is simply a method of allocating the cost of the asset over the periods estimated to benefit from its use (the useful life).

Land normally has an unlimited life and so does not require depreciation, but buildings should be depreciated.

Depreciation of an asset begins when it is available for use.

6 Methods of calculating depreciation

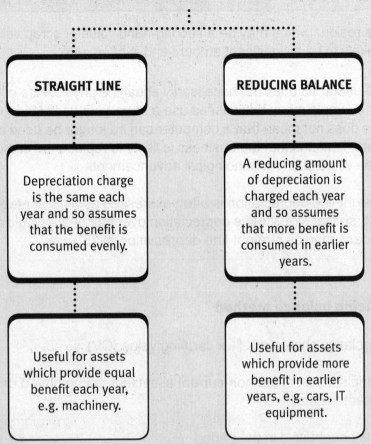

STRAIGHT LINE

Depreciation charge is the same each year and so assumes that the benefit is consumed evenly.

Useful for assets which provide equal benefit each year, e.g. machinery.

REDUCING BALANCE

A reducing amount of depreciation is charged each year and so assumes that more benefit is consumed in earlier years.

Useful for assets which provide more benefit in earlier years, e.g. cars, IT equipment.

Straight-line method

Depreciation charge = (Cost − Residual value)/Useful life

Or X% x cost

Residual value: the estimated disposal value of the asset at the end of its useful life.

Useful life: the estimated number of years during which the business will use the asset.

The residual value may be a second-hand value or scrap value. It is unlikely to be a significant amount and is often zero.

The useful life does not necessarily equal the physical life of the asset. For example many businesses use a three-year useful life for computers. This does not mean that a computer can no longer be used after three years; it means that the business is likely to replace the computer after three years due to technological advancement.

Straight-line depreciation is often expressed as a percentage of original cost, so that straight-line depreciation over four years would alternatively be described as straight-line depreciation at 25% pa.

Reducing balance method

Depreciation charge = X % x carrying value (CV)

CV: original cost of the non-current asset less accumulated depreciation on the asset to date.

Assets bought/sold in the period

If a non-current asset is bought or sold in the period, there are two ways in which the depreciation could be accounted for:

- provide a full year's depreciation in the year of acquisition and none in the year of disposal

- monthly or pro-rata depreciation, based on the exact number of months that the asset has been owned.

Illustration 1 – Reducing balance method

Dev, a trader, purchased an item of plant for $1,000 on 1 August 20X1 which he depreciates on the reducing balance at 20% pa. What is the depreciation charge for each of the first five years if the accounting year end is 31 July?

Solution

Solution

Year	Depreciation charge % x CV	Depreciation charge $	Cumulative depreciation $
1	20% x $1,000	200	200
2	20% x $(1,000 – 200)	160	360
3	20% x $(1,000 – 360)	128	488
4	20% x $(1,000 – 488)	102	590
5	20% x $(1,000 – 590)	82	672

Test your understanding 2

Karen has been running a successful nursery school 'Little Monkeys' since 20X1. She bought the following assets as the nursery grew:

- a new oven for the nursery kitchen at a cost of $2,000 (purchased 1 December 20X4).

- a minibus to take the children on trips for $18,000 (purchased 1 June 20X4).

She depreciates the oven at 10% straight line and the minibus at 25% reducing balance. A full year's depreciation is charged in the year of purchase and none in the year of disposal.

What is the total depreciation charge for the year ended 31 October 20X6?

A $2,531

B $2,700

C $4,231

D $2,731

Test your understanding 3

The following information relates to Bangers & Smash, a car repair business:

	Machine 1	Machine 2
Cost	$12,000	$8,000
Purchase date	1 August 20X5	1 October 20X6
Depreciation method	20% straight line pro rata	10% reducing balance pro rata

What is the total depreciation charge for the years ended 31 December 20X5 and 20X6?

	20X5	20X6
	$	$
A	2,400	2,600
B	1,000	2,600
C	2,400	3,200
D	1,000	3,200

7 Accounting for depreciation

Whichever method is used to calculate depreciation, the accounting remains the same:

Dr Depreciation expense (IS) X

Cr Accumulated depreciation (SFP) X

- The depreciation expense account is an income statement account and therefore is not cumulative.

- The accumulated depreciation account is a statement of financial position account and as the name suggests is cumulative, i.e. reflects all depreciation to date.

- On the statement of financial position it is shown as a reduction against the cost of non-current assets:

	$
Cost	X
Accumulated depreciation	(X)
CV	X

Illustration 2 – Accounting for depreciation

Santa runs a large toy shop in Windsor. In the year ended 31 August 20X5, she bought the following fixed assets:

- A new cash register for $5,000. This was purchased on 1 December 20X4, in time for the Christmas rush, and was to be depreciated at 10% straight line.

- A new delivery van, purchased on 31 March 20X5, at a cost of $22,000. The van is to be depreciated at 15% reducing balance.

Santa charges depreciation on a monthly basis.

- What is the depreciation charge for the year ended 31st August 20X5?

- Show the relevant ledger accounts and statement of financial position presentation at that date.

Solution

Solution

Cash register Depreciation charge: 10% x $5,000 x 9/12

= $375

Delivery van Depreciation charge: 15% x $22,000 x 5/12

= $1,375

Cost (cash register)

	$		$
Cost	5,000	Balance c/f	5,000
	─────		─────
	5,000		5,000
	─────		─────
Balance b/f	5,000		

Cost (delivery van)

	$		$
Cost	22,000	Balance c/f	22,000
	22,000		22,000
Balance b/f	22,000		

Accumulated depreciation (cash register)

	$		$
Balance c/f	375	Depreciation expense 20X5	375
	375		375
		Balance b/f	375

Accumulated depreciation (delivery van)

	$		$
Balance c/f	1,375	Depreciation expense 20X5	1,375
	1,375		1,375
		Balance b/f	1,375

Depreciation expense

	$		$
Accumulated depreciation (cash register)	375		
Accumulated depreciation delivery van)	1,375	Income statement	1,750
	1,750		1,750

Statement of financial position extract at 31 August 20X5

	Cost	Accumulated depreciation	NBV
	$	$	$
Cash register	5,000	(375)	4,625
Delivery van	22,000	(1,375)	20,625
Total	27,000	(1,750)	25,250

Test your understanding 4

Coco acquired two fixed assets for cash on 1 August 20X5 for use in her party organising business:

- a 25-year lease on a shop for $200,000
- a chocolate fountain for $4,000.

The fountain is to be depreciated at 25% pa using the reducing balance method.

A full year of depreciation is charged in the year of acquisition and none in the year of disposal.

Show the ledger account entries for these assets for the years ending 31 October 20X5, 20X6 and 20X7.

8 Consistency and subjectivity when accounting for depreciation

The following are all based on estimates made by the management of a business:

- depreciation method
- residual value
- useful life.

Different estimates would result in varying levels of depreciation and, consequently, profits.

It can be argued that these subjective areas could therefore result in manipulation of the accounts by management.

In order to reduce the scope for such manipulation and increase consistency of treatment, **IAS 16 Property, Plant and Equipment** requires the following:

- Depreciation method should be reviewed at each year end and changed if the method used no longer reflects the pattern of use of the asset.

- Residual value and useful life should be reviewed at each year end and changed if expectations differ from previous estimates.

Illustration 3 – Changes to estimates

Alfie purchased a non-current asset for $100,000 on 1 January 20X2 and started depreciating it over five years. Residual value was taken as $10,000.

At 1 January 20X3 a review of asset lives was undertaken and the remaining useful life was estimated at eight years. Residual value was estimated as nil.

Calculate the depreciation charge for the year ended 31 December 20X3 and subsequent years.

Solution to changes in estimates

Solution

Initial depreciation charge pa	= ($100,000 – $10,000) / 5 years
	= $18,000
CV at date of change	= $100,000 – ($18,000 x 1 year)
	= $82,000
New depreciation charge	= ($82,000 – nil) / 8 years
	= $10,250

chapter 8

Test your understanding 5

Alberto bought a wood-burning oven for his pizza restaurant for $30,000 on 1 January 20X0. At that time he believed that the oven's useful life would be 20 years after which it would have no value.

On 1 January 20X3, Alberto revises his estimations: he now believes that he will use the oven in the business for another 12 years after which he will be able to sell it second-hand for $1,500.

What is the depreciation charge for the year ended 31 December 20X3?

A $2,000

B $2,125

C $1,875

D $2,375

9 Disposal of non-current assets

Profit/loss on disposal

Proceeds (cash or part disposal allowance) > CV at disposal date	= Profit
Proceeds (cash or part disposal allowance) < CV at disposal date	= Loss
Proceeds (cash or part disposal allowance) = CV at disposal date	= Neither profit or loss

Note: A disposals T account is required when recording the disposal of a non-current asset. This is an income statement account which reflects any profit or loss on disposal.

Disposal for cash consideration

This is a three-step process:

(1)   Remove the original cost of the non-current asset from the 'non-current asset' account.

Dr Disposals original cost

Cr NC assets original cost

(2) Remove accumulated depreciation on the non-current asset from the 'accumulated depreciation' account.

Dr Acc'd dep'n acc'd dep'n

Cr Disposals acc'd dep'n

(3) Record the cash proceeds.

Dr Cash proceeds

Cr Disposals proceeds

The balance on the disposals T account is the profit or loss on disposal:

Disposal

Original cost	X	Accumulated depreciation	X
		Proceeds	X
Profit on disposal	ß	Loss on disposal	ß
	X		X

The profit or loss on disposal can also be calculated as proceeds less NBV of asset at disposal.

Test your understanding 6

Percy Throwerp runs a landscape gardening business. On 1 February 20X2, he purchased a sit-on lawnmower costing $3,000. He depreciates it at 10% straight line on a monthly basis. A few years later he decides to replace it with one which has an enclosed cabin for when it rains. He sells the lawnmower to an old friend, Alan Titchmuck, for $2,000 on 31 July 20X5.

How much is charged to Percy's income statement in respect of the asset for the year ended 31 December 20X5?

Disposal through a part exchange agreement (PEA)

A part exchange agreement arises where an old asset is provided in part payment for a new one, the balance of the new asset being paid in cash.

The procedure to record the transaction is very similar to the three-step process seen for a cash disposal. The first two steps are identical, however steps 3 and 4 are as follows:

(3) Record the part exchange allowance (PEA) as proceeds.

   Dr NC assets (= part of cost of new asset) PEA

   Cr Disposals (= sale proceeds of old asset) PEA

(4) Record the cash paid for the new asset.

   Dr NC assets cash

   Cr Cash cash

Again, the balance on the disposals T account is the profit or loss on disposal:

Disposal			
Original cost	X	Accumulated depreciation	X
		Proceeds	X
Profit on disposal	ß	Loss on disposal	ß
	X		X

Disposals

There are two debits to the non-current asset account in respect of the new asset:

- PEA

- cash balance.

Together these are the cost of the new asset. If preferred you can show the total as one debit (however do not forget to record both credits).

Bindi Bobbin runs a business altering and repairing clothes. When she started business on 1 January 20X2, she bought a Soopastitch II sewing machine for $2,500. She depreciates sewing machines using the straight-line method at a rate of 20% pa, and she charges a full year of depreciation in the year of acquisition and none in the year of disposal.

The business has now grown such that she needs a faster machine, and she will upgrade to the Soopastitch V during December 20X5. The Soopastitch salesman has offered her a part exchange deal as follows:

Part exchange allowance for Soopastitch II $750

Balance to be paid in cash for Soopastitch V $4,850

Show the ledger entries for the year ended 31 December 20X5 to reflect this transaction.

10 Revaluation of non-current assets

- Some non-current assets, such as land and buildings may rise in value over time. Businesses may choose to reflect the current value of the asset in their statement of financial position. This is known as revaluing the asset.

- The difference between the CV of the asset and the revalued amount (normally a gain) is recorded in a revaluation reserve in the capital section of the statement of financial position.

- This gain is not recorded in the income statement because it is unrealised, i.e. it is not realised in the form of cash.

- IAS 1 requires that a revaluation gain is disclosed in "other comprehensive income" on the statement of comprehensive income. (this is later covered within chapter 15)

Fair values

If the fair value of a non-current asset can be measured reliably, it can be carried at its fair value at the date of revaluation, less any subsequent depreciation and impairment losses. The revaluation should be repeated regularly to ensure that the fair value of the asset does not differ materially from the carrying amount.

An upward revaluation should be credited to revaluation surplus, unless it reverses a previous downward revaluation which was charged as an expense.

A downward revaluation should be charged as an expense, unless it reverses a previous upward revaluation, when it may be charged against the revaluation surplus for that same asset.

If one asset in a class is revalued, all assets of that class must be revalued. This is to prevent selective revaluation of only those assets that have increased in value.

Illustration 4 – Revaluation of non-current assets

Vittorio owns land which originally cost $250,000. No depreciation has been charged on the land in accordance with IAS 16. Vittorio wishes to revalue the land to reflect its current market value, which he has been advised is $600,000.

What is the double entry to record this revaluation?

Land revaluation

Solution

The land is currently held at cost of $250,000. This needs to be increased by $350,000 to reflect the new valuation of $600,000. Therefore the double entry required is:

Dr Land cost $350,000

Cr Revaluation reserve $350,000

Illustration 5 – Revaluation of non-current assets

Hamish runs a kilt-making business in Scotland. He has run the business for many years from a building which originally cost $300,000 and on which $100,000 total depreciation has been charged to date. Hamish wishes to revalue the building to $750,000.

What is the double entry required to record the revaluation?

Solution to revaluation of NCA's

Solution

The current balances in the accounts are:

Building cost $300,000

Accumulated depreciation $100,000

- The building cost account needs to be raised by $450,000 to $750,000.

- On revaluation, the accumulated depreciation account is cleared out.

Therefore the double entry required is:

Dr Building cost $450,000

Dr Accumulated depreciation $100,000

Cr Revaluation reserve $550,000

The gain of $550,000 reflects the difference between the NBV pre-revaluation of $200,000 and the revalued amount of $750,000.

Cost (building)			
	$		$
Balance b/f	300,000		
Revaluation reserve	450,000	Balance c/f	750,000
	750,000		750,000
Balance b/f	750,000		

Accumulated depreciation (building)

	$		$
Revaluation reserve	100,000	Balance b/f	100,000
	100,000		100,000

Revaluation reserve

	$		$
		Cost (building)	450,000
Balance c/f	550,000	Accumulated depreciation (building)	100,000
	550,000		550,000
		Balance b/f	550,000

Extract from the Statement of comprehensive income: (covered in more detail within chapter 17)

Other comprehensive income:

Gain on property revaluation $450,000

In summary:

Revaluation surplus = Revalued amount – NBV

For a non-depreciated asset:

Dr Non-current asset – cost   revaluation surplus

Cr Revaluation reserve   revaluation surplus

For a depreciated asset:

Dr Accumulated depreciation   depreciation to date

Dr Non-current asset – cost   ß

Cr Revaluation reserve   revaluation surplus

The revaluation gain is disclosed on the face of the statement of comprehensive income under "other comprehensive income" and in the statement of changes in equity (SOCIE).

Test your understanding 8

Max owns a fish-finger factory. The premises were purchased on 1 January 20X1 for $450,000 and depreciation charged at 2% pa straight line.

Max now wishes to revalue the factory premises to $800,000 on 1 January 20X7 to reflect the market value.

What is the balance on the revaluation reserve after this transaction?

A $350,000

B $395,000

C $404,000

D $413,000

11 Depreciation and disposal of a revalued asset

Depreciation of a revalued asset

- When a non-current asset has been revalued, the charge for depreciation should be based on the revalued amount and the remaining useful life of the asset.

- this charge will be higher than depreciation prior to the revaluation.

- the excess of the new depreciation charge over the old depreciation charge should be transferred from the revaluation reserve to accumulated profits (within the capital section of the statement of financial position):

Dr Revaluation reserve X

Cr Accumulated profits X

Illustration 6 – Depreciation of a revalued asset

Eddie owns a retail unit in central Springfield. He bought it 25 years ago for $100,000, depreciating it over 50 years. At the start of 20X6 he decides to revalue the unit to $800,000. The unit has a remaining useful life of 25 years.

What accounting entries should be made in 20X6?

Solution

Solution

On revaluation at start of 20X6

   Dr Retail unit cost $700,000

   Dr Accumulated depreciation $50,000

   Cr Revaluation reserve $750,000

Depreciation for 20X6

   Dr Depreciation expense($800,000/25 yrs) $32,000

   Cr Accumulated depreciation $32,000

Reserves transfer for 20X6

   Dr Revaluation reserve ($32,000 – $2,000) $30,000

   Cr Accumulated profits $30,000

Test your understanding 9

Spartacus United football club's statement of financial position at 31 December 20X7 includes the following information:

	$
Stadium cost	1,500,000
Depreciation	450,000
	1,050,000

Depreciation has been provided at 2% on the straight-line basis.

The stadium is revalued on 30 June 20X8 to $1,380,000. There is no change in its remaining estimated future useful life.

What is the depreciation charge for the year ended 31 December 20X8?

Test your understanding 10

Tiger Trees owns and runs a golf club. Some years ago Tiger purchased land next to the existing course with the intention of creating a smaller nine-hole course. The cost of the land was $260,000. Tiger hasn't yet built the additional course but has revalued this land to $600,000. He has now decided that building the new course is uneconomical and has found a buyer who is willing to pay $695,000 for the land.

What are the ledger entries on disposal?

Disposal of a revalued asset

- The disposal of a revalued asset is recorded as already seen.

12 Disclosure of non-current asset balances in company financial statements

Statement of financial position	Income statement	Notes to the accounts
Aggregate NBV of non-current assets disclosed on the face of the statement of financial position.	Depreciation charge included within relevant expense categories.	• Disclosure of depreciation methods and rates used. • Non-current assets disclosure. • Details of revaluations.

IAS 16 PPE Disclosure

IAS 16 Property Plant and Equipment contains a number of disclosure requirements relating to non-current assets. Here are the main ones:

(1) The measurement bases used for arriving at the carrying amount of the asset (e.g. cost or valuation). If more than one basis has been used, the amounts for each basis must be disclosed.

(2) Depreciation methods used, with details of useful lives or the depreciation rates used.

(3) The gross amount of each asset heading and its related accumulated depreciation (aggregated with accumulated impairment losses) at the beginning and end of the period.

(4) A reconciliation of the carrying amount at the beginning and end of the period, showing:

- additions

- assets classified as held for sale

- disposals

- revaluations

- depreciation.

(5) Any commitments for future acquisition of property, plant and equipment.

(6) If assets are stated at revalued amounts, the following should be disclosed:

– the effective date of the revaluation

– whether an independent valuer was involved

– the methods and assumptions applied in estimating the items' fair value

– the carrying amount that would have been recognised had the assets been carried at cost

– the revaluation surplus, indicating the change for the period.

IAS 38 Intangible assets treatment

Intangible assets

Many businesses invest significant amounts with the intention of obtaining future value on areas such as:

• scientific/technical knowledge

• design of new processes and systems

• licences and quotas

• intellectual property, e.g. patents and copyrights

• market knowledge, e.g. customer lists, relationships and loyalty

• trademarks

All these expenses may result in future benefits to the business, but not all can be recognised as assets.

Objective of IAS 38 Intangible assets

The objective of IAS 38 is to prescribe the specific criteria that must be met before an intangible asset can be recognised in the accounts.

Definition

An intangible asset is an identifiable non-monetary asset without physical substance.

To meet the definition the asset must be identifiable, i.e. separable from the rest of the business or arising from legal rights.

It must also meet the normal definition of an asset:

- controlled by the entity as a result of past events (normally by enforceable legal rights)

- a resource from which future economic benefits are expected to flow (either from revenue or cost saving)

Recognition

To be recognised in the financial statements, an intangible asset must:

- meet the definition of an intangible asset, and
- meet the recognition criteria of the framework:
    - it is probable that future economic benefits attributable to the asset will flow to the entity
    - the cost of the asset can be measured reliably.

If these criteria are met, the asset should be initially recognised at cost.

Disclosure

The notes to the accounts will detail the total intangible non-current assets in the statement of financial position at net book value.

	20XX £000
Development costs	X
Concessions, patents, licences and trade marks	X
Goodwill	X
	X

Chapter summary

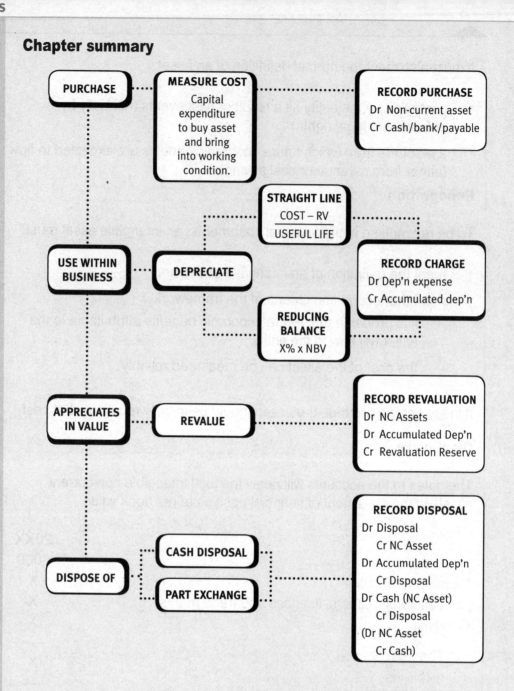

PURCHASE

MEASURE COST
Capital expenditure to buy asset and bring into working condition.

RECORD PURCHASE
Dr Non-current asset
Cr Cash/bank/payable

STRAIGHT LINE

$$\frac{COST - RV}{USEFUL \ LIFE}$$

USE WITHIN BUSINESS

DEPRECIATE

RECORD CHARGE
Dr Dep'n expense
Cr Accumulated dep'n

REDUCING BALANCE
X% x NBV

APPRECIATES IN VALUE

REVALUE

RECORD REVALUATION
Dr NC Assets
Dr Accumulated Dep'n
Cr Revaluation Reserve

DISPOSE OF

CASH DISPOSAL

PART EXCHANGE

RECORD DISPOSAL
Dr Disposal
   Cr NC Asset
Dr Accumulated Dep'n
   Cr Disposal
Dr Cash (NC Asset)
   Cr Disposal
(Dr NC Asset
   Cr Cash)

Test your understanding answers

Test your understanding 1

The correct answer is A

Land and buildings

Office premises: $250,000

Legal fees: $10,000

Total: $260,000

- The cost of the purple paint does not form part of the cost of the office and so should not be capitalised. Instead it should be taken to the income statement as a revenue expense.

Motor vehicles

3 Mercedes E series $116,000

Number plates $210

Delivery charges $180

Total $116,390

- The number plates are one-off charges which form part of the purchase price of any car.
- The road licence fee, drivers' wages and receipts are ongoing expenses, incurred every year. They cannot be capitalised, but should be taken to the income statement as expenses.

Test your understanding 2

The correct answer is D

	20X6
Oven	$
£2,000 x 10%	200
Minibus	
20X4 : 25% x $18,000 = $4,500	
20X5: 25% x $(18,000 – 4,500) = $3,375	
20X6: 25% x $(18,000 – 7,875) = $2,531	2,531
	——
Total depreciation charge	2,731

Test your understanding 3

The correct answer is B

Machine 1 $ $

   20X5: 20% x $12,000 x 5/12 = 1,000

   20X6: 20% x $12,000 = 2,400

Machine 2

   20X6: 10% x $8,000 x 3/12 = 200

Total depreciation charge

   20X5: 1,000

   20X6: $2,400 + $200 2,600

Test your understanding 4

Lease (cost)

	$		$
1.8.X5 Cash	200,000	Balance c/f	200,000
	200,000		200,000
Balance b/f	200,000		

Fountain (cost)

	$		$
1.8.X5 Cash	4,000	Balance c/f	4,000
	4,000		4,000
Balance b/f	4,000		

Depreciation charge – Lease & Fountain

	$		$
X5 accumulated depreciation	9,000	Income statement	9,000
X6 accumulated depreciation	8,750	Income statement	8,750
X7 accumulated depreciation	8,563	Income statement	8,563

Accumulated depreciation – Lease

	$		$
		X5 depreciation charge	8,000
Balance c/f	8,000		
	8,000		8,000
		Balance b/f	8,000
		X6 depreciation charge	8,000
Balance c/f	16,000		
	16,000		16,000
		Balance b/f	16,000
		X7 depreciation charge	8,000
Balance c/f	24,000		
	24,000		24,000
		Balance b/f	24,000

Accumulated depreciation – Fountain

	$		$
		X5 depreciation charge	1,000
Balance c/f	1,000		
	1,000		1,000
		Balance b/f	1,000
		X6 depreciation charge	750
Balance c/f	1,750		
	1,750		1,750
		Balance b/f	1,750
		X7 depreciation charge	563
Balance c/f	2,313		
	2,313		2,313
		Balance b/f	2,313

Annual depreciation workings:

Note, details of the depreciation method and rate for the lease are not given in the question. We are however told that the lease term is 25 years. This suggests that it would be appropriate to use the straight-line method with a useful life of 25 years.

20X5
Lease: $200,000/25 years = 8,000
Fountain: $4,000 x 25% = 1,000

Total: 9,000

20X6
Lease: $200,000/25 years = 8,000
Fountain: $3,000 x 25% = 750

Total: 8,750

20X7
Lease: $200,000/25 years = 8,000
Fountain: $2,250 x 25% = 563

Total: 8,563

Test your understanding 5

The correct answer is A

Initial depreciation charge = $30,000 /20 years = $1,500

CV at date of change = $30,000 – ($1,500 x 3yrs)

   = $25,500

New depreciation charge = $25,500 – $1,500 / 12 years

   = $2,000 pa

Test your understanding 6

(1) Dr Disposals $3,000

Cr Fixtures and fittings cost $3,000

(2) Dr Accumulated depreciation $1,050

Cr Disposals $1,050

Depreciation working:

X2 10% x 3,000 x 11/12 = 275

X3 10% x 3,000 = 300

X4 10% x 3,000 = 300

X5 10% x 3,000 x 7/12 = 175

Total: 1050

(3) Dr Cash $2,000

Cr Disposals $2,000

Disposals:

	$		$
31.7.X5 fixtures and fittings cost	3,000	Accumulated depreciation	1,050
Profit on disposal (ß)	50	Cash proceeds	2,000
	3,050		3,050

The charge to the income statement for the year ended 31 December 20X5 is: $

Depreciation charge for the year 175

Profit/loss on disposal (50)

Note: As depreciation is charged monthly, it is necessary to charge an amount to the income statement for the period 1 January 20X5 to the disposal date 31 July 20X5.

Test your understanding 7

Sewing machine

	$		$
Balance b/f	2,500	Disposal	2,500
New asset			
PEA	750		
Cash	4,850	Balance c/f	5,600
	————		————
	8,100		8,100
	————		————
Balance b/f	5,600		

Accumulated depreciation (Sewing machine)

	$		$
Disposal	1,500	Balance b/f	1,500
		Depreciation	
Balance c/f	1,120	charge X5	1,120
	————		————
	2,620		2,620
	————		————
		Balance b/f	1,120

Depreciation b/f working:

$2,500 x 20% x 3 years = $1,500

Disposals

	$		$
Sewing machine cost	2,500	Sewing machine accumulated depreciation	1,500
		PEA	750
		Loss on disposal (ß)	250
	————		————
	2,500		2,500
	————		————

Depreciation charge

	$		$
Sewing machine accumulated depreciation	1,120	Income statement	1,120

Depreciation charge working:

$5,600 x 20% = $1,120

Test your understanding 8

The correct answer is C

Factory cost

	$		$
Balance b/f	450,000		
Revaluation	350,000	Balance c/f	800,000
	800,000		800,000
	800,000		

Accumulated depreciation (factory)

	$		$
Revaluation (2% x $450,000 x 6 years)	54,000	Balance b/f	54,000
	54,000		54,000

Revaluation reserve

	$		$
		Factory cost	350,000
Balance c/f	404,000	Accumulated depreciation	54,000
	404,000		404,000
		Balance b/f	404,000

Test your understanding 9

Depreciation must continue to be charged on the original cost until the date of revaluation. Thereafter it is charged on the revalued amount:

1 January to 30 June 20X8

2% x $1,500,000 x 6/12

15,000

Note that this is part of the depreciation cleared out on revaluation and so is not part of the accumulated depreciation balance at the year end.

1 July to 31 December 20X8

(1,380,000/34.5 years)x (6/12)

20,000

This amount will form the accumulated depreciation at the year end.

Total depreciation charge

Test your understanding 10

Land (valuation)

	$		$
Balance b/f	600,000	Disposal	600,000

Disposal

	$		$
Land valuation	600,000	Proceeds	695,000
Profit on disposal	95,000		

From trial balance to financial statements

Chapter learning objectives

Upon completion of this chapter you will be able to:

- illustrate the process of adjusting the financial statements for accruals and prepayments, depreciation, irrecoverable debts and the allowance for receivables.

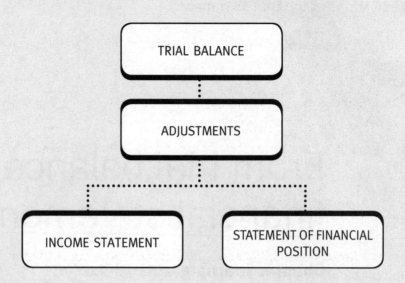

1 Trial balance

In this chapter we will bring together the material from the previous chapters and produce a set of financial statements from a trial balance.

This will involve adjusting for the following items:

- closing inventory
- depreciation
- accruals and prepayments
- irrecoverable debts and the allowance for receivables.

Once these adjustments have been made, the income statement and statement of financial position can be prepared.

When making the adjustments it is important to ensure that each transaction contains the correct double entry.

Purpose of the Trial balance

Purpose of the trial balance

The purpose of the trial balance is

- to check that for every debit entry made, an equal credit entry has been made
- as a first step in preparing the financial statements.

Limitations of the trial balance

Although the trial balance is useful in ensuring that double entry has been maintained, it will not:

- identify errors such as mispostings to the wrong account or a double entry for the wrong amount
- identify where errors have been made, or what those errors are.

2 Adjustments

Here is a reminder of the accounting entries for the adjustments required when preparing the financial statements:

Closing inventory

Dr Inventory (SFP)

Cr Cost of sales (IS)

With the closing inventory at the end of the period.

Depreciation

Dr Depreciation expense (IS)

Cr Accumulated depreciation (SFP)

With depreciation charge for the year for each class of asset.

Accruals

Dr Expenses (IS)

Cr Accrual (Liability) (SFP)

With each accrued expense.

Prepayments

Dr Prepayment (Receivables) (SFP)

Cr Expenses (IS)

With each prepaid expense.

Irrecoverable debts

Dr Irrecoverable debt expense (IS)

Cr Receivables (SFP)

With the total of receivables written off.

Allowance for receivables

Increase in allowance:

Dr Irrecoverable debt expense (IS)

Cr Allowance for receivables (SFP)

With the increase in the allowance for the period.

Decrease in allowance:

Dr Allowance for receivables (SFP)

Cr Irrecoverable debt expense (IS)

With the decrease in the allowance for the period.

Illustration 1 – Preparation of financial statements

In this example, we will account for the period-end adjustments and prepare a set of financial statements from a TB.

The trial balance of Tyndall at 31 May 20X6 is as follows:

Trial balance of Tyndall at 31 May 20X6

	$	$
Capital account		15,258
Drawings by proprietor	5,970	
Purchases	73,010	
Returns inwards	1,076	
Returns outwards		3,720
Discounts	1,870	965
Credit sales		96,520
Cash sales		30,296
Customs duty	11,760	
Carriage inwards	2,930	
Carriage outwards	1,762	
Salesman's commission	711	
Salesman's salary	3,970	
Office salaries	7,207	
Bank charges	980	
Loan interest	450	
Light and heat	2,653	
Sundry expenses	2,100	

	$	$
Rent	3,315	
Insurance	4,000	
Printing and postage	2,103	
Advertising	1,044	
Irrecoverable debts	1,791	
Allowance for receivables		437
Inventory	7,650	
Receivables	10,760	
Payables		7,411
Cash at bank	2,634	
Cash in hand	75	
New delivery van (less trade-in)	2,200	
Motor expenses	986	
Furniture and equipment:		
Cost	8,000	
Depreciation at 1 June 20X5		2,400
Old delivery van:		
Cost	2,000	
Depreciation at 1 June 20X5		1,000
Loan account at 9% (repayable in five years)		5,000
	163,007	163,007

The following information is relevant:

(1) Closing inventory has been valued for accounts purposes at $8,490.

(2) The motor van was sold on 31 August 20X5 and traded in against the cost of a new van. The trade-in price was $1,400 and the cost of the new van was $3,600. No entries have yet been made for this transaction apart from debiting the $2,200 cash paid to the New delivery van account.

(3) Straight-line depreciation is to be provided on a monthly basis at the following annual rates:

Motor vans 25%

Furniture and equipment 10%

(4) Past experience indicates that an allowance for receivables should be made equivalent to 5% of the closing receivables.

(5) An accrual of $372 is required in respect of light and heat.

(6) A quarter's rent to 30 June 20X6 amounting to $900 was paid on 2 April 20X6. Insurance for the year to 31 March 20X7 amounting to $1,680 was paid on 16 April.

Prepare an income statement and a statement of financial position for the year ended 31 May 20X6.

Solution

Solution

Step 1 Inventory

The closing inventory figure of $8,490 must be included in the financial statements. The accounting journal is:

Dr Inventory (SFP) $8,490

Cr Inventory (Cost of sales in IS) $8,490

Step 2 Non-current assets and depreciation

As well as calculating the depreciation for the year, we must also deal with the part-exchange of the van during the year.

Depreciation of van from 1 June 20X5 to 31 August 20X5:

Cost $2,000 x 25% x 3/12 = $125

Disposal of van:

The van has been part-exchanged against the cost of a new van. The trade-in value of $1,400 is equivalent to the disposal proceeds of the van. The new van has a total cost of $3,600 consisting of $1,400 trade-in allowance and $2,200 cash.

The double entry to record the disposal is:

Dr Delivery van accumulated

depreciation account ($1,000 + 125) $1,125

Dr New delivery van cost account $1,400

Cr Delivery van cost account $2,000

Cr Profit on sale of asset $525

This can be shown in the disposal account as follows:

Old delivery van disposal

	$		$
Old delivery van – cost	2,000	Old delivery van – accumulated depreciation	1,125
Profit on disposal	525		
		New delivery van	1,400
	2,525		2,525

Don't forget to add on the depreciation for the first three months of the year when you are calculating the profit on disposal.

Note that this question specifically requires monthly depreciation. Some questions may state that there is no depreciation in the year of acquisition or year of disposal of an asset. Make sure you read the question carefully.

Depreciation of van from 1 September 20X5 to 31 May 20X6:

Cost $3,600 x 25% x 9/12 = $675.

The total depreciation for the year for delivery vans is $800 (675 + 125).

Depreciation on furniture and equipment:

Cost $8,000 x 10% = $800.

Step 3 Irrecoverable debts

* The TB shows us that:
* $1,791 has been written off in the year for irrecoverable debts; and
* the balance on the allowance for receivables is $437.

The closing allowance should be 5% of closing receivables.

$10,760 x 5% = $538.

The charge to the income statement is the movement between the opening and closing allowance.

$538 – $437 = $101 increase in the allowance which is debited to the income statement.

The double entry to record this transactions is:

Dr Irrecoverable debts expense $101

Cr Allowance for receivables $101

The charge in the income statement for irrecoverable debts will amount to $1,892 including the debt already written off ($1,791 + $101).

Step 4 Light and heat

$372 needs to be accrued for light and heat expenses. The double entry is:

Dr Light and heat expense $372

Cr Current liabilities $372

This journal entry ensures that the business has recorded all of its expenses in the period.

Step 5 Rent

The rent has been paid in advance and part of the payment relates to the next accounting period. This must be taken out of expenses for the current period and shown in the statement of financial position as a prepayment.

Rent prepaid (1/3 x $900) = $300

Step 6 Insurance

Insurance has also been paid in advance and must be adjusted.

Insurance prepaid 10/12 x $1,680 = $1,400

Step 7 Prepare the income statement and statement of financial position

	$	$
Sales revenue:		
Credit sales		96,520
Cash sales		30,296
		126,816
Less: Sales returns		(1,076)
		125,740
Opening inventory	7,650	
Purchases	73,010	
Less: Purchase returns	(3,720)	
Carriage inwards	2,930	
Customs duty	11,760	
Closing inventory	(8,490)	
Cost of sales		(83,140)
Gross profit		42,600
Discount received		965
Profit on sale of van		525
		44,090
Less: Expenses:		
Depreciation:		
Van (Step 2)	800	
Equipment (Step 2)	800	
Irrecoverable debts (Step 3)	1,892	
Light and heat ($2,653 + 372)(Step 4)	3,025	
Rent ($3,315 – 300)(Step 5)	3,015	
Insurance ($4,000 – 1,400) (Step 6)	2,600	
Discount allowed	1,870	
Carriage outwards	1,762	
Salesman's commission	711	
Salesman's salary	3,970	

	$	$
Office salary	7,207	
Bank charges	980	
Loan interest	450	
Sundry expenses	2,100	
Printing and postage	2,103	
Advertising	1,044	
Motor expenses	986	
	———	
		(35,315)
		———
Net profit		8,775
		———

Statement of financial position at 31 May 20X6

	Cost	Acc	NBV
	$	$	$
Non-current assets			
Motor van (step 2)	3,600	675	2,925
Furniture and equipment	8,000	3,200	4,800
	———	———	———
	11,600	3,875	7,725
Current assets:			
Inventory		8,490	
Receivables	10,760		
Less: Allowance for receivables (Step 3)	(538)		
	———	10,222	
Prepayments (rent and insurance)		1,700	
Cash at bank		2,634	
Cash in hand		75	
			23,121
			———
			30,846
Capital account:			———
Balance at 1 June 20X5		15,258	
Net profit		8,775	
			24,033
Less: Drawings by proprietor		(5,970)	18,063
Non-current liabilities:			
Loan			5,000

	NBV	Cost	Acc
	$	$	$
Current liabilities			
Payables		7,411	
Accrued expenses		372	
			7,783
			30,846

Test your understanding 1

Kevin Suri carries on business as a retail trader. The trial balance of his business as at 31 December 20X5 was as follows:

	Dr	Cr
	$	$
Capital		225,600
Sales and purchases	266,800	365,200
Inventory at 1 January 20X5	23,340	
Returns	1,200	1,600
Wages	46,160	
Rent	13,000	
Motor expenses	3,720	
Insurance	760	
Irrecoverable debts	120	
Allowance for receivables		
1 January 20X5		588
Discounts	864	1,622
Light and heat	3,074	
Bank overdraft interest	74	
Motor vehicles at cost	24,000	
– aggregate depreciation		
1 Jan 20X5		12,240
Fixtures and fittings at cost	28,000	
– aggregate depreciation		
1 Jan 20X5		16,800
Land	100,000	
Receivables and payables	17,330	23,004

	Dr	Cr
	$	$
Bank	3,412	
Buildings at cost	100,000	
– aggregate depreciation		
1 Jan 20X5		6,000
Drawings	20,800	
	652,654	652,654

You are given the following additional information:

(1) Inventory at 31 December 20X5 was $25,680.

(2) Rent was prepaid by $1,000 and light and heat owed was $460 at 31 December 20X5.

(3) Land is to be revalued to $250,000 at 31 December 20X5.

(4) Following a final review of the receivables at 31 December 20X5, Kevin decides to write off another debt of $130. He also wishes to maintain the allowance for receivables at 3% of the year end balance.

(5) Depreciation is to be provided as follows:

(a) building – 2% annually, straight-line

(b) fixtures & fittings – straight line method, assuming a useful economic life of five years with no residual value

(c) motor vehicles – 30% annually on a reducing balance basis.

A full year's depreciation is charged in the year of acquisition and none in the year of disposal.

Prepare an income statement for the year ended 31 December 20X5 and a statement of financial position as at that date for Kevin Suri.

Chapter summary

```
┌─────────────────────────────┐
│      TRIAL BALANCE          │
│  • Lists out all the        │
│    balances on the          │
│    ledger accounts          │
└─────────────────────────────┘
              ┊
┌─────────────────────────────┐
│        Adjustment           │
│  • Closing inventory        │
│  • Depreciation             │
│  • Accruals and             │
│    prepayments              │
│  • Irrecoverable debts      │
│    and allowance for        │
│    receivables.             │
└─────────────────────────────┘
       ┊                ┊
┌──────────────────┐  ┌──────────────────────┐
│ Income statement │  │ Statement of financial│
│  • Shows the     │  │      position         │
│    financial     │  │  • Shows the financial│
│    performance of│  │    position of the    │
│    the business. │  │    business.          │
└──────────────────┘  └──────────────────────┘
```

Test your understanding answers

Test your understanding 1

Kevin Suri Income statement for the year ended 31 December 20X5

	$	$
Sales		365,200
Returns in		(1,200)
		————
		364,000
Cost of sales		
Opening Inventory	23,340	
Purchases	266,800	
Returns out	(1,600)	
	————	
	288,540	
Closing inventory	(25,680)	
	————	
		(262,860)
		————
Gross profit		101,140
Sundry income		
Discount received		1,622
Decrease in allowance for receivables		72
		————
		102,834
Expenses		
Wages	46,160	
Rent ($13,000 – 1,000)	12,000	
Motor expenses	3,720	
Insurance	760	
Irrecoverable debts ($120 + 130)	250	
Discounts allowed	864	
Light and heat ($3,074 + 460)	3,534	
Bank interest	74	

	$	$
Depreciation		
Buildings (W1)	2,000	
Fixtures and fittings (W1)	5,600	
Motor vehicles (W2)	3,528	
		(78,490)
Net profit		24,344
Other Comprehensive Income		
Revaluation Gain		150,000
Total Comprehensive Income		174,344

Statement of financial position as at 31 December 20X5

	Cost	Acc dep'n	NBV
	$	$	$
Non-current assets			
Land	250,000	–	250,000
Buildings	100,000	8,000	92,000
Fixtures and fittings	28,000	22,400	5,600
Motor vehicles	24,000	15,768	8,232
	402,000	46,168	355,832
Current assets			
Inventory		25,680	
Receivables ($17,330 – 130)	17,200		
Allowance for receivables			
($17,200 X 3%)	(516)		
		16,684	

Prepaid expenses (rent)	1,000
Bank	3,412
	46,776
	402,608

Capital	225,600
Profit	24,344
Revaluation reserve/surplus	
($250,000 – 100,000)	150,000
Drawings	(20,800)
	379,144

Current liabilities

Payables	23,004	
Accrued expenses		
(light and heat)	460	
		23,464
		402,608

Working

	Motor vehicles
Cost	$24,000
Accumulated depreciation	($12,240)
NBV	$11,760
Depreciation rate	x 30%
Annual depreciation charge	$3,528

Books of prime entry and control accounts

Chapter learning objectives

Upon completion of this chapter you will be able to:

- identify the main data sources and records in an accounting system

- describe the contents and purpose of different types of business documentation

- outline the form of accounting records in a typical manual system

- record credit sale and purchase transactions (with and without sales tax) using day books

- post day book totals to the ledger accounts

- explain the division of the ledger into sections

- explain the nature and purpose of control accounts for the accounts receivable and accounts payable ledgers

- account for contras between trade receivables and payables

- record cash transactions using the cash book

- explain the need for a record of petty cash transactions

- illustrate the typical format of the petty cash book

- explain the importance of using the imprest system to control petty cash

- list the necessary controls and security over petty cash that would normally be found in a business

- explain the uses of the journal

- illustrate the use of the journal and the posting of journal entries into ledger accounts.

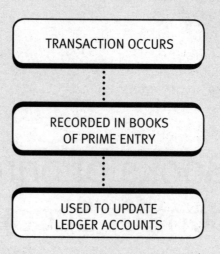

1 Business documentation

The table below summarises the main types of business documentation and sources of data for an accounting system, together with their content and purpose.

	Contents	Purpose
Quotation	Quantity/ description/details of goods required.	To establish price from various suppliers and cross refer to purchase requisition.
Purchase order	Details of supplier, e.g. name, address. Quantity/ description/details of goods required and price. Terms and conditions of delivery, payment, etc.	Sent to supplier as request for supply. To check to the quotation and delivery note.
Sales order	Quantity/ description/details of goods required and price.	Cross checked with the order placed by customer. Sent to the stores/ warehouse department for processing of the order.
Delivery note (goods delivery note – GDN)	Details of supplier, e.g. name and address. Quantity and description of goods	Provided by supplier. Checked with goods received and purchase order.
Goods received note (GRN)	Quantity and description of goods.	Produced by company receiving the goods as proof of receipt. Matched with delivery note and purchase order.

Purchase invoice	Details of supplier, e.g. name and address. Contains details of goods, e.g. quantity, price, value, sales tax, terms of credit, etc.	Issued by supplier as request for payment. Cross checked with delivery note, and purchase order. Statement
Statement	Details of supplier, e.g. name and address. Has details of date, invoice numbers and values, payments made, refunds, amount owing.	Issued by the supplier. Checked with other documents to ensure that the amount owing is correct.
Credit note	Details of supplier, e.g. name and address. Contains details of goods returned, e.g. quantity, price, value, sales tax, terms of credit, etc.	Issued by the supplier. Checked with documents regarding goods returned.
Debit note	Details of the supplier. Contains details of goods returned, e.g. quantity, price, value, sales tax, terms of credit, etc.	Issued by the company receiving the goods. Cross referred to the credit note issued by the supplier.
Remittance advice	Method of payment, invoice number, account number, date, etc.	Sent to supplier with, or as notification of, payment.
Receipt	Details of payment received.	Issued by the selling company indicating the payment received.

2 Accounting records

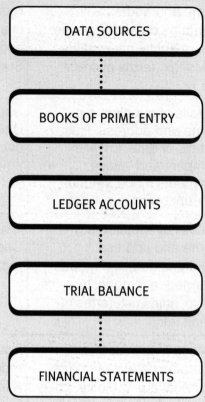

DATA SOURCES

BOOKS OF PRIME ENTRY

LEDGER ACCOUNTS

TRIAL BALANCE

FINANCIAL STATEMENTS

Books of prime entry

- If ledgers were updated each time a transaction occurred, the ledger accounts would quickly become cluttered and errors might be made.

- To avoid this, all transactions are initially recorded in a book of prime entry.

- Several books of prime entry exist, each recording a different type of transaction:

Book of prime entry	Transaction type
Sales day book	Credit sales
Purchases day book	Credit purchases
Sales returns day book	Returns of goods sold on credit
Purchases returns day book	Returns of goods bought on credit
Cash book	All bank transactions
Petty cash book	All small cash transactions
The journal	All transactions not recorded elsewhere

- Entry of a transaction to a book of prime entry does not record the double entry required for that transaction.

- The book of prime entry is, however, the source for double entries to the ledger accounts.

- The double entry arising from the book of prime entry will be recorded periodically (daily, weekly, monthly) depending on the volume of transactions.

3 Ledger accounts and the division of the ledger

In a manual system, ledgers can be thought of as books containing the individual accounts:

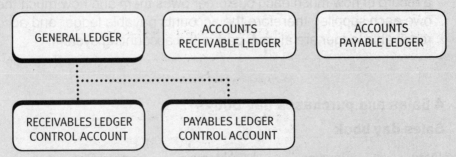

- The **general ledger** contains all accounts or a summary of all accounts necessary to produce the trial balance and financial statements.

- The **accounts receivable ledger** contains an account for each credit customer to show how much each one owes.

  An account to summarise this information, the **receivables control account**, is normally contained within the general ledger.

- The **accounts payable ledger** contains an account for each credit supplier to show how much they are owed.

  An account to summarise this information, the **payables control account**, is normally contained within the general ledger.

Where there are individual accounts in a receivables or payables ledger AND a control account in the general ledger, only one can form part of the double entry system. The other exists for memorandum purposes. It is normally the case that the control accounts form part of the double entry.

Control accounts

Not all businesses maintain a receivables ledger control account and purchases ledger control account, however where they do it is usually these control accounts that form part of the double entry system.

Where control accounts are maintained, they are effective in reducing the time it takes to ascertain the total amount owed by receivables and owed to payables. The scope for making errors when realising these numbers through totalling several individual accounts is also reduced.

Even where control accounts are maintained, a business must still keep a record of how much each customer owes them and how much they owe each supplier, therefore the accounts payable ledger and accounts receivable ledger are always part of the accounting system.

4 Sales and purchases day books

Sales day book

Date	Invoice	Customer	Ledger Ref	$
4.1.X6	1	Jake	RL3	4,500
4.1.X6	2	Bella	RL18	3,000
4.1.X6	3	Fizz	RL6	2,200
4.1.X6	4	Milo	RL1	10,000
4.1.X6	5	Max	RL12	500
				———
Total for 4.1.X6				20,200

The format of the double entry resulting from the sales day book will depend upon whether the individual accounts in the accounts receivable ledger OR the receivables control account in the general ledger is part of the double entry system:

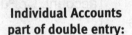

Individual Accounts part of double entry:	Receivables ledger control account part of double entry:
Dr Jake (RL3) $4,500 Dr Bella (RL18) $3,000 Dr Fizz (RL6) $2,200 Dr Milo (RL1) $10,000 Dr Max (RL12) $500 Cr Sales $20,200 The total receivables of $20,200 should then be posted to the memorandum control account (assuming one is maintained).	Dr SLCA $20,200 Cr Sales $20,200 Care must then be taken to update the individual memorandum accounts with the new amounts that Jake, Bella, Fizz, Milo and Max owe.

Purchases day book, sales returns day book and purchases returns day book

The format of the remaining day books is similar to that of the sales day book. The double entries arising are:

	Individual accounts part of double entry	Control accounts part of double entry
Purchases day book	Dr Purchases. Cr Individual accounts in accounts payable ledger.	Dr Purchases. Cr Payables ledger control account. Each entry also posted to individual memorandum accounts in accounts payable ledger.

Sales returns day book	Dr Sales returns. Cr Individual accounts in accounts receivable ledger.	Dr Sales Returns. Cr Receivables ledger control account. Each entry also posted to individual memorandum accounts in accounts Receivables ledger.
Purchases returns day book	Dr Individual accounts in accounts payable ledger. Cr Purchases returns.	Dr Payables ledger control account. Cr Purchases returns. Each entry also posted to individual memorandum accounts in accounts payable ledger.

Format of purchase day book

Format of the purchases day book

Date	Invoice	Customer	Ledger Ref	$
4.1.X6	34	JHarry	RL3	2,700
4.1.X6	11	Ron	RL18	145
4.1.X6	5609	Hermione	RL6	4,675
4.1.X6	2	Neville	RL1	750
4.1.X6	577	Draco	RL12	345
Total for 4.1.X6				8,615

Dr Purchases $8,615

Cr Payables ledger control account $8,615

Individual purchases posted as credits to individual suppliers accounts in accounts payable ledger.

Format of the sales returns day book

Date	Invoice	Customer	Ledger Ref	$
4.1.X6	1	Max	RL12	50
4.1.X6	2	Ernie	RL2	450
4.1.X6	3	Pat	RL20	390
4.1.X6	4	Sam	RL27	670
4.1.X6	5	Milo	RL1	2,300
Total for 4.1.X6				3,860

Dr Sales returns $3,860

Cr Receivables ledger control account $3,860

Individual returns posted as credits to individual customers' accounts in accounts receivable ledger.

Format of the purchases returns day book

Date	Invoice	Customer	Ledger Ref	$
4.1.X6	112	Harry	PL3	600
4.1.X6	56	Cho	PL16	75
4.1.X6	7	Fleur	PL2	800
4.1.X6	890	Neville	PL1	50
4.1.X6	12	Draco	PL12	100
Total for 4.1.X6				1,625

Dr Payables ledger control account $1,625

Cr Purchases returns $1,625

Individual returns posted as debits to individual suppliers accounts in accounts payable ledger.

Illustration 1

Mr Kipper-Ling runs a business providing equipment for bakeries. He always makes a note of sales and purchases on credit and associated returns, but he is not sure how they should be recorded for the purposes of his accounts.

Write up the following credit transactions arising in the first two weeks of August 20X6 into day books and advise Mr Kipper-Ling of the correct double entries assuming that control accounts are maintained as part of the double entry system.

1 August Mrs Bakewell buys $500 worth of cake tins.

1 August Mr Kipper-Ling purchases $2,000 worth of equipment from wholesalers TinPot Ltd.

2 August Mr Kipper-Ling returns goods costing $150 to another supplier, I Cook.

3 August Jack Flap buys $1,200 worth of equipment.

3 August Mrs Bakewell returns $100 worth of the goods supplied to her.

4 August Victoria Sand-Witch buys a new oven for $4,000.

5 August Mr Kipper-Ling purchases $600 worth of baking trays from regular supplier TinTin Ltd.

8 August Mr Kipper-Ling purchases ovens costing $10,000 from Hot Stuff Ltd.

8 August Mr Kipper-Ling returns equipment costing $300 to TinPot Ltd.

9 August Pavel Ova purchases goods costing $2,200.

11 August Mrs Bakewell buys some oven-proof dishes costing $600.

Solution

Solution

Sales day book				Sales returns day book		
Aug	Customer	$	Aug		Customer	$
1	Mrs Bakewell	500				
3	Jack Flap	1,200	3		Mrs Bakewell	100
4	Victoria Sand-Witch	4,000				
						100
9	Pavel Ova	2,200				
11	Mrs Bakewell	600				
		8,500				

Dr Receivables ledger control account	$8,500	Dr Sales returns	$100
Cr Sales	$8,500	Cr Receivables ledger control account	$100

And update the memorandum accounts:

And update the memorandum accounts:

Dr Mrs Bakewell	$1,100	Cr Mrs Bakewell	$100
Dr Jack Flap	$1,200		
Dr Victoria Sand-Witch	$4,000		
Dr Pavel Ova	$2,200		

Purchases day book			Purchases returns day book		
Aug	Supplier	$	Aug	Supplier	$
1	TinPot Ltd	2,000	2	I Cook	150
5	TinTin Ltd	600	8	TinPot Ltd	300
8	Hot Stuff	10,000			
		12,600			450
Dr Purchases		$12,600	Dr Payables ledger control account		$450
Cr Payables ledger control account		$12,600	Cr Purchases returns		$450
And update the memorandum accounts:			And update the memorandum accounts:		
Cr TinPot Ltd	$2,000		Dr I Cook		$150
Cr TinTin Ltd	$600		Dr TinPot Ltd		$300
Cr Hot Stuff	$10,000				

5 Sales tax in day books

If a business is registered for sales tax, the sales and purchases day books must include entries to record the tax.

Illustration 2– Sales tax in day books

Sales day book

Date	Invoice	Customer	Ledger Ref	Gross	Sales tax	Net
				$	$	$
8.7.X6	1	Spencer	J1	587.50	87.50	500.00
10.7.X6	2	Archie	S5	705.00	105.00	600.00
				1,292.50	192.50	1,100.00

Purchases day book

Date	Customer	Ledger Ref	Gross	Sales tax	Net
			$	$	$
8.7.X6	Peggy	Y1	1,762.50	262.50	1,500
10.7.X6	Zena	Z8	352.50	52.50	300
			2,115.00	315.00	1,800

What double entry arises from the day book?

Solution

The double entry for the above transaction will be:

Dr Sales tax $315

Dr Purchases $1,800

Cr Payables ledger control account $2,115

The double entry for the above transaction will be:

Dr Receivables ledger control account $1,292.50

Cr Sales tax $192.50

Cr Sales $1,100.00

Test your understanding 1

The following sales invoices have been issued by Quincy. in July:

Date	Customer	Inv No	Ledger ref.	Sales
8 July	Simpson	1100	A8	$ 411.25 (including sales tax)
10 July	Burns	1101	B5	$ 1,300 (excluding sales tax)

Quincy is registered for sales tax, applied at a rate of 17.5%

What double entry arises from the day book?

		Dr		Cr
A	Receivables ledger control account	$1,711.25	Sales	$2,010.72
	Sales tax	$299.47		
B	Receivables ledger control account	$2,010.72	Sales	$1,711.25
			Sales tax	$299.47
C	Receivables ledger control account	$1,650.00	Sales	$1,938.75
	Sales tax	$288.75		
D	Receivables ledger control account	$1,938.75	Sales	$1,650.00
			Sales tax	$288.75

Control accounts

Control accounts are ledger accounts that summarise a large number of transactions.

Control accounts do form part of the double entry system.

The receivables ledger control account may include any of the following entries:

Receivables ledger control account

Balance b/f	X	Balance b/f	X
Credit sales (SDB)	X	Sales returns (SRDB)	X
		Bank (CB)	X
Bank (CB) dishonoured cheques	X	Irrecoverable debts (journal)	X
Bank (CB) refunds of credit balances	X	Discounts allowed	X
Interest charged	X	Contra	X
Balance c/f	X	Balance c/f	X
	X		X
Balance b/f	X	Balance b/f	X

The payables ledger control account may include any of the following entries:

Payables ledger control account

Balance b/f	X	Balance b/f	X
Bank (CB)	X	Credit purchases (PDB)	X
Purchases returns (PRDB)	X	Bank (CB) refunds of debit balances	X
Discounts received	X		
Contra	X		
Balance c/f	X	Balance c/f	X
	X		X
Balance b/f	X	Balance b/f	X

SDB Sales day book

PDB Purchases day book

SRDB Sales returns day book

PRDB Purchases returns day book

CB Cash book

Note that any entries to the control accounts must also be reflected in the individual accounts within the accounts receivable and payable ledgers.

Recording contra entries

Contra entries

The situation may arise where a customer is also a supplier. Instead of both owing each other money, it may be agreed that the balances are contra'd, i.e. cancelled.

The double entry for this type of contra is:

> Dr Payables ledger control account
>
> Cr Receivables ledger control account

The individual receivable and payable accounts must also be updated to reflect this.

Recording credit balances

Credit balances on the receivables ledger control account

Sometimes the receivables ledger control account may show a credit balance, i.e. we owe the customer money. These amounts are usually small and arise when:

- The customer has overpaid.
- Credit notes have been issued for fully-paid-for goods.
- Payment is received in advance of raising invoices.

The payables ledger control account may show a debit balance for similar reasons.

Test your understanding 2

Jones prepares monthly Receivables and Payables ledger control accounts. At 1 November 2005 the following balances existed in the company's records.

	Dr $	Cr $
Receivables ledger control account	54,000	1,000
Payables ledger control account	200	43,000

The following information is extracted in November 2005 from the company's records:

	$
Credit sales	251,000
Cash sales	34,000
Credit purchases	77,000
Cash purchases	29,000
Credit sales returns	11,000
Credit purchases returns	3,000
Amounts received from credit customers	242,000
Dishonoured cheques	500
Amounts paid to credit suppliers	74,000
Cash discounts allowed	3,000
Cash discounts received	2,000
Irrecoverable debts written off	1,000
Increase in allowances for receivables	1,200
Interest charged to customers	1,400
Contra settlements	800

At 30 November 2005 the balances in the Receivables and Payables ledgers, as extracted, totalled:

	Dr $	Cr $
Receivables ledger balances	To be calculated	2,000
Payables ledger balances	200	To be calculated

Prepare the receivables ledger control account and the payables ledger control account for the month of November 2005 to determine the closing debit and closing credit balances on the receivables ledger control account and payables ledger control account respectively.

6 The cash book

- All transactions involving cash at bank are recorded in the cash book.

- Many businesses have two distinct cash books – a **cash payments book** and a **cash receipts book.**

- A note of cash discounts given and received is also recorded in the cash book. This is to facilitate the recording of discounts in both the general and accounts payable/receivable ledgers.

- It is common for businesses to use a columnar format cash book in order to analyse types of cash payment and receipt.

Illustration 3 – The cash book

The cash payments book

The following is the cash payments book of a small print business.

Date	Detail	Bank	Discount ledger	Payables	Rent
		$	$	$	$
18.7.X6	Mr A	1,400	100	1,400	
18.7.X6	Office	3,000			3,000
18.7.X6	Mr B	210		210	
18.7.X6	Mr C	1,600	80	1,600	
18.7.X6	Shop	400			400
		6,610	180	3,210	3,400

What are the accounting entries arising from the totals in the cash book at the end of the day, assuming control accounts are kept?

Solution to cash payments book

Solution

The cash transactions are recorded in total as follows:

Dr Payables ledger control account $3,210

Dr Rent expense $3,400

Cr Bank $6,610

The discount is recorded as follows:

Dr Payables ledger control account $180

Cr Discounts received $180

Entries must also be made to Mr A, Mr B and Mr C's individual accounts in the accounts payable ledger in order to reflect the payments made and discounts received.

Test your understanding 3

The following is the cash receipts book of the SM Art Gallery.

Date	Detail	Bank received	Discount	Receivables ledger	Bank interest
		$	$	$	$
18.7.X6	C Monet	10,000	500	10,000	
18.7.X6	Interest Acc # 1	20			20
18.7.X6	VV Gogh	25,000		25,000	
18.7.X6	Interest Acc # 2	100			100
18.7.X6	P Picasso	13,700	300	13,700	
		48,820	800	48,700	120

What are the accounting entries arising from the totals in the cash book at the end of the day, assuming control accounts are kept?

7 The petty cash book

- All transactions involving small amounts of cash are recorded in the petty cash book.

- The petty cash system is usually designed to deal with sundry small payments in cash made by a business, e.g. paying the milkman, purchasing biscuits, buying stationery or reimbursing travel expenses.

- The cash receipts will be recorded together with the payments which will be analysed in the same way as a cash book.

The imprest system

The best way of dealing with petty cash is by means of an imprest system, which works as follows.

Step 1

The business decides on the amount of cash to be held as a float.

Dr Petty cash   X

Cr Bank   X

This round sum amount will be referred to as the 'petty cash float'.

Step 2

As the petty cashier makes payments he records these in the petty cash book, which is not part of the double entry system. All expenditure must be evidenced by an expense receipt and the petty cashier will attach an expense voucher to each expense.

Step 3

When the petty cash runs low, a cheque is drawn to return the petty cash to the exact amount of the original float. At this stage the expense vouchers should be produced by the petty cashier to the cheque signatory which will exactly equal the cheque required.

This aspect of control is the essential feature of the petty cash system. At any stage:

Float = Cash in petty cash box + sum total of expense vouchers since last reimbursement

Petty cash

Controls over petty cash

The following controls and security over petty cash should be found in a business:

- Petty cash must be kept in a petty cash box.

- Petty cash box must be secured in a safe.

- Person responsible for petty cash must be reliable and know what he/she is doing.

- All petty cash must be supported by invoices.

- Petty cash vouchers must be signed by the claimant and the person responsible for running the petty cash.

- Regular spot checks must be carried out to ensure that the petty cash is accurate.

Petty Cash Book

In this book the business will record small cash transactions.

- The cash receipts will be recorded together with the payments which will be analysed in the same way as a cash book. An imprest system will be adopted for the petty cash book.

- An amount is withdrawn from the bank account which is referred as a 'petty cash float'.
  This 'float' will be used to pay for the various sundry expenses. The petty cash book cashier will record any payments.

- Any expenditure must be evidenced by an expense receipt and the petty cashier will attach a petty cash voucher to each expense.

- At any point in time the cash together with the expense vouchers should agree to the total float.

- At the end of the period the petty cash float is 'topped up' by withdrawing an amount from the bank totalling the petty cash payment made during the period.

Illustration 4 – The petty cash book

On 1 March 20X9 a petty cash float of $100 is introduced by Dialex. During March the following payments are made out of petty cash:

		$
2 March	Biscuits	10
8 March	Stationery	20
11 March	Bus fare	3
16 March	Train fare	5
25 March	Stationery	40

On 31 March the cash is reimbursed. Write up the petty cash book for the month and show the resulting entries to the general ledger.

Solution

Solution

Received	Date	Details	Voucher	Total	Stationery expenses	Sundry expenses	Travelling
				$	$	$	$
100	1 Mar	Cash book					
	2 Mar	Gateway biscuits	1	10		10	
	8 Mar	Basildon Bond	2	20	20		
	11 Mar	Bus fares	3	3			3
	16 Mar	Rail fares	4	5			5
	25 Mar	Office International	5	40	40		
				78	60	10	8
78	31 Mar	Cash					
		Balance c/f		100			
				178			
	1 Apr	Balance b/f					

No double entry bookkeeping entries are made from the receipts side of the petty cash book – in a good system the only receipt should be the reimbursement of the float, the double entry of which is dealt with in the posting of the cash book.

As regards the payments, the double entry in the general ledger is performed as follows:

Stationery

20X9	$	20X9	$
Mar Petty cash book	60		

Sundry expenses

20X9	$	20X9	$
Mar Petty cash book	10		

Travelling expenses

20X9	$	20X9	$
Mar Petty cash book	8		

8 The journal

The journal is a book of prime entry which records transactions which are not routine (and not recorded in any other book of prime entry), for example:

- year-end adjustments
  - depreciation charge for the year
  - irrecoverable debt write-off
  - record movement in allowance for receivables
  - accruals and prepayments
  - closing inventory
- acquisitions and disposals of non-current assets
- opening balances for statement of financial position items
- correction of errors.

The journal is a clear and comprehensible way of setting out a bookkeeping double entry that is to be made.

Presentation of a journal

A journal should be laid out in the following way:

Dr Non-current asset	X
Cr Cash	X

to record the purchase of a new non-current asset.

A brief narrative should be given to explain the entry.

Test your understanding 4

Igor Romanov runs a Russian restaurant. He is a very good chef but not quite so good at accounting and needs help to record the following transactions:

(1) Closing inventory of 250 bottles of vodka at a cost of $2,750 has not been recorded.

(2) Igor needs to charge depreciation on his restaurant. He holds a 25-year lease which cost him $150,000 ten years ago.

(3) A regular customer, V Shady, keeps a tab behind the bar. He currently owes $350 but was last seen buying a one-way ticket to Moscow. Igor has given up hope of payment and intends to write the debt off.

(4) On the last day of the year Igor bought two new sofas for cash for the bar area of the restaurant. They cost $600 each but the purchase has not been reflected in the accounts.

What journals should Igor post?

Chapter summary

TRANSACTION OCCURS

RECORDED IN BOOKS OF PRIME ENTRY

DAY BOOKS

Used to record credit trading transactions

- Sales
- Purchases
- Sales returns
- Purchases returns.

CASH AND PETTY CASH BOOKS

Used to record all cash transactions.

JOURNAL

Used for all other transactions, e.g. to record

- depreciation
- accruals and prepayments
- closing inventory
- irrecoverable debt write-offs
- movement in allowance for receivables
- correction of errors.

USED TO UPDATE LEDGER ACCOUNTS

GENERAL LEDGER

Contains all accounts or a summary of all accounts.

ACCOUNTS PAYABLE LEDGER

Contains an account for each credit supplier.

ACCOUNTS RECEIVABLE LEDGER

Contains an account for each credit customer.

INCLUDES THE RECEIVABLES LEDGER CONTROL ACCOUNT AND THE PAYABLES LEDGER CONTROL ACCOUNT

For memorandum purposes only where control accounts are maintained.

Test your understanding answers

Test your understanding 1

The correct answer is D

Sales day book

Date	Customer	Invoice	Ledger ref.	Gross	Sales tax	Net
				$	$	$
8 July	Simpson	1100	A8	411.25	61.25	350.00
10 July	Burns	1101	B5	1,527.50	227.50	1,300.00
				1,938.75	288.75	1,650.00

The double entry for the above transaction will be:

Dr	Receivables ledger control account	$1,938.75
Cr	Sales tax	$288.75
Cr	Sales	$1,650.00

KAPLAN PUBLISHING

Test your understanding 2

Receivables ledger control account

	$		$
Balance b/f	54,000	Balance b/f	1,000
Credit sales	251,000	Sales returns	11,000
Dishonoured cheques	500	Cash received	242,000
Interest charged	1,400	Discounts allowed	3,000
		Irrecoverable debts	1,000
		Contra	800
Balance c/f	2,000	Balance c/f	50,100
	308,900		308,900
Balance b/f	50,100	Balance b/f	2,000

Payables ledger control account

	$		$
Balance b/f	200	Balance b/f	43,000
Purchases returns	3,000	Credit purchases	77,000
Cash paid	74,000		
Discounts received	2,000		
Contra	800		
Balance c/f	40,200	Balance c/f	200
	120,200		120,200
Balance b/f	200	Balance b/f	40,200

Test your understanding 3

The cash transactions are recorded in total as follows:

Dr Bank $48,820

Cr Receivables ledger control account $48,700

Cr Interest income $120

The discount is recorded as follows:

Dr Discounts allowed $800

Cr Receivables ledger control account $800

Entries must also be made to Monet, Gogh and Picasso's individual accounts in the accounts receivable ledger in order to reflect the payments received and discounts allowed.

Test your understanding 4

(1) Dr Closing inventory (statement of financial position) $2,750

Cr Closing inventory (cost of sales) $2,750

To record the closing inventory of vodka.

(2) Dr Depreciation expense $6,000 ($150,000/25 yrs)

Cr Accumulated depreciation $6,000

To record depreciation on the restaurant lease.

(3) Dr Irrecoverable debt expense $350

Cr Receivables ledger control account $350

To record the write-off of a debt outstanding from V Shady.

NB Igor must also remember to update V Shady's individual account in the accounts receivable ledger.

(4) Dr Fixtures and Fittings cost $1,200

Cr Cash $1,200

To record the purchase of two sofas for the bar.

Control account reconciliations

Chapter learning objectives

Upon completion of this chapter you will be able to:

- prepare, reconcile and understand the purpose of supplier statements

- identify errors which would be highlighted by performing a control account reconciliation

- perform basic control account reconciliations for receivables and payables, identifying and correcting errors in control accounts and ledgers.

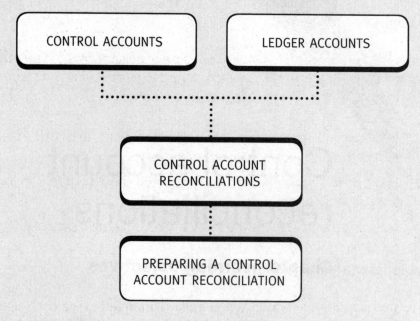

1 Control accounts

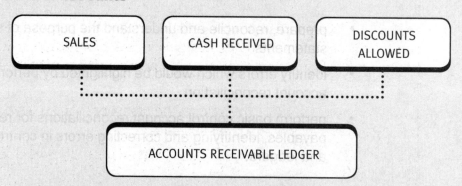

- Control accounts are a means of proving the accuracy of the ledger accounts, such as receivables and payables.

- The diagram above shows the information that is included in the **accounts receivables ledger**.

- If we wanted to check the accuracy of the accounts receivables ledger, one way we can do this is by getting the information from different sources:

  - The sales can be taken from the sales day book.

  - The cash received and discounts allowed are recorded in the cash book.

  - The opening balances can be taken from the prior month's closing balances.

- An alternative way to check the accuracy of the accounts receivables ledger is to compare the sum total of the individual receivables accounts with the balance on the receivables ledger control account.

- Remember, the control account is normally part of the double entry system, whereas the ledger contains memorandum accounts which are not part of the double entry system. Nevertheless, both are updated using the same sources and therefore should agree.

2 Supplier statements

These statements are issued to a business by suppliers to summarise the transactions that have taken place during a given period, and also to show the balance outstanding at the end of the period.

- Their purpose is to ensure that the amount outstanding is accurate and agrees with underlying documentation.

- The payables (individual) ledger account should agree with the total of the supplier statement.

- As such, these are a further way to prove the accuracy of accounting records.

Supplier statement reconciliations

It is also possible to reconcile a supplier statement to the control account.

The purpose for doing this is as follows:

- before any payments are made to suppliers it is important to ensure that the suppliers statement is correct – else we could make over or under payments.

- each invoice and credit note listed on the statement should be checked to the original documentation for accuracy.

- once accuracy has been established, it is then possible to decide which invoices need paying and when by.

Below is an example extract of a statement from a supplier:

STATEMENT					
Date	Transaction	Total $	Current $	30+ $	60+ $
10 May 20X9	Invoice 100	94.50			94.50
1 June 20X9	CN 2008	(24.56)			(24.56)
4 July 20X9	Invoice 110	101.99		101.99	
15 July 20X9	Invoice 156	106.72	106.72		
	TOTALS	278.65	106.72	101.99	69.94
May I remind you that our credit terms are 30 days.					

Here is the payables ledger which corresponds with this supplier:

Nino Ltd

	$			$
1 June 20X9 CN	24.56	10 May 20X9	Invoice 100	94.50
		4 July 20X9	Invoice 110	110.99
		15 July 20X9	Invoice 156	106.72

You can see that the invoice dated 4 July 20X9 in the ledger is of a total $110.99, however in the statement it appears as $101.99.

The purchase invoice itself should be reviewed to check which is the correct amount. If the suppliers statement is incorrect, then a polite telephone call to the supplier should be made or a letter sent explaining the problem.

If it is the ledger that is incorrect then it should be updated.

3 Control account reconciliations

The reconciliation is a working to ensure that the entries in the ledger accounts agree with the entries in the control account. The two should have the same closing balance as ideally they have had exactly the same entries in both accounts.

- A **receivables ledger reconciliation** compares the total of the accounts in the receivables ledger with the balance on the receivables ledger control account.

- A **payables ledger reconciliation** compares the total of the accounts in the payables ledger with the balance on the payables ledger control account.

If there are differences between the control account and the ledger accounts, they must be identified and reconciled. Differences may arise due to:

- errors in the receivables or payables ledger

- errors in the receivables or payables ledger control accounts

- errors in both the control account and ledger account.

Test your understanding 1

Suggest reasons why there might be a difference between the balance on the receivables ledger control account and the total of the list of accounts receivable ledger balances.

4 Preparing a control account reconciliation

The format of a control account reconciliation, in this case for sales is as follows:

Receivables ledger control account

	$		$
Balance given by the examiner	X	Adjustments for errors	X
Adjustments for errors	X	Revised balance c/f	X
	—		—
	X		X

Reconciliation of individual receivables balances with control account balance

	$
Balance as extracted from list of receivables	X
Adjustments for errors	X/(X)
	—
Revised total agreeing with balance c/f on control account	X

- The examiner will provide details of the error(s).

- You must decide for each whether correction is required in the control account, the list of individual balances or both.

- When all errors have been corrected, the revised balance on the control account should agree to the revised total of the list of individual balances.

- Due to the nature of the F3/FFA exam, you will not be asked to produce a full control account reconciliation, however you may be asked for the revised balance on the control account / list of individual balances after one or two errors have been corrected.

Illustration 1 – Preparing a control account reconciliation

Alston's payables ledger control account is an integral part of the double entry system. Individual ledger account balances are listed and totalled on a monthly basis, and reconciled to the control account balance. Information for the month of March is as follows:

(1) Individual ledger account balances at 31 March have been listed out and totalled $19,766.

(2) The payables ledger control account balance at 31 March is $21,832.

(3) On further examination the following errors are discovered:

- The total of discount received for the month, amounting to $1,715, has not been entered in the control account but has been entered in the individual ledger accounts.

- On listing-out, an individual credit balance of $205 has been incorrectly treated as a debit.

- A petty cash payment to a supplier amounting to $63 has been correctly treated in the control account, but no entry has been made in the supplier's individual ledger account.

- The purchases day book total for March has been undercast (understated) by $2,000.

- Contras (set-offs) with the receivables ledger, amounting in total to $2,004, have been correctly treated in the individual ledger accounts but no entry has been made in the control account.

(i) Prepare the part of the payables ledger control account reflecting the above information.

(ii) Prepare a statement reconciling the original total of the individual balances with the corrected balance on the control account.

Solution

Solution

The best way to approach the question is to consider each of the points above in turn and ask to what extent they affect (i) the payables ledger control account and (ii) the listing of payables ledger balances.

Step 1

The total of discount received in the cash book should have been debited to the payables ledger control account and credited to discount received. Thus, if the posting has not been entered in either double entry account it clearly should be. As this has already been entered into the individual ledger accounts, no adjustment is required to the list of balances.

Step 2

Individual credit balances are extracted from the payables ledger. Here, this error affects the ledger accounts balance. No adjustment is required to the control account, only to the list of balances.

Step 3

The question clearly states that the error has been made in the individual ledger accounts. Amendments should be made to the list of balances. Again, no amendment is required to the control accounts.

Step 4

The total of the purchases day book is posted by debiting purchases and crediting payables ledger control account. If the total is understated, the following bookkeeping entry must be made, posting the $2,000 understatement:

Dr Purchases

Cr Payables ledger control account

As the individual ledger accounts in the payables ledger are posted individually from the purchases day book, the total of the day book being understated will not affect the listing of the balances in the payables ledger.

Step 5

Here it is clear that the error affects the control account, not the payables ledger. Correction should be made by the bookkeeping entry:

Dr Payables ledger control account

Cr Receivables ledger control account

Payables ledger control account

20X9	$	20X9	$
Discount received	1,715	31 Mar	
Sales receivable ledger control	2,004	Balance	21,832
Balance c/f	20,113	Purchase	2,000
	23,832		23,832

Reconciliation of individual balances with control account balance

	Cr $
Balances as extracted	19,766
Credit balance incorrectly treated 2 x $205	410
Petty cash payment	(63)
Net total agreeing with control account	20,113

Test your understanding 2

Rayneydaze is a business selling umbrellas branded with corporate logos. The umbrellas are sold in bulk lots on credit. The accountant is carrying out a reconciliation of the receivables ledger control account balance, which is $172,120 to the total of the balances on the individual accounts in the receivables ledger, which is $176,134.

The following has been found:

(1) A contra item of $1,500 has not been entered in the receivables ledger control account.

(2) A cheque for $555 from a customer has been dishonoured. The correct double entry has been posted but the individual accounts have not been updated.

(3) A payment of $322 from a customer has incorrectly been entered in the accounts receivable ledger as $233.

(4) Discounts allowed totalling $120 have not been entered in the control account.

(5) Cash received of $800 has been debited to the individual customer's account in the accounts receivable ledger.

(6) Total credit sales of $4,500 to a large accountancy firm, Close & Counter have been posted correctly to the ledger account but not recorded in the control account.

Correct the receivables ledger control account and reconcile this to the sum total of the individual accounts in the accounts receivable ledger.

Test your understanding 3

Tonga received a statement from a supplier, Cook, showing a balance of $14,810. Tonga's Payables ledger shows a balance due to Cook of $10,000. Investigation reveals the following:

(1) Cash paid to Cook of $4,080 has not been allowed for by Cook.

(2) Tonga's recorded the fact that a $40 cash discount was not allowed by Cook, but forgot to record this in the payables ledger.

What discrepancy remains between Tonga and Cook's records after allowing for these items?

A $9,930

B $9,850

C $770

D $690

Chapter summary

CONTROL ACCOUNTS

- Control accounts include a summary of transactions that have occurred in the period.
- They are a means of checking that the information in the ledger accounts is correct.
- They are part of the double entry system.

LEDGER ACCOUNTS

- Ledger accounts include a separate account for each credit customer/ credit supplier.
- They are memorandum accounts and not part of the double entry system.

CONTROL ACCOUNT RECONCILIATIONS

- These are a means of checking that the balance on the control account agrees with the balance on the ledger account.
- There may be errors in the ledger account, the control account or both.

PREPARING A CONTROL ACCOUNT RECONCILIATION

- Compare the balance on the ledger account with the control account.
- Review the list of errors to see which account needs amending.
- Set up a T account for the control accounts.
- Prepare a reconciliation for the ledger account.

Test your understanding answers

Test your understanding 1

The following are reasons why the accounts receivable control account may not agree with the ledger account:

- The sales day book, sales returns day book or cash receipts book have been incorrectly totalled.
- A total from a book of prime entry has been transferred to the control account as a different figure.
- An individual entry from a book of prime entry has been transferred to the individual customer's account as a different figure.
- An entry in the control account or the individual customer's account has been omitted or posted to the wrong side of the account.
- The double entry for a day book total has been incorrectly made.
- An individual customer's account has been incorrectly balanced.
- The list of accounts receivable ledger balances has been incorrectly totalled.
- An entry has been made in either the control account or the individual customer's account but not in both.
- An individual customer's balance has been omitted from the list of balances.

Test your understanding 2

Receivables ledger control account

	$		$
Balance b/f	172,120	Contra (1)	1,500
Credit sales (6)	4,500	Discounts (4)	120
		Balance c/f	175,000
	176,620		176,620
Balance b/f	175,000		

Receivables ledger reconciliation

Balance per accounts receivable ledger	176,134
Dishonoured cheque (2)	555
Misposting (3)	(89)
Cash received (5)	(1,600)
Revised balance	175,000

Test your understanding 3

The correct answer is D.

	Cook $	Tonga $	
Difference			
Balance per question	14,810	10,000	
Adjustment	(4,080)	40	
Revised balance	10,730	10,040	690

Bank reconciliations

Chapter learning objectives

Upon completion of this chapter you will be able to:

- describe the purpose of bank reconciliations
- identify the main differences between the cash book and the bank statement
- identify the bank balance to be reported in the final accounts
- correct cash book errors or omissions
- prepare bank reconciliation statements
- derive bank statement and cash book balances from given information.

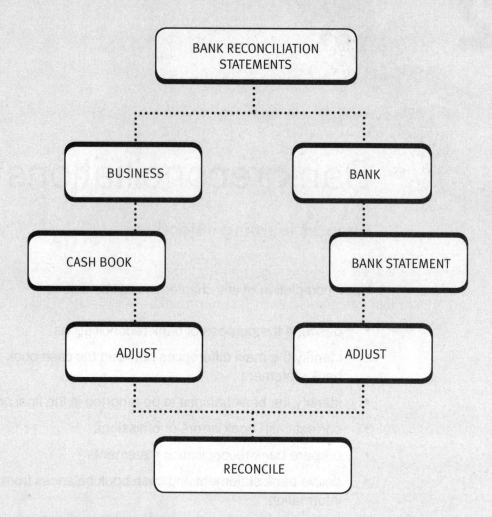

1 The bank reconciliation

The objective of a bank reconciliation is to reconcile the difference between:

- the cash book balance, i.e. the business' record of their bank account, and

- the bank statement balance, i.e. the bank's records of the bank account.

Note that debits and credits are reversed in bank statements because the bank will be recording the transaction from its point of view, in accordance with the business entity concept.

Reasons to prepare a bank reconciliation statement

Nature and purpose of a bank reconciliation statement.

The cash book records all transactions with the bank. The bank statement records all the bank's transactions with the business.

The contents of the cash book should be exactly the same as the record provided by the bank in the form of a bank statement, and therefore our records should correspond with the bank statement.

This is in fact so, but with three important provisos:

(1) The ledger account maintained by the bank is the opposite way round to the cash book. This is because the bank records the balance in favour of an individual as a credit balance, i.e. a liability of the bank to the individual. From the individual's point of view it is, of course, an asset, i.e. a debit balance in his cash book.

(2) Timing differences must inevitably occur. A cheque payment is recorded in the cash book when the cheque is despatched. The bank only records such a cheque when it is paid by the bank, which may be several days later.

(3) Items such as interest may appear on the bank statement but are not recorded in the cash book as the cashier is unaware that they have arisen.

The existence of the bank statement provides an important check on the most vulnerable of a company's assets – cash. However, the differences referred to above make it essential to reconcile the balance on the ledger account with that of the bank statement.

The reconciliation is carried out frequently, usually at monthly intervals.

2 Differences between the bank statement and the cash book

When attempting to reconcile the cash book with the bank statement, there are three differences between the cash book and bank statement:

- unrecorded items
- timing differences
- errors

Cash book adjustments

Unrecorded items

These are items which arise in the bank statements before they are recorded in the cash book. Such 'unrecorded items' may include:

- interest
- bank charges
- dishonoured cheques.

They are not recorded in the cash book simply because the business does not know that these items have arisen until they see the bank statement.

The cash book must be adjusted to reflect these items.

Test your understanding 1

On which side of the cash book should the following unrecorded items be posted?

- bank charges
- direct debits/standing orders
- direct credits
- dishonoured cheques
- bank interest.

Bank reconciliation adjustments

Timing differences

These items have been recorded in the cash book, but due to the bank clearing process have not yet been recorded in the bank statement:

- Outstanding/unpresented cheques (cheques sent to suppliers but not yet cleared by the bank).
- Outstanding/uncleared lodgements (cheques received by the business but not yet cleared by the bank).

The bank statement balance needs to be adjusted for these items:

	$
Balance per bank statement	X
Less: Outstanding/unpresented cheques	(X)
Add: Outstanding/uncleared lodgements	X
Balance per cash book (revised)	X

Errors in the cash book

The business may make a mistake in their cash book. The cash book balance will need to be adjusted for these items.

Errors in the bank statement

The bank may make a mistake, e.g. record a transaction relating to a different person within our business' bank statement. The bank statement balance will need to be adjusted for these items.

Outstanding payments and receipts

Outstanding or unpresented cheques

Suppose a cheque relating to a payment to a supplier of Poorboy is written, signed and posted on 29 March. It is also entered in the cash book on the same day. By the time the supplier has received the cheque and paid it into his bank account, and by the time his bank has gone through the clearing system, the cheque does not appear on Poorboy's statement until, say, 6 April. Poorboy would regard the payment as being made on 29 March and its cash book balance as reflecting the true position at that date.

Outstanding deposits

In a similar way, a trader may receive cheques by post on 31 March, enter them in the cash book and pay them into the bank on the same day. Nevertheless, the cheques may not appear on the bank statement until 2 April. Again the cash book would be regarded as showing the true position. Outstanding deposits are also known as outstanding lodgements.

3 Proforma bank reconciliation

Cash book

Bal b/f	X	Bal b/f	X
Adjustments	X	Adjustments	X
Revised bal c/f	X	Revised bal c/f	X
	X		X
Revised bal b/f	X	Revised bal b/	X

Bank reconciliation statement as at .....

	$
Balance per bank statement	X
Outstanding cheques	(X)
Outstanding lodgements	X
Other adjustments to the bank statement	X/(X)
Balance per cash book (revised)	X

- Beware of overdrawn balances on the bank statement.

- Beware of debits/credits to bank statements.

- Beware of aggregation of deposits in a bank statement.

- **Note that the bank balance on the statement of financial position is always the balance per the revised cash book.**

Test your understanding 2

In preparing a company's bank reconciliation statement, the accountant finds that the following items are causing a difference between the cash book balance and bank statement balance:

(1) Direct debit $530.

(2) Lodgements not credited $1,200.

(3) Cheque paid in by the company and dishonoured $234.

(4) Outstanding cheques $677.

(5) Bank charges $100.

(6) Error by bank $2,399 (cheque incorrectly credited to the account.

Which of these items will require an entry in the cash book?

A   3, 4 and 6

B   1, 3 and 5

C   1, 2 and 4

D   2, 5 and 6

Test your understanding 3

The following information has been extracted from the records of N Patel:

Bank account

		$			Chq no	$
1Dec	Balance b/f	16,491	1 Dec	Alexander	782	857
2 Dec	Able	962	6 Dec	Burgess	783	221
	Baker	1,103	14 Dec	Barry	784	511
10 Dec	Charlie	2,312	17 Dec	Cook	785	97
14 Dec	Delta	419	24 Dec	Hay	786	343
21 Dec	Echo	327	29 Dec	Rent	787	260
23 Dec	Cash sales	529				
30 Dec	Fred	119	31 Dec	Balance c/f		19,973
		22,262				22,262

High Street Bank

Bank Statement – N. Patel

Date	Details	With-drawals	Deposits	Balance
		$	$	$
1 December	Balance b/f			17,478
2 December	780	426		
2 December	781	737		16,315
2 December	Deposit		176	16,491
5 December	782	857		
5 December	Bank charges	47		15,587
6 December	Deposit		2,065	17,652
10 December	Standing order (rates)	137		17,515
11 December	783	212		17,303
13 December	Deposit		2,312	19,615
17 December	784	511		19,104
17 December	Deposit		419	19,523
23 December	Deposit		327	19,850
24 December	Deposit		528	20,378
28 December	786	343		20,035
30 December	310923	297		19,738
31 December	Balance c/f			19,738

(a) Prepare a bank reconciliation statement at 1 December.

(b) Update the cash book for December.

(c) Prepare a bank reconciliation statement at 31 December.

Test your understanding 4

The following is a summary of Ami's cash book as presented to you for the month of December 20X6:

	$		$
Receipts	1,469	Balance b/f	761
Balance c/f	554	Payments	1,262
	———		———
	2,023		2,023
	———		———

All receipts are banked and payments made by cheque.

On investigation you discover:

(1) Bank charges of $136 entered on the bank statement had not been entered in the cash book.

(2) Cheques drawn amounting to $267 had not been presented to the bank for payment.

(3) A cheque for $22 had been entered as a receipt in the cash book instead of as a payment;

(4) A cheque drawn for $6 had been incorrectly entered in the cash book as $66.

What balance is shown on the bank statement at 31 December 20X6?

A $913

B $941 overdraft

C $941

D $407 overdraft

Chapter summary

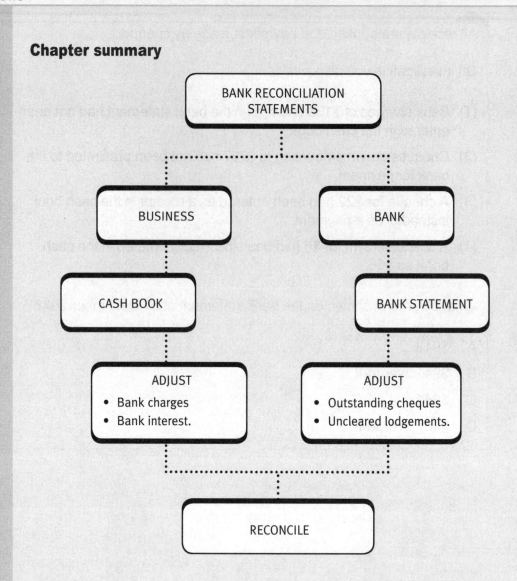

BANK RECONCILIATION STATEMENTS

BUSINESS

BANK

CASH BOOK

BANK STATEMENT

ADJUST
- Bank charges
- Bank interest.

ADJUST
- Outstanding cheques
- Uncleared lodgements.

RECONCILE

Test your understanding answers

Test your understanding 1

Cash book

	$		$
Bank interest	X	Bank charges	X
Direct credits	X	Direct debits/ standing orders	X
		Dishonoured cheques	X

Test your understanding 2

The correct answer is B

Test your understanding 3

Bank reconciliation statement as at 1December	$
Balance per bank statement	17,478
Less: Outstanding cheques ($426 + 737)	(1,163)
Add: Outstanding lodgements	176
Balance per cash book	
	16,491

Bank

	$		$
Balance b/f	19,973	Deposit difference ($529 – 528)	1
Error – cheque 783 ($221–212)	9	Bank charges	47
		Rates – s/order	137
		Revised balance c/f	19,797
	19,982		19,982
Revised balance b/f	19,797		

Bank reconciliation statement as at 31 December	$
Balance per bank statement	19,738
Less: Outstanding cheques ($97 + 260)	(357)
Add: Outstanding lodgements (Fred)	119
Bank error (Cheque 310923)	297
Balance per cash book	
	19,797

Test your understanding 4

The correct answer is D

Cash book

	$		$
Adjustment re cheque (4)	60	Balance b/f	554
Balance c/f	674	Bank charges (1)	136
		Adjustment re paid cheque entered as receipt (3)	44
	734		734
		Balance b/f	674

Bank reconciliation statement as at 31 December 20X6

	$
Balance per bank statement at 31 December 20X6 (derived)	(407) O/D
Less: Cheques issued but not yet presented (2)	(267)
Balance per cash book at 31 Dec 20X6	
	(674) O/D

13

Correction of errors and suspense accounts

Chapter learning objectives

Upon completion of this chapter you will be able to:

- identify the types of error which may occur in bookkeeping systems
- identify errors which would not be highlighted by the extraction of a trial balance
- identify errors leading to the creation of a suspense account.
- describe the purpose of a suspense account
- prepare journal entries to correct errors and clear out a suspense account
- prepare statements correcting profit for errors discovered.

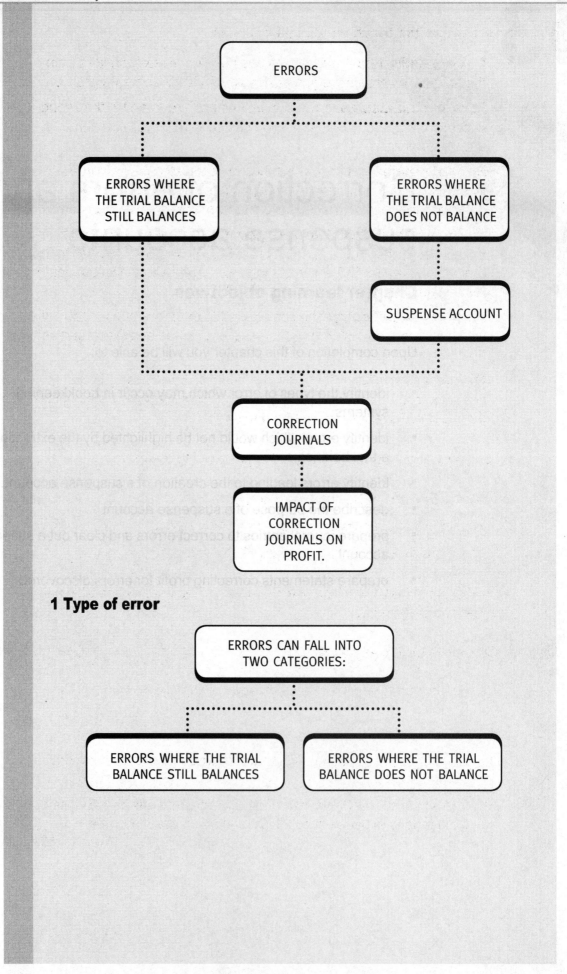

1 Type of error

Errors where the trial balance still balances

- **Error of omission:** A transaction has been completely omitted from the accounting records, e.g. a cash sale of $100 was not recorded.

- **Error of commission:** A transaction has been recorded in the wrong account, e.g. rates expense of $500 has been debited to the rent account in error.

- **Error of principle:** A transaction has conceptually been recorded incorrectly, e.g. a non-current asset purchase of $1,000 has been debited to the repair expense account rather than an asset account.

- **Compensating error:** Two different errors have been made which cancel each other out, e.g. a rent bill of $1,200 has been debited to the rent account as $1,400 and a casting error on the sales account has resulted in sales being overstated by $200.

- **Error of original entry:** The correct double entry has been made but with the wrong amount, e.g. a cash sale of $76 has been recorded as $67.

- **Reversal of entries:** The correct amount has been posted to the correct accounts but on the wrong side, e.g. a cash sale of $200 has been debited to sales and credited to bank.

When correcting these errors, a good approach is to consider:

(1) What was the double entry? ('did do').

(2) What should the double entry have been? ('should do').

(3) Therefore what correction is required? ('to correct').

Always assume that if one side of the double entry is not mentioned, it has been recorded correctly.

Test your understanding 1

Provide the journal to correct each of the following errors:

(1) A cash sale of $100 was not recorded.

(2) Rates expense of $500, paid in cash has been debited to the rent account in error.

(3) a non-current asset purchase of $1,000 on credit has been debited to the repairs expense account rather than an asset account.

> (4) A rent bill of $1,200 paid in cash has been debited to the rent account as $1,400 and a casting error on the sales account has resulted in sales being overstated by $200.
>
> (5) A cash sale of $76 has been recorded as $67.
>
> (6) A cash sale of $200 has been debited to sales and credited to cash.

Errors where the trial balance does not balance

- Single sided entry – a debit entry has been made but no corresponding credit entry or vice versa.

- Debit and credit entries have been made but at different values.

- Two entries have been made on the same side.

- An incorrect addition in any individual account, i.e. miscasting.

- Opening balance has not been brought down.

- Extraction error – the balance in the trial balance is different from the balance in the relevant account.

If there is a difference on the trial balance, then a suspense account is used to make the total debits equal the total credits:

	$	$
Non-current assets	5,000	
Receivables	550	
Inventory	1,000	
Cash	200	
Payables		600
Loan		2,000
Capital		4,000
Suspense account		150
	6,750	6,750

The balance on the suspense account must be cleared before final accounts can be prepared.

Corrections to any of the six errors mentioned above will affect the suspense account.

2 Suspense accounts

A suspense account is an account in which debits or credits are held temporarily until sufficient information is available for them to be posted to the correct accounts.

Suspense accounts are often encountered and must be dealt with according to the usual rules of double entry bookkeeping.

There are two main reasons why suspense accounts may be created:

- On the extraction of a trial balance the debits are not equal to the credits and the difference is put to a suspense account.

- When a bookkeeper performing double entry is not sure where to post one side of an entry he may debit or credit a suspense account and leave the entry there until its ultimate destination is clarified.

Approach to questions:

- Take the approach as before.

- Use the suspense account to make the 'did do' Dr = the 'did do' Cr and then part of the correction journal will be to reverse this suspense account entry.

E.g. The purchase of a non-current asset costing $100 has been recorded by debiting $10 to the non-current assets account and crediting $100 to cash.

What was the double entry? ('Did do')	What should the double entry have been? ('Should do')	Correcting journal	
Dr NCA	$10 Dr NCA	$100 Dr NCA	$90
Dr suspense	$90 Cr Cash	$100 Cr Suspense	$90
Cr Cash	$100		

- Where an opening balance has not been brought down, journal it in and send the opposite entry to suspense.

- The correction journal must always include an equal debit and credit.

Test your understanding 2

The debit side of a company's TB totals $1,200 more than the credit side. Which of the following errors would fully account for the difference?

A   The petty cash balance of $1,200 has been omitted from the TB

B   A receipt of $1,200 for commission receivable has been omitted from the records

C $600 paid for plant maintenance has been correctly entered into the cash book and credited to the plant cost account

D   Discount received of $600 has been debited to the discount allowed account

Test your understanding 3

Bond's TB failed to agree and a suspense account was opened for the difference. Bond does not maintain control accounts for sales and purchases. The following errors were found in Bond's accounting records:

(1)   In recording the sale of a non-current asset, cash received of $33,000 was credited to the disposals account as $30,000.

(2)   An opening accrual of $340 had been omitted.

(3)   Cash of $8,900 paid for plant repairs was correctly accounted for in the cash book but was credited to the plant cost account.

(4)   A cheque for $12,000 paid for the purchase of a machine was debited to the machinery account as $21,000.

Which of the errors will require an entry to the suspense account to correct them?

A   1, 3 and 4 only

B   All

C   1 and 4 only

D   2 and 3 only

Suspense accounts

On extracting a trial balance, the accountant of ETT discovered a suspense account with a debit balance of $1,075 included therein; she also found that the debits exceeded the credits by $957. She posted this difference to the suspense account and then investigated the situation. She discovered:

(1) A debit balance of $75 on the postage account had been incorrectly extracted on the list of balances as $750 debit.

(2) A payment of $500 to a credit supplier, X, had been correctly entered in the cash book, but no entry had been made in the supplier's account.

(3) When a motor vehicle had been purchased during the year the bookkeeper did not know what to do with the debit entry so he made the entry Dr Suspense, Cr Bank $1,575.

(4) A credit balance of $81 in the sundry income account had been incorrectly extracted on the list of balances as a debit balance.

(5) A receipt of $5 from a credit customer, Y, had been correctly posted to his account but had been entered in the cash book as $625.

(6) The bookkeeper was not able to deal with the receipt of $500 from the owner's own bank account, and he made the entry Dr Bank and Cr Suspense.

(7) No entry has been made for a cheque of $120 received from a credit customer M.

(8) A receipt of $50 from a credit customer, N, had been entered into his account as $5 and into the cash book as $5.

What journals are required to correct the errors and eliminate the suspense account?

Solution

Solution

Process of clearing a suspense account

The starting position we have is as follows (once we have posted our $957):

Suspense account

	$		$
Balance b/f	1,075	Trial balance difference	957

We now need to work our way through the information given in numbered points 1 to 8 to try and clear this suspense account.

You need to ask yourself the following questions for each point:

(a) what was the double entry that has been made?

(b) what should the double entry have been?

(c) what is the journal we need to correct this?

(1) (a) They have posted Dr postage 750, Cr bank 75, so the other Dr of 675 will automatically go to the suspense a/c.

   (b) It should have been : Dr postage 75, Cr bank 75 .

   (c) correction = Dr suspense a/c 675, Cr postage 675

(2) (a) They have posted Dr suspense a/c 500, Cr cash 500.

   (b) It should have been: Dr payables (X) 500, Cr cash 500

   (c) correction = Dr payables (X) 500, Cr suspense a/c 500

(3) (a) They have posted: Dr suspense a/c 1575, Cr cash 1575.

   (b) It should have been Dr Motor vehicles cost 1575, Cr bank 1575

   (c) correction = Dr motor vehicles 1575, Cr suspense a/c 1575

(4)(a) They have posted Dr sundry income 81, Dr bank 81 Cr suspense a/c 162

   (b) should have been: Dr bank/cash 81. Cr sundry income 81

   (c) Correction = Dr suspense a/c 162, Cr sundry income 162

(5) (a) They have posted Dr cash 625, Cr receivables 5, so Cr suspense a/c 620

   (b) Should have been Dr cash 5, Cr receivables 5

   (c) Correction = Dr suspense a/c 620, Cr cash 620

(6) (a) They have posted Dr bank 500, Cr suspense a/c 500

   (b) Should have been: Dr bank 500, Cr capital 500

   (c) correction = Dr suspense a/c 500, Cr capital 500

(7) (a) They have posted nothing

   (b) They should have posted Dr bank 120, Cr receivables (M) 120

   (c) Correction = Dr bank 120, Cr receivables (M) 120

(8) (a) They have posted Dr cash 5, Cr receivables 5

   (b) Should have been Dr cash 50, Cr receivables 50

   (c) Correction = Dr cash 45, Cr receivables 45

Now you can post all of the journals that you have listed under the (c) corrections which affect the suspense a/c.

Then you can balance off your suspense a/c and it should balance on both the debit and credit sides. Hence, this will clear your suspense a/c and leave it with a nil balance.

Once you have done so, you should get the following result:

Suspense Account

	$		$
Balance b/f	1,075	Trial balance difference	957
Postage (1)	675	Payable X (2)	500
Sundry income (4)	162	Motor vehicle cost (3)	1,575
Cash (5)	620		
Capital (6)	500		
	-----		-----
	3,032		3,032

3 Adjustments to profit

The correction journal may result in a change in profit, depending on whether the journal debits or credits the income statement:

Dr Statement of financial position account Cr Statement of financial position account	No impact on profit
Dr Income statement account Cr Income statement account	No impact on profit
Dr Income statement account Cr Statement of financial position account	Profit decreases
Dr Statement of financial position account Cr Income statement account	Profit increases

For this purpose the suspense account is defined as a statement of financial position account.

Test your understanding 4

The following correction journals have been posted by Boris Brokovitch, a self-employed plumber:

(1) Dr Suspense $4,000

    Cr Rent $4,000

(2) Dr Payables $2,500

    Cr Suspense $2,500

(3) Dr Loan interest $1,000

     Cr Loan $1,000

(4) Dr Suspense $650

     Cr Sundry income $650

(5) Dr Suspense $6,000

     Cr Cash $6,000

Boris' draft profit figure prior to the posting of these journals is $355,000.

What is the revised profit figure?

A $354,000
B $358,650
C $356,150
D $358,000

What affect will these correction journals have on the Statement of financial position?

4 Statement of comprehensive income

Your correction journals may also affect the Statement of comprehensive income. The only correction journals which would affect this would be revaluation journals.

Chapter summary

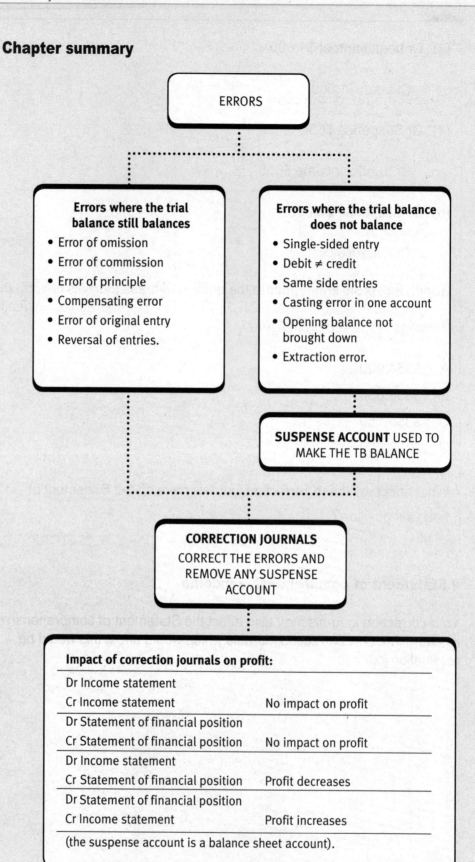

ERRORS

Errors where the trial balance still balances
- Error of omission
- Error of commission
- Error of principle
- Compensating error
- Error of original entry
- Reversal of entries.

Errors where the trial balance does not balance
- Single-sided entry
- Debit ≠ credit
- Same side entries
- Casting error in one account
- Opening balance not brought down
- Extraction error.

SUSPENSE ACCOUNT USED TO MAKE THE TB BALANCE

CORRECTION JOURNALS
CORRECT THE ERRORS AND REMOVE ANY SUSPENSE ACCOUNT

Impact of correction journals on profit:

Dr Income statement	
Cr Income statement	No impact on profit
Dr Statement of financial position	
Cr Statement of financial position	No impact on profit
Dr Income statement	
Cr Statement of financial position	Profit decreases
Dr Statement of financial position	
Cr Income statement	Profit increases

(the suspense account is a balance sheet account).

Test your understanding answers

Test your understanding 1

	What was the double entry?	What should the double entry have been?	Correcting journal
(1)		Dr cash $100 Cr sales $100	Dr cash $100 Cr sales $100 to record both sides of the sale correctly
(2)	Dr rent $500 Cr cash $500	Dr rates $500 Cr cash $500	Dr rates $500 to record the rates expense correctly Cr rent $500 to reverse the incorrect debit to the rent account
(3)	Dr repairs $1,000 Cr payables $1,000	Dr NC asset $1,000 Cr payables $1,000	DR NC asset $1,000 to record the asset correctly Cr repairs $1,000 to reverse the incorrect debit to the repairs account
(4)	Dr rent $1,400 Cr cash $1,200	Dr rent $1,200 Cr cash $1,200	Cr rent $200 to reverse the extra £200 debited to the rent account Dr sales $200 to correct the casting error
(5)	Dr cash $67 Cr sales $67	Dr cash $76 Cr sales $76	Dr cash $9 Cr sales $9 to record the extra $9 sales not previously recorded
(6)	Dr sales $200 Cr cash $200	Dr cash $200 Cr sales $200	Dr cash $400 Cr sales $400 to firstly reverse the error of $200 and then record the sale of $200 correctly in both accounts

Test your understanding 2

The correct answer is D

A and C would result in the credit side of the TB being $1,200 higher than the debit side.

B would have no effect on the TB since neither the debit nor the credit side of the transaction has been accounted for.

Test your understanding 3

The correct answer is B

An entry to the suspense account is required wherever an account is missing from the trial balance or the initial incorrect entry did not include an equal debit and credit.

Test your understanding 4

Income statement profits

The correct answer is B

	Increase $	Decrease $	$
Draft profit			355,000
1 Rent	4,000		
2 No impact			
3 Loan interest		1,000	
4 Sundry income	650	―――	
	―――		
5 No impact			
			3,650
			―――
Revised profit			358,650

Statement of financial position

Journal 1
The Dr entry would go towards clearing any suspense a/c balance.

Journal 2
The Dr payables would decrease the current liabilities. The Cr suspense a/c would go towards clearing the account balance.

Journal 3
The Cr loan would increase the loan liability balance. It does not state whether it is current or non-current.

Journal 4
The Dr suspense a/c would work towards clearing any balance left.

Journal 5
Dr suspense a/c would completely clear the balance in this account. The Cr cash would decrease the cash balance held, which is a current asset.

14

Incomplete records

Chapter learning objectives

Upon completion of this chapter you will be able to:

- explain and illustrate the calculation of profit or loss as the difference between opening and closing net assets

- explain techniques used in incomplete record situations:
  - calculation of opening capital
  - use of ledger total accounts to calculate missing figures.
  - use of cash and/or bank summaries
  - use of given gross profit percentage to calculate missing figures.

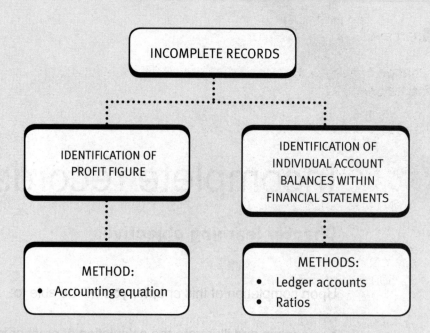

1 Incomplete records

When you are preparing a set of accounts, it is likely that you may not have all of the information available to you to complete a set of financial statements.

It is likely that you may have an incomplete ledger or control accounts system.

If this is the case, you will have to use the best information that is available to you and 'guestimate' any missing figures.

There are a number of different ways which we can use to calculate missing figures and balances, such as:

- Accounting equation method
- Opening capital calculations
- Balancing figure approach
- Ratios – mark up and margin
- Lost inventory methods

2 Identification of profit figure using the accounting equation

If a business has recorded very little information of its transactions it may only be possible to calculate net profit for the year. This can be done using the accounting equation as follows:

Net assets = Capital + Profit – Drawings

Therefore:

Change in net assets = Capital introduced + Profit for the period – Drawings for the period.

NB: Net assets = Assets – Liabilities

Test your understanding 1

Andy Carp's statement of financial position at 31 December 2004 shows that his fishing business has net assets of $5,000. The statement of financial position as at 31 December 20X5 shows that the business has net assets of $8,000. Andy's drawings for the year amounted to $2,500 and he didn't introduce any further capital in that year.

What profit is made by Andy Carp in the year ended 31 December 2005?

A $5,500

B $500

C $10,500

D $7,500

NB: Net assets = Assets – Liabilities

3 Identification of individual account balances within financial statements

- In most cases a business will keep limited accounting records from which it is possible to prepare a full set of financial statements. You may be asked to calculate any of the balances within these financial statements.

- In these types of questions the opening asset and liability balances will be given together with details of transactions during the year.

- Opening capital can be calculated as:

Opening assets – Opening liabilities

- Two further methods may be used to identify other missing figures:

    (1) Use of ledger accounts to find a balancing figure

    (2) Use of ratios.

4 The balancing figure approach

The balancing figure approach, using ledger accounts, is commonly used in the following way:

Ledger account	Missing figure
Receivables	Credit sales, Money received from receivables
Payables	Credit purchases, Money paid to payables
Cash at bank	Drawings, Money stolen
Cash in hand	Cash sales, Cash stolen

Cash at bank

	$		$
Cash received from customers	X	Cash paid to suppliers	X
Bankings from cash in hand	X	Expenses	X
Sundry income	X	Drawings	X
		Money stolen	X
	__	Balance c/f	X
	X		__
Balance b/f	__		X

Cash in hand

	$		$
Cash sales	X	Cash purchases	X
Sundry income	X	Sundry Expenses	X
	__	Bankings	X
	X	Money stolen	X
		Balance c/f	X
			__
Balance b/f			X

In the case of receivables and payables, you may need to use total receivables and total payables accounts where information given cannot be split between cash and credit sales and purchases:

Total receivables

	$		$
Balance b/f	X	Total cash received	X
Total sales	X	in respect of sales	
(cash and credit)	—	(from cash and credit customers)	
	X	Balance c/f	X
	—		—
Balance b/f	X		X

Total payables

	$		$
		Balance b/f	
Total cash paid in	X	Total purchases	X
respect of purchases		(cash and credit)	
(cash purchases and payments to credit suppliers)	—		—
Balance c/f	X		X
	—		—
		Balance b/f	

Test your understanding 2

Suppose that opening receivables for B Rubble's business are $30,000. There have been total receipts from customers of $55,000 of which $15,000 relates to cash sales and $40,000 relates to receipts from receivables. Discounts allowed in the year totalled $3,000 and closing receivables were $37,000.

What are total sales for the year?

A $65,000

B $50,000

C $47,000

D $62,000

Test your understanding 3

The opening payables of Dick Dastard-Lee's business are $15,000.
Total payments made to suppliers during the year were $14,000.
Discounts received were $500 and closing payables were $13,000.

What are total purchases for the year?

A $16,500

B $16,000

C $12,000

D $12,500

Questions may require you to calculate 'missing' income statement figures, for example rent and rates values, from a list of information including payments and opening/closing accruals and prepayments.

To calculate the missing value for each expense use either:

- T-accounts, or
- Equations

Test your understanding 4

The following information relates to Ivor Big-Head's business:

On 1 January	Electricity accrued	$250
	Rent prepaid	$300
Cash paid in the year	Electricity	$1,000
	Rent	$2,000
On 31 December	Electricity accrued	$300
	Rent prepaid	$400

What are the income statement charges for electricity and rent for the year?

	Electricity	Rent
	$	$
A	1,050	2,100
B	1,050	1,900
C	950	1,900
D	950	2,100

Test your understanding 5

On 1 January Elma Fudd's bank account is overdrawn by $1,367. Payments in the year totalled $8,536 and on 31 December the closing balance is $2,227 (positive).

What are total receipts for the year?

A $4,942

B $7,676

C $9,396

D $12,130

Test your understanding 6

On 1 January, Daisee Chain's business had a cash float of $900. During the year cash of $10,000 was banked, $1,000 was paid out as drawings and wages of $2,000 were paid. On 31 December the float was $1,000.

How much cash was received from customers for the year?

A $12,900

B $14,900

C $13,100

D $6,900

5 Ratios – mark up and margin

Gross profit can be expressed as a percentage of either sales or cost of sales:

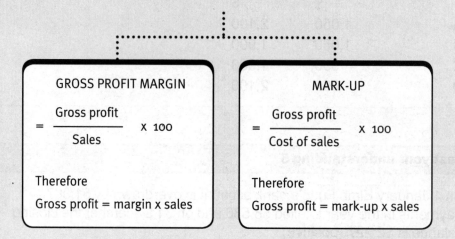

GROSS PROFIT MARGIN

$$= \frac{\text{Gross profit}}{\text{Sales}} \times 100$$

Therefore

Gross profit = margin x sales

MARK-UP

$$= \frac{\text{Gross profit}}{\text{Cost of sales}} \times 100$$

Therefore

Gross profit = mark-up x sales

E.g.

Sales $5,000

Cost of sales ($4,000)

Gross profit $1,000

- Gross profit margin = (1,000/5,000) x 100 = 20%
- Mark up = (1,000/4,000) x 100 = 25%

Test your understanding 7

Padraig O'Flaherty has sales of $1,000. He makes a margin of 25%.

What is the cost of sales figure?

A $200

B $800

C $750

D $250

Test your understanding 8

Ratios

Lorna McDuff has cost of sales of $600 and a 25% mark up.

What is her sales figure?

A $750

B $800

C $250

D $200

Using margin and mark up

An exam question will often provide you with margin and cost of sales or mark up and sales. You will then be required to calculate the remaining figures in the income statement. This can be done using the following 'relationship' columns:

Margin 25%			Mark up 25%		
Sales	2	100%	Sales	3	100 + ratio
Cost of sales	3	100 – ratio	Cost of sales	2	100%
Gross profit	1	Ratio	Gross profit	1	Ratio

Therefore, if we know the mark up or margin percentage and one of the figures in the income statement, we can calculate the remaining figures in the income statement.

Test your understanding 9

Jethro Longhorn can tell you the following with regard to his business:

Margin 5%

Opening inventory $800

Closing inventory $600

Purchases $2,840

Complete Jethro's income statement with the above figures.

6 Cost of lost inventory

- In incomplete record questions, inventory may have been lost – probably due to a fire or flood.

- Closing inventory that has not been lost is subtracted from cost of sales because by definition, the inventory has not been sold in the year.

- Lost inventory has not been sold in the year and therefore also needs subtracting within cost of sales.

- Therefore, to work out the cost of lost inventory, complete the trading account from the information given and then lost inventory can be calculated as a balancing figure.

Test your understanding 10

Jack Spratt provides the following information about his business:

Margin	20%
Sales	$100,000
Opening inventory	$10,000
Purchases	$82,000
Closing inventory after fire	$3,000

What is the cost of inventory lost in the fire?

A $12,000

B $9,000

C $69,000

D $5,667

Double entries for inventory and lost inventory

Actual closing inventory is posted by:

Dr Inventory (SFP)   X

Cr Income statement X

Lost inventory will still be credited to the income statement so that it is removed from cost of sales. However, the debit side of the entry will depend on whether or not the lost inventory has been insured:

If insured: Dr Insurance company (Current asset)

                  Cr Income statement   (Cost of sales)

If not insured: Dr Income statement   (Expense)

                  Cr Income statement   (Cost of sales)

Test your understanding 11

Fred lost his entire inventory in a fire. His unsigned insurance policy is still in the pocket of his good suit. Fred has supplied you with the following information:

Mark up 25%

Sales $10,000

Opening inventory $2,000

Purchases $7,500

Prepare Fred's income statement and show the journal to record closing inventory.

---

7 Reconstruction of full financial statements

Although you will not face an exam question of this length, the following illustration will help you to see how a full set of financial statements can be reconstructed using the methods within this chapter.

Illustration 1 – Reconstruction of full financial statements

Malcolm is a retailer, selling stationery. He does not keep a full set of records. The following records have been extracted from his books.

	30 September 2004 $	30 September 2005 $
Fixtures and fittings: Cost	20,000	To be determined
Accumulated depreciation	8,000	To be determined
Motor vehicles: Cost	22,000	To be determined
Accumulated depreciation	4,180	To be determined
Inventory	18,000	33,900
Receivables	10,000	12,000
Allowances for receivables	500	To be determined
Prepayments – Rates	400	450
Bank	2,000	(15,500)
Cash	600	600
Payables	4,000	4,600
Accruals – Light and heat	250	300

He also has the following cash and bank transactions for the year ended 30 September 2005.

	Cash	Bank
	$	$
Balance b/f	600	2,000
Receipts:		
Cash sales	15,000	
From receivables		140,000
Loan received (long-term)		30,000
Sale proceeds of a motor vehicle sold during the year		8,200
Cash banked		15,000
	_____	_____
	15,600	195,200
Payments:		
Payables		110,000
Rates		9,000
Light and heat		2,000
Telephone		1,500
Loan interest		1,500
Insurance		1,000
Rent		20,000
Wages and salaries		25,000
Withdrawals		15,000
Purchase of fixtures		5,000
Purchase of new motor vehicle		20,000
Sundry expenses		700
Cash paid into bank	15,000	
Balance c/f	_____	_____
	600	(15,500)
	_____	_____

The following further information is available:

(1) The loan was received at the beginning of the year and is entitled to 5% interest pa.

(2) The motor vehicle disposed of during the year had cost $10,000 and the accumulated depreciation on it as at 30 September 2004 was $1,900.

(3) Discount received during the year amounted to $500.

(4) Goods amounting to $1,000 at cost were withdrawn by Malcolm during the year.

(5) The depreciation policy is as follows:

    (a) Fixtures and fittings, 20% pa on a straight-line basis.

    (b) Motor vehicles, 10% pa on a reducing-balance basis.

(6) The allowance for receivables is to be provided at 5% pa on the closing receivables.

    (a) Prepare Malcolm's income statement for the year ended 30 September 2005.

    (b) Prepare Malcolm's statement of financial position as at 30 September 2005.

Completing a full set of financial statements

Solution

(a) Malcolm's income statement for the year ended 30 September 2005

	$	$
Sales: Cash		15,000
– Credit (W1)		142,000
		157,000
Less: Cost of sales		
Opening Inventory	18,000	
Purchases (W2)	111,100	
Goods withdrawn	(1,000)	
	128,100	
Less: Closing inventory	(33,900)	
		(94,200)
Gross profit		62,800
Add: Discount received	500	
Profit on sale of motor vehicle (W3)	100	
		600
		63,400
Less: Increase in allowances for receivables (W4)	(100)	
Rates (9,000 + 400 – 450)	(8,950)	
Light and heat (2,000 + 300 – 250)	(2,050)	
Telephone	(1,500)	
Loan interest	(1,500)	
Insurance	(1,000)	
Rent	(20,000)	
Wages and salaries	(25,000)	

	$	$
Depreciation:		
Motor vehicles (W6)	(2,972)	
Fixtures and fittings (W5)	(5,000)	
Sundry expenses	(700)	
		(68,772)
Net loss		(5,372)

(b) Malcolm's statement of financial position as at 30 September 2005

	Cost	Accumulated depreciation	Net book value (NBV)
	$	$	$
Non-current assets: Fixtures and fittings (W5)	25,000	(13,000)	12,000
Motor vehicles (W6)	32,000	(5,252)	26,748
	57,000	18,252)	38,748
Current assets			
Inventory		33,900	
Receivables	12,000		
Less: Allowances for receivables	(600)		
		11,400	
Rates prepaid		450	
Cash		600	
			46,350
			85,098
Capital (W7)			56,070
Less: Net loss			(5,372)
			50,698
Less: Drawings (W8)			(16,000)
			34,698

Non-current liabilities		
Loan		30,000
Current liabilities		
Payables	4,600	
Lighting and heating accrued	300	
Bank overdraft	15,500	
		20,400
		85,098

(W1)

Receivables

	$		$
Balance b/f	10,000	Bank	140,000
Credit sales (derived)	142,000	Balance c/f	12,000
	152,000		152,000

(W2)

Payables

	$		$
Discount received	500	Balance b/f	4,000
Bank	110,000	Credit purchases (derived)	111,100
Balance c/f	4,600		
	115,100		115,100

(W3)

	$	$
Disposal proceeds		8,200
Less: Net book value:		
Cost	10,000	
Accumulated depreciation	(1,900)	
		8,100
Profit on disposal		100

(W4) **Allowances for receivables**

	$
– Required (5% x $12,000)	600
– B/f	(500)
Increase in allowance	100

(W5) **Fixtures and fittings**

	Cost	Accumulated depreciation	NBV
	$	$	$
Balance b/f	20,000	(8,000)	12,000
Additions	5,000	–	5,000
	25,000	(8,000)	17,000
Charge for the year:			
20% x $25,000		(5,000)	(5,000)
		(13,000)	12,000
	25,000		

(W6) **Motor vehicles**

	Cost	Accumulated depreciation	NBV
	$	$	$
Balance b/f	22,000	(4,180)	17,820
Disposals	(10,000)	1,900	(8,100)
	12,000	(2,280)	9,720
Additions	20,000		20,000
	32,000	(2,280)	29,720
Charge for the year:			
10% x $29,720		(2,972)	(2,972)
Balance c/f	32,000	(5,252)	26,748

(W7) **Capital as at 30 September 2004**

	$	$
Fixtures and fittings ($20,000 – 8,000)		12,000
Motor vehicles ($22,000 – 4,180)		17,820
Inventory		18,000
Receivables ($10,000 – 500)		9,500
Rates prepaid		400
Bank		2,000
Cash		600
		60,320
Payables	4,000	
Light and heat accrued	250	
		(4,250)
		56,070

(W8) **Drawings**

	$
Bank	15,000

Chapter summary

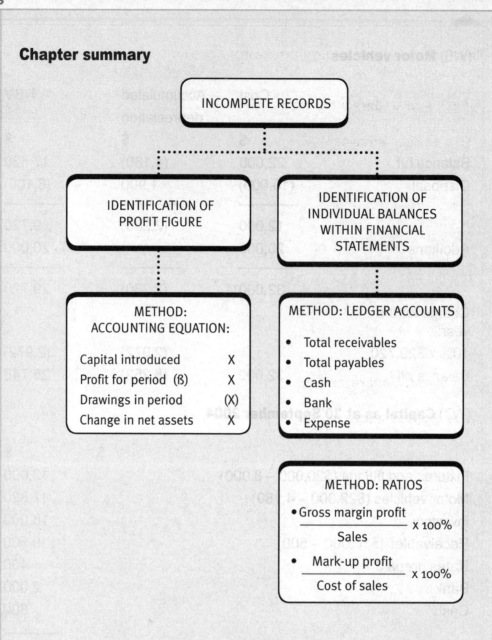

Test your understanding answers

Test your understanding 1

The correct answer is A

Change in net assets = Capital introduced + Profit for the year- Drawings for the year

$8,000 – $5,000 = 0 + Profit for the year – $2,500

Profit = $3,000 + $ 2,500

= $5,500

Test your understanding 2

The correct answer is A

Receivables

	$		$
Balance b/f	30,000	Bank	40,000
Credit sales (ß)	50,000	Discount allowed	3,000
		Balance c/f	37,000
	80,000		80,000
Balance b/f	37,000		

Receivables

Total sales = $50,000 + $15,000 = $65,000

OR

Total receivables

	$		$
Balance b/f	30,000	Bank	55,000
		(total cash rec'd)	
Total sales (ß)	65,000	Discount allowed	3,000
		Balance c/f	37,000
	95,000		95,000

Test your understanding 3

The correct answer is D

Total payables

	$		$
Bank	14,000	Balance b/f	15,000
Discount received	500	Purchases (ß)	12,500
Balance c/f	13,000		
	27,500		27,500
		Balance b/f	13,000

Test your understanding 4

The correct answer is B

Income statement (extracts):

Expenses

Electricity (−250 + 1,000 + 300) = $1,050

Rent (300 + 2,000 − 400) = $1,900

Test your understanding 5

The correct answer is D

Bank

	$		$
Receipts (ß)	12,130	Balance b/f	1,367
		Payments	8,536
		Balance c/f	2,227
	12,130		12,130
Balance b/f	2,227		

Test your understanding 6

The correct answer is C

Cash in till

	$		$
Balance b/f	900	Bank	10,000
Receipts	13,100	Drawings	1,000
		Wages	2,000
		Balance c/f	1,000
	14,000		14,000
Balance c/f	1,000		

Test your understanding 7

The correct answer is C

Gross profit: $1,000 x 25% = $250

Cost of sales:

	$
Sales	1,000
Cost of sales (ß)	(750)
Gross profit	250

Test your understanding 8

The correct answer is A

Gross profit: $600 x 25% = $150

Sales:

	$
Sales (ß)	750
Cost of sales	(600)
Gross profit	150

Test your understanding 9

	$	$	%
Sales:		3,200	100
Cost of sales:	800		
Opening inventory	2,840		
Purchases	(600)		
		(3,040)	(95)
Gross profit:		160	5

Test your understanding 10

The correct answer is B

	$	$	%
Sales:		100,000	100
Cost of sales:			
Opening inventory	10,000		
Purchases	82,000		
Closing inventory	(3,000)		
Inventory lost (ß)	(9,000)		
		(80,000)	(80)
Gross profit:		20,000	20

Test your understanding 11

	$	$	%
Sales:		10,000	125
Cost of sales:			
Opening inventory	2,000		
Purchases	7,500		
Inventory lost (ß)	(1,500)		
		(8,000)	(100)
Gross profit:		2,000	25
Dr Income statement (expense):		1,500	
Cr Income statement (cost of sales):		1,500	

Being the recording of uninsured inventory destroyed by the fire.

15

Company accounts

Chapter learning objectives

Upon completion of this chapter you will be able to:

- explain the difference between a sole trader and a limited liability company

- illustrate the IAS1 required presentation of financial statements

- identify items requiring separate disclosure on the face of the income statement

- explain the capital structure of a limited liability company

- explain and illustrate the share premium account

- define a rights issue and its advantages and disadvantages

- record a rights issue in ledger accounts and show the effect in the statement of financial position

- define a bonus (capitalisation) issue and its advantages and disadvantages

- record a bonus issue in ledger accounts and show the effect in the statement of financial position

- explain and illustrate other reserves which may appear in a company statement of financial position

- explain why the heading, retained earnings, appears in a company statement of financial position

- explain how finance is raised by borrowing rather than by the issue of shares

- calculate and record finance costs in the ledger accounts and the financial accounts

- explain the requirements of IAS as regards current assets and liabilities
- explain the impact of tax on company profits and illustrate the ledger account required to record it
- record tax in the income statement and statement of financial position of a company
- explain and illustrate the recording of dividends.

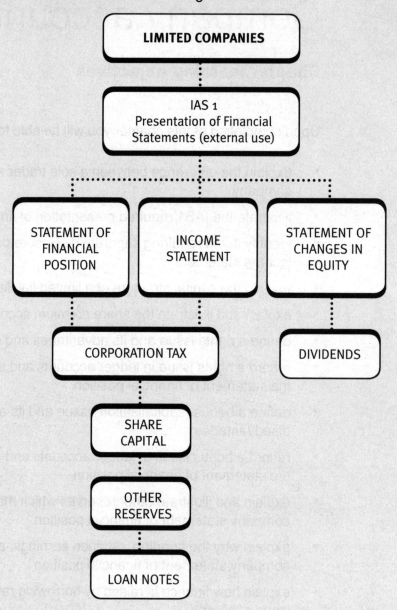

1 Characteristics of limited companies

	Limited liability company	Sole trader
Separate legal entity	A limited company is a separate legal entity, i.e. in the eyes of the law it is a person in its own right and is distinct from its owners.	A sole trader is legally not separate from his business even though he is treated as such for accounting purpose
Liability	A company is fully liable for its own debts. This means that if the company goes into liquidation, the owners (shareholders) of the company are liable only for amounts that they have not yet paid for their shares. Thus the shareholders are said to have limited liability.	If a sole trader goes into liquidation then he is personally liable for any outstanding debts of his business.
Ownership and management	A company is owned by shareholders. The managers of the company are called directors and are appointed by the shareholders. The directors may or may not be shareholders in the company. Thus most shareholders do not play a part in the day-to-day running of the company.	A sole trader is generally both the owner and manager of his or her business.
Formalities	Formalities involved vary from country to country, but frequently require public availability of financial statements and an annual audit by qualified auditors.	No such formalities exist for sole traders.

Advantages of a limited company

The advantages of operation as a limited company rather than as a sole trader can be as follows:

- The liability of the shareholders is limited to the capital already introduced by them.

- There is a formal separation of the business from the owners of the business, which may be helpful to the running of the business. For example, if several members of a family are the shareholders in a company, but only two of the family are directors, it is clear to all concerned who is running the company.

- Ownership of the business can be shared between people more easily than in other forms of business organisation, e.g. a partnership.

- Shares in the business can be transferred relatively easily.

- There may be tax advantages.

The disadvantages of operation as a limited company rather than as a sole trader can be as follows:

- The costs of formation of the company.

- Costs of complying with companies' legislation, including the audit requirement, if any.

- Directors of a company are subject to greater legislative duties than others running an unincorporated business.

- It is difficult/expensive to return capital surplus to the business's requirements back to the shareholders.

- There may be tax disadvantages.

2 IAS 1 presentation of financial statements

IAS 1 incorporates the recommended formats for company published accounts. The following financial summaries are required:

- statement of financial position

- income statement

- statement of comprehensive income (only examinable where a revaluation of non-current assets has occurred)

- statement of changes in equity

- notes to the accounts

- a statement of cash flows and supporting notes

3 Statement of financial position

There are many similarities to the statement of financial position of a sole trader, although some items will require further explanation.

Note that IAS 1 requires an asset or liability to be classified as current if:

- it will be settled within 12 months of the statement of financial position date, or

- it is part of the enterprise's normal operating cycle.

Statement of financial position for XYZ at 31 December XXXX

	$m	$m
Non-current assets		
Property, plant and equipment		
Investments	X	
Intangibles	X	
		X
Current assets		
Inventories	X	
Trade and other receivables	X	
Prepayments	X	
Cash	X	
		X
Total assets		**X**
Equity		
Ordinary share capital	X	
Irredeemable preference share capital	X	
Share premium	X	
Reserves:		
Accumulated profits	X	
		X
Non-current liabilities		
Loan notes		X
Current liabilities		
Trade and other payables	X	
Overdrafts	X	
Tax payable	X	
		X
Total equity and liabilities		**X**

Current assets and current liabilities

The suggested statement of financial position format makes a distinction between current and non-current assets and liabilities. IAS 1 sets down the rules to be applied in making this distinction.

Current assets

An asset should be classified as a current asset if it is:

*   part of the enterprise's operating cycle
*   held primarily for trading purposes
*   expected to be realised within 12 months of the statement of financial position date; or
*   cash or a cash equivalent.

All other assets should be classified as non-current assets.

Note that this definition allows inventory or receivables to qualify as current assets under (a) above, even if they may not be realised into cash within twelve months.

Current liabilities

The rules for current liabilities are similar to those for current assets.

A liability should be classified as a current liability if:

*   it is expected to be settled in the normal course of the enterprise's operating cycle
*   it is held primarily for the purpose of being traded
*   it is due to be settled within 12 months of the statement of financial position date or
*   the company does not have an unconditional right to defer settlement for at least 12 months after the statement of financial position date.

All other liabilities should be classified as non-current liabilities.

4 Income statement

Income statement

A recommended format for the Income statement is as follows:

XYZ Group
Income statement for the year ended 31 December 20X2

	$
Revenue	X
Cost of sales	(X)
	—
Gross profit	X
Distribution costs	(X)
Administrative expenses	(X)
	—
Profit from operations	X
Finance costs	(X)
	—
Profit before tax	X
tax expense	(X)
	—
Net profit for the period	X
	—

Disclosure notes

Notes are printed and published as part of the financial statements. Their contents are normally specified by an accounting standard.

Workings are confidential. They will not be published.

Cost categories

Note that all expenses are classified under one of three headings:

- **Cost of sales**

  This is calculated as for a sole trader. However the calculation should be shown in a note to the accounts rather than on the face of the income statement.

- **Distribution costs**

  These are all expenses relating to selling or delivering products or services.

- **Administrative expenses**

  This includes all expenses not classified within cost of sales or distribution costs.

  Some expenses such as depreciation will be split across all three expense categories.

5 Statement of comprehensive income

The suggested format is as follows.

Statement of comprehensive income for XYZ for the year ended 31 December XXXX

	$m
Revenue	X
Cost of sales	(X)
Gross profit	X
Distribution costs	(X)
Administrative expenses	(X)
Profit from operations	X
Finance costs	X
Profit before tax	X
Tax expense	(X)
Net profit for the period	X
Other comprehensive income:	
Gain/loss on property revaluation	X
Total comprehensive income for the year	**X**

Exceptional items

There are certain circumstances where large one-off items require separate disclosure on the face of the Statement of comprehensive income, these are:

- restructuring or the reorganisation of the entity
- disposal of items of property, plant and equipment
- disposal of investment
- write downs of inventory or property, plant and equipment

These will be clearly shown in the question and should be shown on a separate line on the Statement of comprehensive income.

Relationship between the income statement and statement of financial position

The link between the statement of financial position and income statement is shown below:

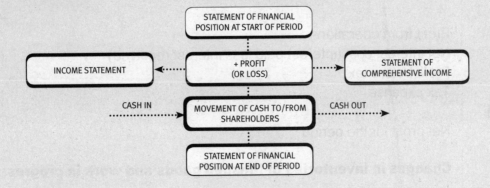

Income statement

The income statement may be presented in one of two ways.

(1) The **function of expenditure** or **cost of sales** method shows expenses classified under the headings: cost of sales, distribution costs and administrative expenditure.

(2) The **nature of expenditure** method analyses expenses according to their nature:

	$m	$m
Sales revenue		X
Other operating income		X
Changes in inventories of finished goods and work in progress	(X)	
Raw materials and consumables used	(X)	
Staff costs	(X)	
Depreciation and amortisation expense	(X)	
Other operating expenses	(X)	
		(X)
Profit from operations		X
Net interest cost (interest paid less interest received)		(X)
Profit before tax		X
Tax expense		(X)
Net profit for the period		X

Changes in inventories of finished goods and work in progress

This is simply the difference between the opening and closing amounts and could thus be a debit or a credit in the statement – if inventories have risen it will be a credit and if they have fallen a debit. Note that raw materials inventories are included below rather than here.

Raw materials and consumables used

This is purchases of raw materials adjusted for opening and closing inventories.

6 Statement of changes in equity

This statement is included within the accounts to provide further information on certain statement of financial position accounts, namely share capital and reserves.

Statement of changes in equity for XYZ Ltd

	Share capital $m	Share premium $m	Revaluation reserve $m	Accumulated profits $m	Total $m
Balance at 1 January	X	X	X	X	X
Equity shares issued	X	X			X
Revaluation surplus			X		X
Net profit				X	X
Dividends				(X)	(X)
	X	X	X	X	X

7 Share capital

A company is owned via shares.

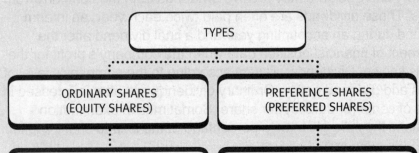

ORDINARY SHARES (EQUITY SHARES)	PREFERENCE SHARES (PREFERRED SHARES)
• Carry voting rights. • Shareholders receive a dividend at the discretion of the company directors. • Dividend is paid out of profits after the preference shareholders receive their dividend.	• Do not generally carry voting rights. • Shareholders receive a fixed dividend (calculated as % x nominal value of shares held). • Dividend is paid out in priority to ordinary dividend.

Cumulative preference shares	Non-cumulative preference shares
If the dividend is not paid in a given year, it is still owed to the shareholders in the following year (and must be paid ahead of any ordinary dividend).	If the dividend is not paid in a given year, then in the following year, only that year's preference dividend need be paid before an ordinary dividend.

- Redeemable preference shares are preference shares which are repayable by the company at a specified future date. On this date the shares are cancelled and the shareholders repaid.

  These shares have the characteristics of debt. They are therefore classified as a liability on the statement of financial position.

- Irredeemable preference shares are preference shares which are not redeemable. They remain in existence indefinitely.

  These shares are classified as equity on the statement of financial position.

Share capital

The share capital of a company may be divided into various classes. The company's internal regulations define the respective rights attached to the various shares, e.g. as regards dividend entitlement or voting at company meetings. In practice it is usually only larger companies which have different classes of share capital.

Ordinary shares are the normal shares issued by a company. The ordinary shareholders are the real owners of the business

Ordinary shareholders may receive dividends from the company from its profits. These dividends are often paid twice each year, an interim dividend during an accounting year and a final dividend after the statement of financial position date when the company's profit for the year is known. Dividends will vary according to the company's level of profits and dividend policy. Ordinary dividends are often expressed in terms of cents (or dollars) per share. Sometimes in examination questions they are given as a percentage of the issued share capital.

No dividend may be paid on the ordinary shares until the preference share dividend has been paid in full.

Preference shares are shares carrying a fixed rate of dividend, the holders of which have a prior claim to any company profits available for distribution.

Special categories of preference shares include:

- Participating preference shares – where shareholders are entitled to participate together to a specified extent in distributable profits and surpluses on liquidation

- Redeemable preference shares – the terms of issue specify that they are repayable by the company.

Share capital values

- Each share has a nominal or par value, often $1, 50c or 25c. This value is often used as a means of calculating dividends to shareholders (paid as a percentage of the nominal value).

- Shares are issued by the company at an issue price. This is at least equal to the nominal value of the share, but often exceeds it.

Market value of shares

The market value of a share fluctuates according to the success and perceived expectations of a company. If a company is listed on the stock exchange, the value is determined by reference to recent transactions between buyers and sellers of shares. This value does not feature in the financial statements.

Share capital terminology

- **Authorised** share capital is the nominal value of the maximum number of shares that a company can have in issue at any particular point in time.

- **Issued** share capital is the share capital that has actually been issued to shareholders. The number of issued shares is used in the calculation of dividends.

- **Called-up** share capital is the amount of the nominal value paid by the shareholder plus any further amounts that they have agreed to pay in the future.

- **Paid up** share capital is the amount of the nominal value which has been paid at the current date.

Accounting for the issue of shares

A company will generally issue shares at above par (nominal) value.

The double entry to record an ordinary or irredeemable preference share issue is:

Dr Cash   Issue price x no. shares

Cr Share capital (SFP)   Nominal value x no. shares

Cr Share premium   ß

Both the share capital and share premium accounts are shown on the statement of financial position within the 'Share Capital and Reserves' section.

The double entry to record a redeemable preference share issue is:

Dr Cash   Issue price x no. shares

Cr Liability   Issue price x no. of shares

Test your understanding 1

Bourbon issues 200,000 25c shares at a price of $1.75 each.

Show this transaction using ledger accounts.

8 Rights issues

A **rights issue** is:

the offer of new shares to existing shareholders in proportion to their existing shareholding at a stated price (normally below market values).

The **advantages** are:

*   A rights issue is the cheapest way for a company to raise finance through the issuing of further shares.
*   A rights issue to existing shareholders has a greater chance of success compared with a share issue to the public.

The **disadvantages** are:

*   A rights issue is more expensive than issuing debt.
*   It may not be successful in raising the finance required.

A rights issue is accounted for in the same way as a normal share issue.

Test your understanding 2

Upon incorporation in 20X4, The Jammy Dodger, a limited liability company, issues 1,000 50c shares at nominal value. Needing further funds, in 20X5 it makes a rights issue of 1 for 5 at $0.75. This offer is fully taken up.

What accounting entries are required in 20X4 and 20X5? Illustrate the relevant section of the statement of financial position at year end 20X5.

9 Bonus issues

A **bonus (or capitalisation or scrip)** issue is:

the issue of new shares to existing shareholders in proportion to their existing shareholding. No cash is received from a bonus issue.

The **advantages** are:

- Issued share capital is divided into a larger number of shares, thus making the market value of each one less, and so more marketable.

- Issued share capital is brought more into line with assets employed in the company.

The **disadvantages** are:

- the admin costs of making the bonus issue.

As no cash is received from a bonus issue, the issue must be funded from reserves. Any reserve can be used, though a non-distributable reserve such as the share premium account would be used in preference to reserves which can be distributed:

Dr Share premium   Nominal value

(or other reserve)

Cr Share capital   Nominal value

Test your understanding 3

Ginger Knut, a limited liability company, has 20,000 50c shares in issue (each issued for $1.25) and makes a 1 for 4 bonus issue, capitalising the share premium account.

What are the balances on the share capital and share premium accounts after this transaction?

	SC	SP
	$	$
A	15,000	10,000
B	12,500	12,500
C	25,000	Nil
D	22,500	2,500

Test your understanding 4

Rich T is a limited liability company with 200,000 25c shares in issue. At 1 January the balance on the share premium account is $75,000. The following transactions occur in the year ended 31 December 20X6:

31 January There is a fully taken-up 2 for 5 rights issue. The issue price is $1.80.

12 August There is a 1 for 10 bonus issue made using the share premium account.

What are the balances on the share capital and share premium accounts on 31 December 20X6?

	SC	SP
	$000	$000
A	308	111
B	77	84
C	154	93
D	77	192

10 Other reserves

Any balances representing profits or surpluses owed to the shareholders are called reserves.

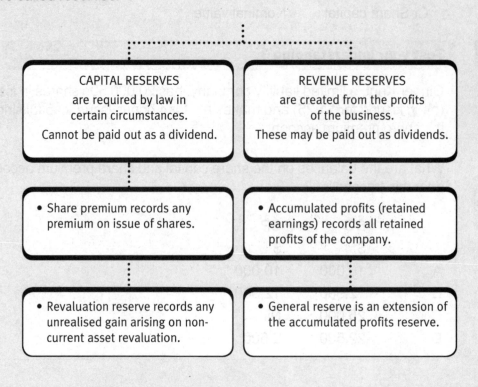

CAPITAL RESERVES
are required by law in certain circumstances.
Cannot be paid out as a dividend.

REVENUE RESERVES
are created from the profits of the business.
These may be paid out as dividends.

- Share premium records any premium on issue of shares.

- Accumulated profits (retained earnings) records all retained profits of the company.

- Revaluation reserve records any unrealised gain arising on non-current asset revaluation.

- General reserve is an extension of the accumulated profits reserve.

Retained earnings

Accumulated profits (retained earnings) appear in the capital and reserves section of the statement of financial position in the same way that the profits of a sole trader are added to capital.

Retained profits are due (although generally not paid out) to the shareholders of the company. It follows that they should be presented as part of the liability to the shareholders.

11 Loan notes (loan stock)

- A limited company can raise funds by issuing loan notes .

- A loan note is a document that is evidence of a debt.

- A person will buy a loan note for a set nominal value, e.g. $100. He or she is effectively loaning $100 to the company.

- The nominal value of the loan note will be repayable after a certain number of years.

- In the meantime, the loan note-holder will receive an annual fixed amount of interest based on the nominal value.

- The interest incurred is included in 'finance cost' in the income statement.

Test your understanding 5

Custard Creameries is an incorporated business which needs to raise funds to purchase plant and machinery. On 1 March 20X5 it issues $150,000 10% loan notes, redeemable in 10 years' time. Interest is payable half yearly at the end of August and February.

What accounting entries are required in the year ended 31 December 20X5? Show relevant extracts from the statement of financial position.

12 Corporation tax

- Companies are charged corporation tax on their profits.

- Accounting for tax is initially based on estimates, since a company's tax bill is not finalised and paid until nine months after its year end.

- This means that a company will normally under– or over-provide for tax in any given year

- Tax will therefore appear in the year-end financial statements as:
  - A charge to profits in the income statement being
    - Current year estimated tax + previous year's under-provision; or
    - Current year estimated tax – previous year's over-provision.
- A year end liability in the statement of financial position being the current year's estimated tax.

Test your understanding 6

Garry Baldy commenced trade on 1 January 20X4 and estimates that the tax payable for the year ended 31 December 20X4 is $150,000.

In September 20X5, the accountant of Garry Baldy receives and pays a tax demand for $163,000 for the year ended 31 December 20X4. At 31 December 20X5 he estimates that the company owes $165,000 for corporation tax in relation to the year ended 31 December 20X5.

Draw up the tax charge and income tax payable accounts for the years ended 31 December 20X4 and 20X5 and detail the amounts shown in the statement of financial position and income statement in both years.

Test your understanding 7

Choccychip estimated last year's tax charge to be $230,000. As it happened, their tax advisor settled with the tax authorities at $222,000.

This year, Choccychip estimate their tax bill to be $265,000, but they are a little confused as to how this should be reflected in the financial statements. Which of the following is correct for the end of the current year?

	Statement of financial position liability ($)	Income statement tax charge ($)
A	257,000	265,000
B	273,000	265,000
C	265,000	257,000
D	265,000	273,000

13 Dividends

- Dividends are the share of profits paid out to shareholders.
- Dividends on preference shares are a fixed amount.
- Dividends on ordinary shares are expressed as an amount per share e.g. 10c per share or 10% of nominal value

Preference dividends

In line with the statement of financial position presentation of preference shares:

- redeemable preference share dividends are classified as **finance costs**
- irredeemable preference share dividends are classified as **dividends**.

Preference dividends

The return is calculated as a percentage of the nominal value of the preference share capital. If, at the year-end, the company has not paid all of the dividends due to preference share holders, the company will show the amount owing as a current liability on the statement of financial position under the heading 'proposed dividends' or 'interest accrual'.

Ordinary dividends

A company may pay a mid-year or interim dividend. The double entry is:

Dr Retained earnings (and disclose in statement of changes in equity)   X
Cr Bank   X

At the end of the year companies may propose or declare a dividend to the ordinary shareholders (i.e. tell the shareholders the amount of a dividend to be paid after the year-end). This is a **final dividend**. These dividends have to be approved at the annual general meeting (AGM) and therefore cannot be a liability pre year-end and will not be examined.

Test your understanding 8

Cracker, a company, has share capital as follows:

Ordinary share capital (50c shares) $200,000

8% Irredeemable Preference share capital $50,000

The company pays an interim dividend of 12.5c per share to its ordinary shareholders and pays the preference shareholders their fixed dividend. Before the year end the company declares a final dividend of 36.5c per share to its ordinary shareholders.

Calculate the amounts shown in the statement of changes in equity (SOCIE) and statement of financial position (SFP) in relation to dividends for the year.

	SOCIE	SFP
	$000	$000
A	200	150
B	54	nil
C	200	146
D	101	72

14 Preparation of company accounts

You will not be asked to produce a full set of accounts in the F3/FFA examination, although you may be required to provide certain balances.

The following example will, however, help you to fully understand the preparation of company accounts.

Test your understanding 9

Preparation of company accounts

The trial balance of Penguin, a company as at 31 December 20X5 was as follows:

	Dr $	Cr $
Sales and purchases	20,000	50,000
Inventory	8,000	
Distribution costs	8,000	
Administration expenses	15,550	
Receivables and payables	10,000	20,000
Fundamental reorganisation costs	2,400	
Cash at bank	8,100	
Ordinary shares 50c		8,000
10% irredeemable preference shares $1		9,000
10% loan notes		8,000
Non-current assets at net book value	35,000	
Share premium		3,000
Accumulated profits at 1 January 20X5		3,000
Loan note Interest	400	
Preference dividend	450	
Interim ordinary dividend	1,600	
Tax		500
Suspense		8,000
	109,500	109,500

The following is to be taken into account.

(1) A building whose net book value is currently $5,000 is to be revalued to $11,000.

(2) A final ordinary dividend of 10c per share is to be proposed.

(3) The balance on the corporation tax account represents an overprovision of tax for the previous year. Tax for the current year is estimated at $3,000.

(4) Closing inventory is $12,000.

(5) The balance on the suspense account represents the proceeds from the issue of 4,000 ordinary shares.

Prepare the following statements for the year ended 31 December 20X5:

(1) statement of comprehensive income

(2) statement of financial position

(3) statement of changes in equity

(4) an income statement (hence ignoring the revaluation)

Chapter summary

Chart flow:

LIMITED COMPANIES
- Separate legal entity
- Limited liability
- Management vs ownership
- Formalities

IAS 1 PRESENTATION OF FINANCIAL STATEMENTS (EXTERNAL USE)

- **STATEMENT OF FINANCIAL POSITION**
- **INCOME STATEMENT**
- **STATEMENT OF CHANGES IN EQUITY**

Corporation tax
Show full liability in statement of financial position
Show charge adjusted for previous year's under–/overprovision in income statement.

Dividends
Disclose preference dividend plus ordinary dividend paid or declared before year end.

Share capital
Issue of shares
Rights issue
Bonus issue.

Other reserves
Revenue
Capital.

LOAN NOTES

Test your understanding answers

Test your understanding 1

Cash

	$		$
Share capital / share premium	350,000		

Share capital

	$		$
		Cash	50,000

Share premium

	$		$
		Cash	300,000

Working

Nominal value: 200,000 x 25 = $50,000

Funds raised: 200,000 x $1.75 = $350,000

Test your understanding 2

20X4 Dr Cash $500

      Cr Share capital $500

20X5 For every five shares a shareholder owns, he or she is are entitled to buy another one. The offer is fully taken up, meaning that 200 new shares are issued.

    Dr Cash (200 x 75c) $150
    Cr Share capital (200 x 50c) $100
    Cr Share premium $50

Statement of financial position

Capital and reserves:

	$
Share capital – 50c ordinary shares	600
Share premium	50
Accumulated profit	X

Test your understanding 3

The correct answer is B

- For every four shares held, a new share is issued.
- Therefore 5,000 new shares are issued

    Dr Share premium (5,000 x 50c) $2,500

    Cr Share capital $2,500

Statement of financial position

Capital and reserves:

	$
Share capital – 50c ordinary shares (20,000 x 50c) + $2,500	12,500
Share premium (20,000 x ($1.25 – $0.5)) – $2,500	12,500
Accumulated profit	X

Test your understanding 4

The correct answer is D

Share capital

	$		$
		Balance b/f	50,000
		Rights issue (cash)	20,000
Balance c/f	77,000	Bonus issue	7,000
	77,000		77,000
		Balance b/f	77,000

Share premium

	$		$
		Balance b/f	75,000
Bonus issue (SC)	7,000	Rights issue (cash)	124,000
Balance c/f	192,000		
	199,000		199,000
		Balance b/f	192,000

Statement of financial position

Capital and reserves:	$
Share capital – 25c ordinary shares	77,000
Share premium	192,000
Accumulated profit	X

Workings

Rights issue: (200,000/5) x 2 = 80,000 new shares

   Proceeds: 80,000 x $1.80 = $144,000

   Nominal value: 80,000 x 25c =$20,000

Bonus issue: (280,000/10) x 1 = 28,000 new shares

Nominal value: 28,000 x 25c = $7,000

Test your understanding 5

1 March 20X5	Dr Cash		$150,000
	Cr 10% Loan notes		$150,000
31 August 20X5	Dr Finance cost		$7,500
	Cr Cash		$7,500
	$150,000 x 10% x 6/12 = $7,500		
31 December 20X5	Dr Finance cost		$5,000
	Cr Interest accrual		$5,000
	$150,000 x 10% x 4/12 = $5,000		

Statement of financial position

	$
Non-current liabilities	
10% Loan notes	150,000
Current liabilities	
Trade payables	X
Loan note interest payable	5,000

Test your understanding 6

Tax payable (statement of financial position)

	$		$
		20X4	
		income statement	150,000
	150,000		150,000
Sept X5 Bank	163,000	20X5 Balance b/f	150,000
		Under-provision b/f	13,000
		20X5 income	
Balance c/f	165,000	statement (ß)	165,000
	328,000		328,000
		20X6 Balance b/f	165,000

Tax charge (income statement)

	$		$
20X4 tax payable	150,000	Income statement	150,000
	150,000		150,000
20X5 Under-provision	13,000		
	165,000		178,000
Tax payable			
	178,000		178,000

The income statement tax charge in 20X5 is increased to reflect the under-provision made in 20X4.

Statement of financial position

	20X4 $000	20X5 $000
Corporation tax liability	150	165

Income statement

Tax expense	150	178

Test your understanding 7

The correct answer is B

- The liability in the statement of financial position= the estimated amount payable for the current year.

- The tax charge in the income statement = the estimated amount payable for the current year – last year's overprovision.

Test your understanding 8

The correct answer is C

No. of ordinary shares = $200,000/50c = 400,000

Ordinary dividend
Interim   400,000 x 12.5c $50,000

Preference dividend

   50,000 x 8% = $4,000

Statement of changes in equity

	$
Retained earnings at start of year	X
dividends ($50,000 + $4,000)	(54,000)
At end of year	X

NOTE: The final dividend cannot be accounted for until approved at the AGM and therefore cannot be a liability pre year-end.

Penguin

Statement of comprehensive income for the year ended 31 December 20X5

	$
Sales revenue	50,000
Cost of sales ($8,000 + 20,000 – 12,000)	(16,000)
Gross profit	34,000
Distribution costs	(8,000)
Administrative expenses	(15,550)
Operating profit	10,450
Fundamental reorganisation costs	(2,400)
	8,050
Interest payable (10% x 8,000)	(800)
Profit before taxation	7,250
Taxation (*3,000 – 500)	(2,500)
Profit after taxation	4,750
Other Comprehensive income	
Revaluation Gain	6,000
Total Comprehensive Income	10,750

Statement of financial position at 31 December 20X5

	$	$
Tangible assets ($35,000 + 6,000)		41,000
Current assets		
Inventory	12,000	
Trade receivables	10,000	
Cash at bank and in hand	8,100	
		30,100
Total assets		71,100
Capital and reserves		
Ordinary share capital		10,000
($8,000 + 2,000)		
10% preference share capital		9,000
Share premium account		9,000
($3,000 + 6,000)		
Revaluation reserve		6,000
Accumulated profits		5,250
		39,250
Non-current liabilities		
10% loan notes		8,000
Current liabilities		
Trade payables	20,000	
Proposed preference		
dividends (900 – 450)	450	
Taxation	3,000	
Loan note interest	400	
		23,850
		71,100

Income statement for the year ended 31 December 20X5

	$
Revenue	50,000
Cost of sales	(16,000)
Gross profit	34,000
Distribution costs	(8,000)
Administrative expenses	(15,550)
Profit from operations	10,450
Fundamental reorganisation costs	(2,400)
Finance costs	(800)
Profit before tax	7,250
tax expense	(2,500)
Net profit for the period	4,750

Statement of changes in equity
for the year ended 31 December 20X5

	Ordinary share capital	Share premium	Reval- uation Reserve	Accum profits	Total
	$	$	$	$	$
Balance at 1 Jan 20X5	8,000	3,000	–	3,000	14,000
Surplus on revaluation of building			6,000		6,000
Net gains and losses not recognised in the income statement			6,000		6,000
Net profit for the year				4,750	4,750
Dividends					
–Preference (10% x 9,000)				(900)	(900)
–Ordinary Interim				(1,600)	(1,600)
Issue of share capital (4000 shares = $8,000 thus issue price is $2 which is made up the nominal value of $0.50 and share premium of $1.50)	2,000	6,000			8,000
Balance at 31 December 20X5	10,000	9,000	6,000	5,250	30,250

Accounting standards

Chapter learning objectives

Upon completion of this chapter you will be able to:

- recognise the difference between tangible non-current assets and intangible non-current assets

- identify types of intangible non-current assets.

- define research and development

- explain the accounting treatment of research and development costs in accordance with IAS 38

- calculate the amounts to be capitalised as development expenditure or expensed from given information.

- explain the purpose of amortisation

- calculate the amortisation charge and account for it correctly

- define an event after the reporting period date.

- account for both adjusting and non-adjusting events correctly in the financial statements

- classify events as adjusting or non-adjusting.

- define provision, contingent liability and contingent asset.

- classify items as provision, contingent asset or contingent liability from information given

- account for provisions, contingent liabilities and contingent assets correctly

- calculate provisions and changes in provisions and account for these changes correctly

- report provisions in the final accounts

- explain what is meant by an accounting policy and the provisions of IAS 8 regarding changes in accounting policy

- identify the appropriate accounting treatment for a change in a material accounting policy according to IAS 8

- describe the provisions of IAS 8 which govern financial statements regarding material errors which result in prior period adjustments

- explain the requirements of IAS 18 governing revenue recognition.

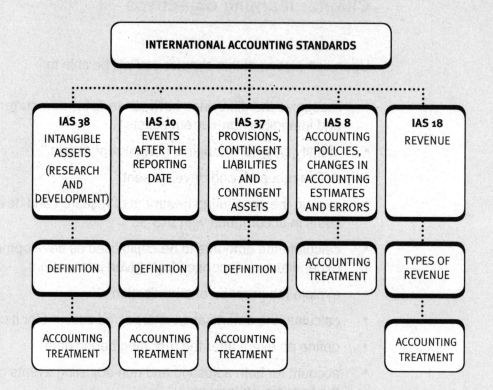

Some other examples of intangible assets which you may come across are brands, quotas and patents.

1 Intangible non-current assets

Non-current assets are assets used within the business on an ongoing basis in order to generate revenue.

They can be split into two distinct types:

Tangible non-current assets

Normally have physical substance, e.g land and buildings.

Normally involve expenditure being incurred.

Cost of the tangible non-current asset is capitalised.

Depreciation is a reflection of the wearing out of the asset.

Intangible non-current assets

Do not normally have physical substance, e.g. copyright.

Can be purchased or may be created within a business without any expenditure being incurred, i.e. internally generated, e.g. brands.

Purchased intangible non-current assets are capitalised. Generally, internally generated assets may not be capitalised.

Amortisation is a reflection of the wearingout of the (capitalised) asset.

Examples:
- Development costs
- Goodwill
- Trade marks
- Licences
- Patents
- Copyrights
- Franchises

Test your understanding 1

Willis Ltd purchased a patent, with a useful economic life of ten years for $20,000 on 1 January 20X9.

Prepare extracts of the financial statements for the year ended 31 December 20X9?

2 Research and development (IAS 38)

Research can be defined as original and planned investigation undertaken with the prospect of gaining new scientific or technical knowledge and understanding.

Development can be defined as the application of research findings or other knowledge to a plan or design for the production of new or substantially improved materials, devices, products, processes, systems or services before the start of commercial production or use.

Test your understanding 2

Which of the following should be classified as development?

(1) Braynee Ltd has spent $300,000 investigating whether a particular substance, flubber, found in the Amazon rainforest is resistant to heat.

(2) Cleverclogs Ltd has incurred $120,000 expenses in the course of making a new waterproof and windproof material with the idea that it may be used for ski-wear.

(3) Ayplus Ltd has found that a chemical compound, known as XYX, is not harmful to the human body.

(4) Braynee Ltd has incurred a further $450,000 using flubber in creating prototypes of a new heat-resistant suit for stuntmen.

    A   All of them

    B   1 and 3

    C   2 and 4

    D   2 only

Accounting treatment of research and development

Where a company undertakes research and development, expenditure is being incurred with the intention of producing future benefits.

The accounting issue is therefore whether these costs should be expensed to the income statement or capitalised as an intangible asset on the statement of financial position to match to future benefits arising.

Research

- All research expenditure should be written off to the income statement as it is incurred. This is in compliance with the prudence concept.

- Research expenditure does not directly lead to future benefits and therefore it is not possible to follow the matching concept.

- Any capital expenditure on research equipment should be capitalised and depreciated as normal.

2.1 Development

- Development expenditure must be capitalised as an intangible asset provided that certain criteria are met:
    - **S**eparate project
    - **E**xpenditure identifiable and reliably measured
    - **C**ommercially viable
    - **T**echnically feasible
    - **O**verall profitable
    - **R**esources available to complete

- If the above criteria are not met, development expenditure must be written off to the income statement as it is incurred.

- Once expenditure has been treated as an expense, it cannot be reinstated as an asset.

Subsequent treatment of capitalised development expenditure

- The asset should be amortised over the period that is expected to benefit. This ensures that costs are matched to the revenue in the income statement.

- Amortisation should commence with commercial production. It should be charged over the period of benefit, and also in proportion to the revenue generated.

- Each project should be reviewed at the year end to ensure that the 'SECTOR' criteria are still met. If they are no longer met, the previously capitalised expenditure must be written off to the income statement immediately.

If a policy of capitalisation is adopted, it should be applied to all projects that meet the criteria.

IAS 38 Intangible assets

Development

An intangible asset arising from development (or from the development phase of an internal project) should be recognised if, and only if, an enterprise can demonstrate all of the following:

- the technical feasibility of completing the intangible asset so that it will be available for use or sale

- its intention to complete the intangible asset and use or sell it

- its ability to use or sell the intangible asset

- how the intangible asset will generate probable future economic benefits. Among other things, the enterprise should demonstrate the existence of a market for the output of the intangible asset or the intangible asset itself or, if it is to be used internally, the usefulness of the intangible asset.

- the availability of adequate technical, financial and other resources to complete the development and to use or sell the intangible asset

- its ability to measure reliably the expenditure attributable to the intangible asset during its development.

The amount to be included is the cost of the development. Note that expenditure once treated as an expense cannot be reinstated as an asset.

Amortisation

If the useful life of an intangible asset is finite, its capitalised development costs must be amortised once commercial exploitation begins.

The amortisation method used should reflect the pattern in which the asset's economic benefits are consumed by the enterprise. If that pattern cannot be determined reliably, the straight-line method should be used.

An intangible asset with an indefinite useful life should not be amortised. An asset has an indefinite useful life if there is no foreseeable limit to the period over which the asset is expected to generate net cash inflows for the business.

Illustration – Accounting for development costs

Brightspark Ltd is developing a new product, the widget. This is expected to be sold over a three-year period starting in 20X6. The forecast data is as follows:

	20X5 $000	20X6 $000	20X7 $000	20X8 $000
Net revenue from other activities	400	500	450	400
Net revenue from widgets	–	450	600	400
Development costs	(900)	–	–	–

Show how the development costs should be treated if:

(a) the costs do not qualify for capitalisation

(b) the costs do qualify for capitalisation .

Solution to accounting for development costs

Solution

(a) Profit treating development costs as expenses when incurred

	20X5 $000	20X6 $000	20X7 $000	20X8 $000
Net revenue from other activities	400	500	450	400
Net revenue from widgets	–	450	600	400
Development costs	(900)	–	–	–
Net profit/(loss)	(500)	950	1,050	800

(b) Net profit amortising development costs over life of widgets

	20X5 $000	20X6 $000	20X7 $000	20X8 $000
Net revenue from other activities	400	500	450	400
Net revenue from widgets	–	450	600	400
Development costs of widgets	–			
(W)		(279.3)	(372.4)	(248.3)
Net profit	400	670.7	677.6	551.7

Amortisation working:

20X6: (450/1450) x $900,000 = $279,300
20X7: (600/1450) x $900,000 = $372,400
20X8: (400/1450) x $900,000 = $248,300

Test your understanding 3

This year, Deep Blue Sea Ltd has developed a new material from which the next generation of wetsuits will be made. This special material will ensure that swimmers are kept warmer than ever. The costs incurred meet the capitalisation criteria and by the 31 December 20X5 year end $250,000 has been capitalised.

The wetsuits are expected to generate revenue for five years from the date that commercial production commences on 1 January 20X6. What amount is charged to the income statement in the year ended 31 December 20X6?

A   nil

B $250,000

C $100,000

D $50,000

IAS 38 Disclosure

Disclosure

The financial statements should disclose the following for capitalised development costs:

* the amortisation method used and the expected period of amortisation

* a reconciliation of the carrying amounts at the beginning and end of the period, showing new expenditure incurred, amortisation and amounts written off because a project no longer qualifies for capitalisation

* amortisation during the period.

In addition, the financial statements should also disclose the total amount of research and development expenditure recognised as an expense during the period.

3 Events after the reporting period date (IAS 10)

Events after the reporting period date can be defined as those material events which occur between the statement of financial position date and the date on which the financial statements are approved.

Adjusting and non-adjusting events

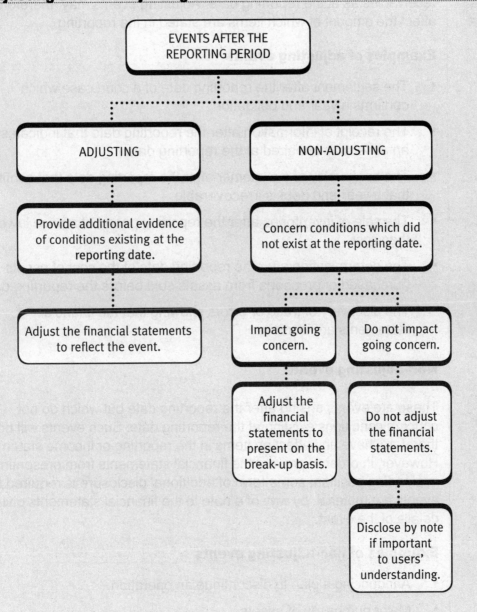

EVENTS AFTER THE
REPORTING PERIOD

ADJUSTING

NON-ADJUSTING

Provide additional evidence
of conditions existing at the
reporting date.

Concern conditions which did
not exist at the reporting date.

Adjust the financial statements
to reflect the event.

Impact going
concern.

Do not impact
going concern.

Adjust the
financial
statements to
present on the
break-up basis.

Do not adjust
the financial
statements.

Disclose by note
if important
to users'
understanding.

Adjusting and non adjusting events

Adjusting events

These events provide additional evidence of conditions existing at the reporting date. For example, irrecoverable debts arising one or two months after the reporting date may help to quantify the allowance for receivables as at the reporting date. Adjusting events may, therefore, affect the amount at which items are stated in the reporting.

Examples of adjusting events

- The settlement after the reporting date of a court case which confirms a year end obligation.

- The receipt of information after the reporting date that indicates that an asset was impaired at the reporting date.

- The bankruptcy of a customer after the reporting date that confirms that a year-end debt is irrecoverable.

- The sale of inventories after the reporting period at a price lower than cost.

- The determination after the reporting date of the cost of assets purchased or proceeds from assets sold before the reporting date.

- The discovery of fraud or errors showing that the financial statements are incorrect.

Non-adjusting events

These are events arising after the reporting date but which do not concern conditions existing at the reporting date. Such events will not, therefore, have any effect on items in the reporting or income statement. However, in order to prevent the financial statements from presenting a misleading position, some form of additional disclosure is required if the events are material, by way of a note to the financial statements giving details of the event.

Examples of non-adjusting events

- Announcing a plan to discontinue an operation.

- Major purchases of assets.

- The destruction of assets after the reporting date by fire or flood.

- Entering into significant commitments or contingent liabilities (see section 4).

- Commencing a court case arising out of events after the reporting date.

Proposed dividends

It is not acceptable to include dividends declared after the reporting date as liabilities at the year end.

If dividends are declared before the year end, they must be shown in the statement of changes in equity and accrued for in the reporting period update.

Test your understanding 4

Which of the following are adjusting events for BigCo Ltd? The year end is 30 June 20X6 and the accounts are approved on 18 August 20X6.

(1) Sales of year-end inventory on 2 July 20X6 at less than cost.

(2) The issue of new ordinary shares on 4 July 20X6.

(3) A fire in the main warehouse occurred on 8 July 20X6. All stock was destroyed.

(4) A major credit customer was declared bankrupt on 10 July 20X6

(5) All of the share capital of a competitor, TeenyCo Ltd was acquired on 21 July 20X6.

(6) On 1 August 20X6, $500,000 was received in respect of an insurance claim dated 13 February 20X6.

A   1,4 and 6

B   1,2,4 and 6

C   1,2,5 and 6

D   1,4,5 and 6

Disclosure

Where there are material non-adjusting events, a note to the financial statements should explain:

*   the nature of the event

*   an estimate of the financial effect.

Disclosure in the accounts

In respect of each event after the reporting that must be disclosed as above, the following information should be stated by way of notes in the financial statements:

(1) (a) the nature of the event

(2) (b) an estimate of the financial effect, or a statement that such an estimate cannot be made.

The date on which the financial statements were authorised for issue, and who gave the authorisation, should be disclosed in the financial statements.

If the owners or others have the power to amend the financial statements after issue, that fact should be disclosed.

4 Provisions, contingent liabilities and assets (IAS 37)

A provision can be defined as a Liability of uncertain timing or amount.

Contingent liability

A contingent liability is:

(1) a possible obligation that arises from past events and whose existence will be confirmed only by the occurrence or non-occurrence of one or more uncertain future events not wholly within the control of the enterprise; or

(2) a present obligation that arises from past events but is not recognised because:

  – it is not probable that an outflow of resources embodying economic benefits will be required to settle the obligation; or

  – the amount of the obligation cannot be measured with sufficient reliability.

A contingent asset is a possible asset that arises from past events and whose existence will be confirmed only by the occurrence or non-occurrence of one or more uncertain future events not wholly within the control of the enterprise.

Accounting for contingent liabilities and assets

The requirements of IAS 37 as regards contingent liabilities and assets are summarised in the following table:

Probability of Occurrence	Contingent liabilities	Contingent assets
Virtually certain	Provide	Recognise
Probable	Provide	Disclose in note
Possible	Disclose in note	Ignore
Remote	Ignore	Ignore

- Note that the standard gives no guidance as the meaning of the terms in the left-hand column. One possible interpretation is as follows:

  Virtually certain > 95%

  Probable 51% – 95%

  Possible 5% – 50%

  Remote < 5%

Provisions and criteria

A provision is made where all of the following conditions are met:

- A present obligation (legal or constructive) exists as the result of a past event.
- There is a probable transfer of economic benefits.
- A reliable estimate of the amount can be made.

A legal present obligation is an obligation that derives from:

- the terms of a contract
- legislation
- any other operation of law.

A constructive obligation is an obligation that derives from an entity's actions where:

- The entity has in some way indicated that it will accept certain responsibilities.
- The entity has created an expectation on the part of other parties that it will meet those responsibilities.

Illustration

A retail store has a policy of refunding purchases by dissatisfied customers, even though it is under no legal obligation to do so. Its policy of making refunds is generally known.

Should a provision be made at the year end?

Solution

The policy is well known and creates a valid expectation.

There is a constructive obligation.

It is probable some refunds will be made.

These can be measured using expected values.

Conclusion: A provision is required.

Test your understanding 5

The draft financial statements of Madras, a limited liability company, for the year ended 31 December 20X6 is currently under review. The following points have been raised:

(i) An ex-employee has started an action against the company for wrongful dismissal. The company's legal team have stated that the ex-employee is not likely to succeed. The following estimates have been given by the lawyers relating to the case:

   (a) Legal costs (to be incurred whether the claim is successful or not) $ 5,000

   (b) Settlement of claim if successful $15,000
   Total $ 20,000

   Currently no provision has been made by the company in the financial statements.

(ii) The company has a policy of refunding the cost of any goods returned by dissatisfied customers, even though it is under no legal obligation to do so. This policy of making refunds is generally known. At the year end returns totalling $4,800 have been made.

(iii) A claim has been made against a company for injury suffered by a pedestrian in connection with building work by the company. Legal advisers have confirmed that the company will probably have to pay damages of $100,000 but that a counterclaim made against the building subcontractors for $50,000 would probably be successful.

State with reasons what adjustments, if any, should be made by the company in the financial statements.

Accounting entries for provisions

A provision should initially be accounted for at the best estimate of the probable outflow:

   Dr relevant expense account

   Cr provision

Movement in provisions

Provisions should be reviewed at each statement of financial position date and adjusted to reflect the current best estimate.

Increase in provision:	Dr Relevant expense account
	Cr Provision
Decrease in provision:	Dr Provision
	Cr Relevant expense account

Disclosure

Reporting provisions in the final accounts

Provisions are reported as a liability.

They may be classed as current or non-current, depending upon the subject matter of the provision.

Disclosure

- Where the requirement is to provide for a contingent liability, the liability is reflected in the financial statements, but called a provision in order to highlight the uncertainty surrounding it
- The movement in this provision is recorded in the financial statements each year.
- When disclosure is made by note, the note should state:
  - the nature of the contingency
  - the uncertain factors that may affect the future outcome
  - an estimate of the financial effect, or a statement that such an estimate cannot be made.

5 Accounting policies, changes in accounting estimates and errors (IAS 8)

The main issues covered by this standard are:

- changes in accounting estimates
- changes in accounting policy
- correction of prior period errors.

Changes in accounting estimates

- These result in the adjustment of the carrying amount of an asset or liability, e.g. revising the useful life of a non-current asset from five years to seven years.

- Any necessary change should be included in the current income statement under the same heading as the previous estimate, with a note giving details of the change if it has a material effect.

Changes in accounting policies

- Accounting policies are the specific principles, bases, conventions, rules and practices applied by an entity in preparing and presenting financial statements.

- The consistency theory means that a company's accounting policies will generally remain the same from year to year. There may, however, be circumstances where the policies do have to change:
  - If required by a standard or interpretation.
  - If the change will result in a more reliable and relevant presentation of events in financial statements.

- The change is applied retrospectively by adjusting the opening balance of accumulated profit; this is reflected in the statement of changes in equity. Comparative information for previous years is also restated.

A change in accounting policy occurs if there has been a change in:

- recognition, e.g. an expense is now recognised rather than an asset

- presentation, e.g. depreciation is now included in cost of sales rather than administrative expenses, or

- measurement basis, e.g. stating assets at replacement cost rather than historical cost.

Fundamental errors

- E.g. discovery of a major fraud which occurred last year

- If a fundamental error from a prior period is reflected in the accounts, this must be corrected.

- The correction involves adjusting the opening balance of accumulated profits; this is reflected in the statement of changes in equity. Comparative information for prior years should also be restated if practical.

Test your understanding 6

Entity Ltd was incorporated 3 years ago and has depreciated vehicles using the reducing balance method at 35%. It now wishes to change this to allow a fairer presentation to the straight line method over a period of 4 years. In addition certain freehold properties had not been depreciated during the first 2 years. The directors are now of the opinion that all property, plant & equipment should now be depreciated.

Are the above proposals a change in accounting policy or a change in accounting estimate?

6 Revenue (IAS 18)

IAS 18 Revenue defines when revenue from various sources may be recognised. It deals with revenue arising from three types of transaction or event:

- sale of goods
- rendering of services
- interest, royalties and dividends from the assets of the enterprise.

Sale of goods

Revenue from the sale of goods should be recognised when all the following conditions have been satisfied:

(a) All the significant risks and rewards of ownership have been transferred to the buyer.

(b) The seller retains no effective control over the goods sold.

(c) The amount of revenue can be reliably measured.

(d) The benefits to be derived from the transaction are likely to flow to the enterprise.

(e) The costs incurred or to be incurred for the transaction can be reliably measured.

KAPLAN PUBLISHING

Revenue recognition

Conditions (a) and (b) are usually met at the time when legal ownership passes to the buyer, but there are four examples in IAS 18 where the seller retains significant risks:

- when the seller has an obligation for unsatisfactory performance beyond normal warranty provisions

- when the receipt of the cash for the sale is contingent upon the buyer selling the goods on and receiving cash

- when the goods are to be installed at the buyer's site and this has not yet been completed

- when the buyer has the right to cancel the contract.

Revenue and associated costs are recognised simultaneously in accordance with the matching concept.

Rendering of services

The provision of a service is likely to be spread over a period of time.

IAS 18 states that revenue from services may be recognised according to the stage of completion of the transaction at the statement of financial position date.

As with the sale of goods, conditions must be satisfied:

(a) The amount of the revenue can be measured reliably.

(b) The benefits from the transaction are likely to flow to the enterprise.

(c) The stage of completion of the work can be measured reliably.

(d) The costs incurred or to be incurred for the transaction can be reliably measured.

When a partly completed service is in its early stages, or the outcome of the transaction cannot be reliably estimated, revenue should be recognised only up to the amount of the costs incurred to date, and then only if it is probable that the enterprise will recover in revenue at least as much as the costs.

If it is probable that the costs of the transaction will not be recovered, no revenue is to be recognised.

Other revenues

Interest, royalties and dividends

Provided the amount of revenue can be reliably measured and the receipt of the income is reasonably assured, these items should be recognised as follows:

- Interest should be recognised on a time-proportion basis taking account of the yield on the asset.

- Royalties should be recognised on an accruals basis in accordance with the relevant agreement.

- Dividends should be recognised when the shareholder's right to receive payment has been established.

Disclosure

- The accounting policy for revenue recognition, including the methods used to determine the stage of completion of service transactions.

- The amount of revenue recognised for each of the five categories above.

- The amount, if material, in each category arising from exchanges of goods or services.

Chapter summary

```
                    INTERNATIONAL ACCOUNTING STANDARDS
```

| IAS 38 INTANGIBLE ASSETS (RESEARCH AND DEVELOPMENT) | IAS 10 EVENTS AFTER THE REPORTING PERIOD | IAS 37 PROVISIONS, CONTINGENT LIABILITIES AND CONTINGENT ASSETS | IAS 8 ACCOUNTING POLICIES, CHANGES IN ACCOUNTING ESTIMATES AND ERRORS | IAS 18 REVENUE |

Research: original and planned investigation to gain new scientific or technical knowledge and understanding.

Development: application of research findings or other knowledge to a plan or design for the production of new or substantially improved materials, devices, products, processes, systems or services before the start of commercial production or use.

Those material events which occur between the reporting date and the date on which the financial statements are approved.

Adjusting event: amend financial statements to reflect event.

Non-adjusting event: do not amend financial statements unless event impacts going concern. Disclose non-adjusting event if material.

Provision: a liability of uncertain timing or amount.

Contingent liability: a possible obligation that arises from past events.

Contingent asset: possible assets arising from past events.

Change to accounting policy applied retrospectively (i.e. financial statements altered to show the position as if the new policy had always been in place).

Change to accounting estimates accounted for prospectively (i.e. previous years' results not amended).

Adjust opening balances to correct fundamental **errors** of prior years.

- Sale of goods
- Rendering of services.
- Interest, royalties and dividends.

Recognition criteria depend on type of revenue.

Research costs expensed to income statement.

Development costs capitalised on balance sheet if SECTOR criteria met.

Development costs expensed to income statement if SECTOR criteria not met.

	Cont. liability	Cont. asset
Virtually certain	Provide	Recognise
Probable	Provide	Disclose
Possible	Disclose	Ignore
Remote	Ignore	Ignore

Test your understanding answers

Test your understanding 1

Income statement extract

Amortisation $2,000
($20,0000 / 10 years)

Statement of financial position extract

Intangible assets $18,000
($20,000 – $2,000)

Test your understanding 2

The correct answer is C

Both 1 and 3 involve researching materials, without any form of commercial production in mind.

Test your understanding 3

The correct answer is D

Amortisation will be charged for each of the five years that revenue is generated.

As there is no reliable pattern of this revenue, amortisation will be charged on the straight-line basis.

Therefore the amortisation charge for each of the years ended 31 December 20X6 – 20Y0 will be:

$250,000/5 years = $50,000

KAPLAN PUBLISHING

Test your understanding 4

The correct answer is A

(1)	Sales of year end inventory at less than cost	Adjusting	Closing inventory must be valued at the lower of cost and net realisable value. The post-year-end sale provides evidence of the net realisable value. Therefore closing inventory must be adjusted to reflect the reduction in value.
(2)	Share issue	Non-adjusting	
(3)	Fire in warehouse	Non-adjusting	If this is BigCo's only or main warehouse and the fire affects going concern, the event will be reclassified as adjusting.
(4)	Bankruptcy of major customer	Adjusting	The bankruptcy of the customer provides evidence of their inability to pay their debt at the year-end. The amount outstanding from the customer at 30 June 20X6 should therefore be written off in the year end accounts.
(5)	Acquisition of TeenyCo Ltd	Non-adjusting	
(6)	Receipt of insurance monies	Adjusting	The receipt of insurance monies provides evidence of a year-end asset. The amount subsequently received should be reflected as such in the year-end accounts.

Test your understanding 5

(i)   IAS 37 defines a contingency as an obligation or an asset that arises from past events whose existence will be confirmed only by the occurrence or non-occurrence of one or more uncertain future events not wholly within the control of the enterprise. A provision should be made if:

(a) There is an obligation.

(b) A transfer is probable.

(c) There is a reliable estimate.

The legal costs of $5,000 should therefore be provided for since they will have to be paid whatever the outcome of the case. However, the claim is not likely to succeed and so no provision should be made. A disclosure note should be made for the potential loss of $15,000.

(ii) IAS 37 states that an obligation can be legal or constructive. In this case the policy of refunds has created a constructive obligation. A provision for $4,800 should therefore be made.

(iii) As the success of the claim for damages of $100,000 is probable, it constitutes a present obligation as a result of a past obligating event, and would therefore be accounted for as a provision. The success of the counterclaim for $50,000 is also considered probable and would therefore need to be disclosed as a contingent asset (reimbursement). Only if it were considered virtually certain would the counterclaim be recognised as an asset in the statement of financial position.

Test your understanding 6

The change to the vehicle depreciation is a change in accounting estimate. It does not involve a change to recognition, presentation or measurement basis. The change to the freehold property in that depreciation is now to be charged is a change in accounting policy. The measurement basis of freehold property is now changed.

Statement of cash flows

Chapter learning objectives

Upon completion of this chapter you will be able to:

- explain the differences between profit and cash flows

- explain the need for management to control cash flows

- explain the value of a statement of cash flows to users of financial statements

- explain the inward and outward flows of cash in a typical company

- calculate cash flows from operating activities using the indirect method

- calculate cash flows from operating activities using the direct method

- calculate the cash flows from investing activities

- calculate the cash flows from financing activities

- prepare extracts from statement of cash flows from given information.

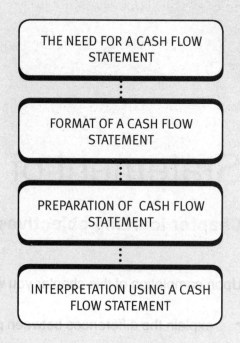

THE NEED FOR A CASH FLOW STATEMENT

FORMAT OF A CASH FLOW STATEMENT

PREPARATION OF CASH FLOW STATEMENT

INTERPRETATION USING A CASH FLOW STATEMENT

1 The need for a statement of cash flows

Profit and liquidity

The accounting concepts of accruals and matching are used to compute a profit figure which shows the additional wealth created for the owners of a business during an accounting period. However, it is important for a business to generate cash as well as to make profits. The two do not necessarily go hand in hand.

Objectives of IAS 7

The Objectives of IAS 7 are to ensure that companies:

• Report their cash generation and cash absorption for a period by highlighting the significant component of cash flow in a way that facilitates comparison of the cash flow performance different businesses.

• provide information that assists in the assessment of their liquidity, solvency and financial adaptability.

The importance of statements of cash flow

Statement of cash flow are an important statement for the users of accounts because:

- They help users to assess liquidity and solvency – an adequate cash position is essential in the short term both to ensure the survival of the business and to enable debts and dividends to be paid.

- They help users to assess financial adaptability – will the company be able to take effective action to alter its cash flows in response to any unexpected events?

- They help users assess future cash flows – an adequate cash position in the longer term is essential to enable asset replacement, repayment of debt and fund further expansion.

- Cash flow means survival – a company may be profitable but, if it does not have an adequate cash position, it may not be able to survive.

- They help to highlight where cash is being generated – the statement of cash flow will clearly detail cash that is being generated from the core activities of the business and other non-operating activities.

- Cash flows are objective – a cash flow is a matter of fact whereas the calculation of profit is subjective.

- they help to indicate problems early.

Profit

Profit represents the increase in net assets in a business during an accounting period. This increase can be in cash or it may be 'tied up' in other assets, for example:

- non-current assets may have been purchased

- there may be an increased amount of receivables

- there may be increased investment in inventory

- the liabilities of the business may have decreased, i.e. more cash has been spent this year in paying off suppliers more quickly than was the case last year.

The benefits of a statement of cash flows

A statement of cash flows is needed as a consequence of the above differences between profits and cash. It helps to:

- provide additional information on business activities

- assess the current liquidity of the business

- allow the user to see the major types of cash flows into and out of the business

- estimate future cash flows

- determine cash flows generated from trading transactions rather than other cash flows.

The drawbacks of a statement of cash flow

The drawbacks of a statement of cash flows

- The statement of cash flows is backward looking. Users of the accounts are particularly interested in the future.

- No interpretation of the statement of cash flows is provided within the accounts. Users are required to draw their own conclusions as to the relevance of the figures contained within it.

- Non-cash transactions, e.g. a bonus issue of shares are not highlighted on the face of the statement of cash flows (although they are disclosed elsewhere within the accounts). These are of interest to users as they will impact future cash flows.

2 Format of a statement of cash flows

IAS 7 Statement of cash flows requires companies to prepare a statement of cash flows within their financial statements. The cash flow must be presented using standard headings.

Statement of cash flows for the period ended ...

	$000	$000
Cash flows from operating activities		
Cash generated from operations	2,550	
Interest paid	(270)	
Dividends paid	(300)	
Income taxes paid	(420)	
	———	
Net cash from operating activities		1,560
Cash flows from investing activities		
Purchase of property, plant and equipment	(900)	
Proceeds of sale of equipment	20	
Interest received	200	
Dividends received	200	
	———	
Net cash used in investing activities		(480)
Cash flows from financing activities		
Proceeds of issue of shares	1,210	
Repayment of loans	(2,000)	
	———	
Net cash used in financing activities		(790)
		———
Net increase in cash and cash equivalents		290
Cash and cash equivalents at the beginning of the period		120
		———
Cash and cash equivalents at the end of the period		410
		———

Key points

Key points:

- Operating activities are the principal revenue-producing activities of the business. This section of the statement begins with cash generated from operations. This figure can be calculated using either the direct or indirect method.

- Investing activities are cash spent on non-current assets, proceeds of sale of non-current assets and income from investments.

- Financing activities include the proceeds of issue of shares and long-term borrowings made or repaid.

- Net increase or decrease in cash and cash equivalents is the overall increase (or decrease) in cash and cash equivalents during the year. After adding the cash and cash equivalents at the beginning of the year, the final balance of cash and cash equivalents at the end of the year emerges.

- Cash means cash in hand and deposits available on demand.

- Cash equivalents means short-term highly liquid investments that are readily convertible to known amounts of cash and which are subject to an insignificant risk of changes in value. (Investments are thus not cash equivalents unless they have these two attributes of being readily convertible and with little or no risk of change in value.)

IAS 7 notes

IAS 7 requires a note to the statement of cash flows giving details of the make-up of cash and cash equivalents:

Cash and cash equivalents

	At end of year $000	At beginning of year $000
Cash on hand and balance at banks	40	25
Short-term investments	370	95
	410	120

3 Cash generated from operations

There are two methods of calculating cash from operations – the direct or indirect method. The method used will depend upon the information provided within the question.

Direct method

This method uses information contained in the ledger accounts of the company to calculate the cash from operations figure as follows:

	$	$
Cash sales		X
Cash received from debtors		X
		–––
		X
Less:		
Cash purchases	X	
Cash paid to credit suppliers	X	
Cash expenses	X	
	–––	
		(X)
		–––
Cash generated from operations		X

Examples of using direct method

Example of calculations using direct method

The gross cash flows necessary for the direct method can be derived:

(1) from the accounting records of the entity by totalling the cash receipts and payments directly, or

(2) from the opening and closing statement of financial positions and income statement for the year by constructing summary control accounts for:

- – sales (to derive cash received from customers)
- – purchases (to derive cash payments to suppliers)
- – wages (to derive cash paid to and on behalf of employees).

Example using control accounts

The statement of financial positions of a business are:

	Last year $	This year $
Non-current assets	153,364	149,364
Inventories		
Receivables	265,840	346,000
Cash		165,166
	419,204	660,530

	Last year $	This year $
Share capital	200,000	200,000
Reserves		141,640
	200,000	341,640
Current liabilities	219,204	318,890
	4,19,204	6,60,530

Extracts from the income statement for the year are:

	$	$
Sales revenue		1,589,447
Cost of sales		
Purchases (no inventory)	1,105,830	
Wages and salaries	145,900	
		(1,251,730)
Administration		
Purchases	96,077	
Salaries	100,000	
		(196,077)
Operating profit and retained profit for the year		141,640

Additional information

(1) Payables consist of

	Last year	This year
	$	$
Payables ledger		
Re non-current assets		46,000
Other	210,564	258,240
Wages accrued	8,640	14,650

(2) Purchase invoices relating to the acquisition of non-current assets totalling $80,000 have been posted to the payables ledger during the year.

Calculate the net cash flow from operating activities using the direct method.

Solution

	$
Operating activities	
Cash received from customers (W1)	1,509,287
Cash payments to suppliers (W2)	(1,154,231)
Cash paid to and on behalf of employees (W3)	(239,890)
Net cash inflow from operating activities	115,166

Workings

(W1)

Receivables ledger control account

	$		$
Balance b/f	265,840	Cash receipts (ß)	1,509,287
Sales revenue	1,589,447	Balance c/f	346,000
	1,855,287		1,855,287

(W2)

Payables ledger control account (excluding non-current asset purchases)

	$		$
Cash paid (ß)	1,154,231	Balance b/f	210,564
Balance c/f	258,240	Purchases	
		– Cost of sales	1,105,830
		– Administration	96,077
	1,412,471		1,328,471

Tutorial note: information relating to non-current assets is not included in the payables ledger control account above in order to compute cash paid to suppliers of operating costs.

(W3)

Wages control

	$		$
Net wages paid (ß)	239,890	Balance b/f	8,640
Balance c/f	14,650	Cost of sales	145,900
		Administration	100,000
	254,540		254,540

Indirect method

This method reconciles between profit before tax (as reported in the income statement) and cash generated from operations as follows:

	$
Profit before tax	X
Finance cost	X
Investment income	(X)
Depreciation charge	X
Loss/(profit) on disposal of non-current assets	X/(X)
(Increase)/decrease in inventories	(X)/X
(Increase)/decrease in trade receivables	(X)/X
Increase/(decrease) in trade payables	X/(X)
Cash generated from operations	X

This working begins with the profit before tax as shown in the income statement. The remaining figures are the adjustments necessary to convert the profit figure to the cash flow for the period.

Depreciation – Added back to profit because it is a non-cash expense

Interest expense – Added back because it is not part of cash generated from operations (the interest actually paid is deducted later)

Increase in trade receivables – Deducted because this is part of the profit not yet realised into cash but tied up in receivables

Decrease in inventories – Added on because the decrease in inventories liberates extra cash

Decrease in trade payables – Deducted because the reduction in payables must reduce cash

In order to prepare a statement of cash flows, information from the current and prior year statement of financial position and the current year income statement is used. The following financial statements provide the source data for the requirements of Test your understanding 1 throughout this chapter:

Test your understanding 1

Requirement 1

Statement of cash flows source data

Statement of financial position of Geronimo at 31 December

	20X6	20X5
	$000	$000
Non-current assets	1,048	750
Accumulated depreciation	(190)	(120)
	858	630
Current assets		
Inventory	98	105
Trade receivables	102	86
Dividend receivable	57	50
Cash	42	18
	299	259
Total assets	1,157	889
Capital and reserves		
Share capital	200	120
Share premium	106	80
Revaluation reserve	212	12
Accumulated profits	283	226
	801	438
Non-current liabilities		
Loan	200	300
Current liabilities		
Trade payables	47	52
Dividend payable	30	27
Interest accrual	3	5
Tax	76	67
	156	151
Total liabilities	1,157	889

Income statement of Geronimo at 31 December 20X6

	$000
Sales revenue	1,100
Cost of sales	(678)
Gross profit	422
Operating expenses	(309)
Operating profit	113
Investment income – interest	15
– dividends	57
Finance charge	(22)
Income tax	(71)
Net profit for year	92

Operating expenses include a loss on disposal of non-current assets of $5,000.

- During the year plant which originally cost $80,000 and with depreciation of $15,000 was disposed of.

Calculate the cash generated from operations using the indirect method.

4 Cash from operating activities

Cash flows may include:

- interest paid
- dividends paid
- income taxes paid.

Calculation of interest/income taxes paid

The cash flow should be calculated by reference to:

- the charge to profits for the item (shown in the income statement); and
- any opening or closing payable balance shown on the statement of financial position.

A T account working may be useful:

e.g. Interest payable

	$		$
		Interest accrual b/f	X
Cash paid (ß)	X	Income statement	
		Interest charge	X
Interest accrual c/f	X		
	——		——
	X		X
	——		——

If there is no change to the opening or closing then it should be the statement of financial position payable amount.

Calculation of dividends paid

The cash flow should again be calculated by reference to the charge to profits and the opening or closing dividend payable shown in the statement of financial position.

Note that the charge to profits for dividends is not shown in the income statement. It can, however, be derived using an accumulated profits T account working.

Test your understanding 2

Requirement 2

Identify and calculate the remaining amounts to be shown under the heading 'Cash flows from operating activities' within Geronimo's statement of cash flows.

5 Cash from investing activities

Cash inflows may include:

- interest received
- dividends received
- proceeds of sale of equipment.

Cash outflows may include:

- purchase of property, plant and equipment.

Calculation of interest and dividends received

Again, the calculation should take account of both the income receivable shown in the income statement and any relevant receivables balance from the opening and closing statement of financial positions.

A T account working may be useful:

e.g. Interest receivable

	$		$
Interest receivable b/f	X		
Income statement interest receivable	X	Cash received (ß)	X
		Interest receivable c/f	X
	___		___
	X		X
	___		___

Test your understanding 3

Requirement 3

Identify and calculate the dividends and interest received to be shown under the heading ' cash flow from investing activities' within Geronimo's statement of cash flows .

Calculation of purchase of property, plant and equipment and proceeds of sale of equipment

These amounts are often the trickiest to calculate within a statement of cash flows. It is therefore recommended that T account workings are used.

The following T accounts will be required for each class of assets:

- cost account
- accumulated depreciation account
- disposals account (where relevant).

Data provided in the source financial statements should then be entered into these T accounts and the required cash flows found – often as balancing figures.

NB If there is evidence of a revaluation, remember to include the uplift in value on the debit side of the cost T account.

In some cases, insufficient detail is provided to produce separate cost and accumulated depreciation accounts. Instead, a net book value account should be used:

Net book value(NBV)

	$		$
NBV b/f	X		
Additions at NBV (= cash to purchase PPE)	X	Disposals at NBV	X
Revaluation	X	Depreciation charge for year	X
		Net book value c/f	X
	X		X

 Test your understanding 4

Requirement 4

Identify and calculate the cash outflow to purchase property, plant and equipment and the proceeds from the sale of equipment to be shown under the heading 'Cash flows from investing activities' within Geronimo's statement of cash flows.

6 Cash from financing activities

Cash inflows may include:

- proceeds of issue of shares
- proceeds of issue of loans/debentures.

Cash outflows may include:

- repayment of loans/debentures.

Calculation of proceeds of issue of shares

This cash inflow is derived by comparison of the sum brought forward and sum carried forward balances on two accounts:

- share capital
- share premium.

Calculation of proceeds of issue of loans/repayment of loans

This cash flow is derived by simply subtracting the brought forward balance from the carried forward.

Test your understanding 5

Requirement 5

Identify and calculate each of the amounts to be shown under the heading 'Cash flows from financing activities' within Geronimo's statement of cash flows.

Test your understanding 6

Requirement 6

Complete the following proforma statement of cash flows for Geronimo using your answers to Test your understanding 1 requirements 1–5.

Statement of cash flows for Geronimo for year ended 31 December 20X6

	$000	$000
Cash flows from operating activities		
Cash generated from operations		
Interest paid		
Dividends paid		
Tax paid		
		_____
Net cash from operating activities		
Cash flows from investing activities		
Proceeds of sale of equipment		
Purchase of property, plant and equipment		
Interest received		
Dividends received		
	_____	
Net cash used in investing activities		
Cash flows from financing activities		
Proceeds of issue of shares		
Repayment of loans		
	_____	
Net cash used in financing activities		
Net increase in cash and cash equivalents		
		_____
Cash and cash equivalents at beginning of period		
		_____
Cash and cash equivalents at end period		

Test your understanding 7

You are given below, in summarised form, the accounts of Algernon, a limited company, for 20X6 and 20X7.

	20X6 SFP			20X7 SFP		
	Cost	Dep'n	Net	Cost	Dep'n	Net
	$	$	$	$	$	$
Plant	10,000	4,000	6,000	11,000	5,000	6,000
Buildings	50,000	10,000	40,000	90,000	11,000	79,000
			46,000			85,000
Investments at cost			50,000			80,000
Land			43,000			63,000
Inventory			55,000			65,000
Receivables			40,000			50,000
Bank			3,000			
			237,000			343,000
Ordinary shares of $1 each			40,000			50,000
Share premium			12,000			14,000
Revaluation reserve (land)			–			20,000
Accumulated profit			45,000			45,000
10% Loan notes			100,000			150,000
Payables			40,000			60,000
Bank			–			4,000
			237,000			343,000

Income statement

	20X6	20X7
	$	$
Sales	200,000	200,000
Cost of sales	(100,000)	(120,000)
	100,000	80,000
Expenses	(50,000)	(47,000)
	50,000	33,000
Interest	(10,000)	(13,000)
Net profit for year	40,000	20,000

Notes:

A $20,000 dividend has been paid in the year.

(a) Prepare a statement of cash flows for Algernon for 20X7, to explain as far as possible the movement in the bank balance. The statement of cash flows should be prepared using the direct method.

(b) Using the summarised accounts given, and the statement you have just prepared, comment on the position, progress and direction of Algernon.

Test your understanding 8

Part of a company's statement of cash flows is shown below:

	$000
Operating profit	1,255
Loss on disposal	(455)
Increase in receivables	(198)
Increase in payables	340

The following criticisms of the extract have been made:

(1) The loss on disposal should have been added, not deducted.

(2) Increase in receivables should have been added, not deducted.

(3) Increase in payables should have been deducted, not added.

Which of the criticisms is valid?

A   1, 2 and 3

B   1 only

C   2 and 3 only

D   none of them

Test your understanding 9

Which of the following could appear in a company's statement of cash flows?

(1) Proposed dividend

(2) Dividends received

(3) Bonus issue of shares

(4) Surplus on revaluation of non-current assets

A   1 and 2

B   1,2 and 3

C   2 only

D   2 and 3

Test your understanding 10

The following details are provided to the accountant of Caddyshack Ltd, which has an operating profit of $469,850 in the year ended 31 December 20X6:

(1) Depreciation of $37,400 has been charged to the income statement; this included an amount of $7,600 which was the loss on disposal of a non-current asset.

(2) The following extract of the statement of financial position at 31 December 20X5 and 20X6 have been provided:

	31 December 20X6 $000	31 December 20X5 $000
Inventory	145	167
Trade receivables	202	203
Prepayments	27	16
Trade payables	196	212
Interest accrual	6	28

What is the cash generated from operations?

A $511,250

B $510,850

C $501,250

D $503,250

Chapter summary

The need for a statement of cash flows

- Helps to assess liquidity of a company.
- Helps to assess future cash flows.
- User can see cash flows in and out of the business.

Format of a statement of cash flows

IAS 7 requires the cash flow statement to have three headings:

- Operating activities
- Investing activities
- Financing activities.

Preparation of a statement of cash flows

The cash movement is simply the movement between the current and previous year's balance in the statement of financial position. Watch out for trickier areas such as taxation, and non-current assets where a working will need to be done.

Interpretation using a statement of cash flows

The cash flow provides useful information including:

- how a business spends and receives cash
- whether operating activities yield a positive cash flow
- whether the business has the ability to generate cash in the future.

Test your understanding answers

Test your understanding 1

Requirement 1

	$000
Net profit before taxation	163
Finance charge	22
Investment income	(72)
Depreciation (W1)	85
Loss on disposal of plant	5
Decrease in inventory	7
Increase in trade receivables	(16)
Decrease in trade payables	(5)
Cash generated from operations	189

(W1)

Accumulated depreciation

	$000		$000
Disposals	15	balance b/f	120
Balance c/f	190	Depreciation charge (ß)	85
	205		205

Test your understanding 2

Requirement 2

Interest paid

Interest payable

	$000		$000
		Interest accrual b/f	5
Cash paid (ß)	24	Income statement	
Interest accrual c/f	3	finance charge	22
	27		27

Dividends paid

Accumulated profits

	$000		$000
		Balance b/f	226
Dividend (ß)	35	Retained profit shown in income statement	92
Balance c/f	283		
	318		318

Dividend payable

	$000		$000
		Dividend payable b/f	27
Cash paid (ß)	32	Dividend (accumulated profits)	35
Dividend payable c/f	30		
	62		62

Income tax payable

	$		$
		Tax payable b/f	67
Cash paid (ß)	62	Income statement tax charge	71
Tax payable c/f	76		
	___		___
	138		138
	___		___

Test your understanding 3

Requirement 3

There is no balance for interest receivable at the start or end of the year; therefore interest received must equal interest receivable in the income statement

Interest received $15,000

Dividends received

Dividends receivable

	$		$
Dividends receivable b/f	50	Cash received (ß)	50
Income statement dividends receivable	57	Dividends receivable c/f	57
	___		___
	X		X
	___		___

Requirement 4

(see Solution to Requirement 1 for accumulated depreciation account.)

PPE Cost

	$000		$000
Balance b/f	750		
Additions (= Cash to purchase PPE)	178	Disposals	80
Revaluation	200	Balance c/f	1,048
	1,128		1,128

Disposals

	$000		$000
Cost	80	Accumulated depreciation	15
		Loss on disposal	5
		Proceeds (ß)	60

Requirement 5

	20X6	20X5	
	$000	$000	$000
Share capital	200	120	
Share premium	106	80	
	306	200	
Proceeds of share issue			106

Repayment of loan

- Balance on loan account was $300,000 in 20X5; in 20X6 it is $200,000.

- Therefore $100,000 has been repaid.

Test your understanding 6

Requirement 6

Statement of cash flows for Geronimo for year ended 31 December 20X6

	$000	$000
Cash flows from operating activities		
Cash generated from operations	189	
Interest paid	(24)	
Dividends paid	(32)	
Tax paid	(62)	
	___	
		71
Net cash from operating activities		
Cash flows from investing activities		
Proceeds of sale of equipment	60	
Purchase of property, plant and equipment	(178)	
Interest received	15	
Dividends received	50	
	___	
Net cash used in investing activities		(53)
Cash flows from financing activities		
Proceeds of issue of shares	106	
Repayment of loans	(100)	
	___	
Net cash used in financing activities		6
		___
Net increase in cash and cash equivalents		24
Cash and cash equivalents at beginning of period		18
		___
Cash and cash equivalents at end of period		42
		___

Statement of Cashflows for Algernon for year ended 31 December 2007

	$	$
Cash flows from operating activities		
Cash receipts from customers (W1)	190,000	
Cash paid to suppliers and employees (W2)	(155,000)	
	————	
Cash generated from operations	35,000	
Interest paid	(13,000)	
Dividends paid	(20,000)	–
Net cash from operating activities		2,000
Cash flows from investing activities		
Purchase of tangible non-current assets (1,000 + 40,000)	(41,000)	
Purchase of investments	(30,000)	
Net cash used for investing activities		(71,000)
Cash flows from financing activities		
Issue of shares (10,000 + 2,000)	12,000	
Loan notes	50,000	
	————	
Net cash from financing activities		62,000
Net decrease in cash and cash equivalents		(7,000)
Cash and cash equivalents at 1 January 20X7		3,000
		————
Cash and cash equivalents at 31 December 20X7		(4,000)
		————

	31 December	
	20X6	20X7
	$	$
Balance at bank	3,000	(4,000)
	————	————

Workings

(W1) Receipts from sales

Receivables control

	$		$
Balance b/f	40,000	Cash receipts (ß)	190,000
Sales revenue	200,000	Balance c/f	50,000
	240,000		240,000

(W2) Payables and wages control

Payable and wages control

	$		$
Cash paid (ß)	155,000	Balance b/f	40,000
Depreciation	2,000	Purchases re cost of sales (W3)	130,000
Balance c/f	60,000		
		Expenses	47,000
	217,000		217,000

(W3) Cost of sales

Cost of sales

	$		$
Opening inventory	55,000	Cost of sales	120,000
Purchases and wages (ß)	130,000	Closing inventory	65,000
	185,000		185,000

Tutorial note Little information has been given as to the nature of the costs of the company; for example, no information is supplied on wages and salaries. The payments figure thus includes all cash outflows relating to trading activities. Depreciation would have been charged in either cost of sales or expenses and this needs to be adjusted for. It does not matter whether the adjustment is shown in the payables control or the cost of sales accounts.

(b) Algernon has invested substantially in buildings, investments, inventory and receivables in the year. The finance has come from new share capital in part but mainly from loans. The equity to assets ratio of the company has thus decreased. The working capital has been financed by an equal increase in trade payables.

The profits have been fully distributed as dividends despite the halving of profits from last year. It might have been wiser to cut back on dividends in the period of expansion until the benefits of the expansion are seen in the form of higher profits.

Test your understanding 8

The correct answer is B

A loss on disposal should be added back to profit as it is a non-cash expense.

Test your understanding 9

The correct answer is C

Dividends received involve a cash receipt. The other transactions do not involve a movement of cash.

Test your understanding 10

The correct answer is D

	$
Operating profit	469,850
Depreciation and loss on disposal	37,400
Decrease in inventory	22,000
Decrease in trade receivables	1,000
Increase in prepayments	(11,000)
Decrease in trade payables	(16,000)
	503,250

Note that the movement in the interest accrual is not part of the reconciliation as this is dealt with within the Interest paid line of the statement of cash flows.

Consolidated statement of financial position

Chapter learning objectives

Upon completion of this chapter you will be able to:

- prepare a consolidated statement of financial position for a simple group (parent and one subsidiary)

- deal with pre- and post-acquisition profits

- deal with non-controlling interests (at fair value)

- describe the required accounting treatment of consolidated goodwill

- apply the required accounting treatment of consolidated goodwill

- explain the consolidation of other reserves (e.g. share premium and revaluation)

- account for the consolidation of other reserves

- account for the effects of intra-group trading in the statement of financial position

- explain why it is necessary to use fair values

- Acquisitions of subsidiaries part way through the financial year.

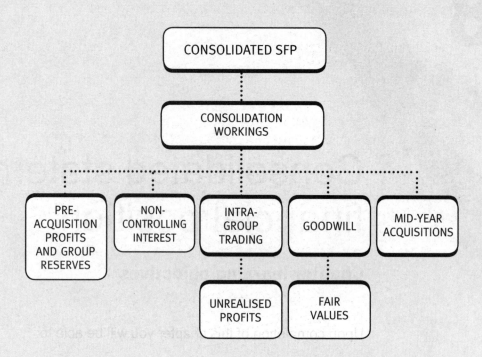

1 Principles of the consolidated statement of financial position

The concept of group accounts

What is a group?

If one company owns more than 50% of the ordinary shares of another company:

- this will usually give the first company 'control' of the second company

- the first company (the parent company, P) has enough voting power to appoint all the directors of the second company (the subsidiary company, S)

- P is, in effect, able to manage S as if it were merely a department of P, rather than a separate entity

- in strict legal terms P and S remain distinct, but in economic substance they can be regarded as a single unit (a 'group').

Definitions

IAS 27 Consolidated and Separate Financial Statements uses the following definitions:

- **subsidiary** – an entity that is controlled by another entity (known as the parent)

- **control** – the power to govern the financial and operating policies of an entity so as to obtain benefits from its activities

Requirements for consolidated financial statements

IAS 27 outlines the circumstances in which a group is required to prepare consolidated financial statements.

Consolidated financial statements should be prepared when the parent company has control over the subsidiary. Control is usually established based on ownership of more than 50% of voting power, but other forms of control are possible.

IAS 27 gives four other situations in which control exists – when the parent has power:

- over more than half the voting rights by virtue of an agreement with other investors

- to govern the financial and operating policies of the entity under a statute or an agreement

- to appoint or remove the majority of the members of the board of directors

- to cast the majority of votes at a meeting of the board of directors.

Exclusion of individual companies from the group accounts

Subsidiary exclusion

An undertaking required to produce group accounts may have (or be required) to exclude certain subsidiaries on the following basis:

Severe restrictions on control

Subsidiaries to be excluded if the holding company no longer has control. An example of this is a foreign investment where the overseas government has imposed restrictions.

Interest held exclusively for resale

IFRS 5 provides that an investment in a subsidiary which is held with an intention to resell in the near future (approximately within one year) should not be consolidated.

Method of preparing a consolidated statement of financial position

(1) The investment in the subsidiary (S) shown in the parent's (P's) statement of financial position is replaced by the net assets of S.

(2) The cost of the investment in S is effectively cancelled with the ordinary share capital and reserves of the subsidiary.

This leaves a consolidated statement of financial position showing:

- the net assets of the whole group (P + S)

- the share capital of the group which always equals the share capital of P only and

- the retained profits, comprising profits made by the group (i.e. all of P's historical profits + profits made by S post-acquisition).

Illustration 1 – Simple CSFP

Statements of financial position at 31 December 20X4

	P	S
	$000	$000
Non-current assets	60	50
Investment in S at cost	50	
Current assets	40	40
	150	90
Ordinary share capital ($1 shares)	100	40
Retained earnings	30	10
Current liabilities	20	40
	150	90

P acquired all the shares in S on 31 December 20X4 for a cost of $50,000.

Prepare the consolidated statement of financial position at 31 December 20X4.

Solution

Approach

(1) The balance on 'investment in subsidiary account' in P's accounts will be replaced by the underlying assets and liabilities which the investment represents, i.e. the assets and liabilities of S.

(2) The cost of the investment in the subsidiary is effectively cancelled with the ordinary share capital and reserves of S. This is normally achieved in consolidation workings (discussed in more detail below). However, in this simple case, it can be seen that the relevant figures are equal and opposite ($50,000), and therefore cancel directly.

This leaves a consolidated statement of financial position showing:

- the net assets of the whole group (P + S)

- the share capital of the group, which equals the share capital of P only – $100,000

- retained earnings comprising profits made by the group. Here this will only include the $30,000 retained earnings of the parent company. S is purchased on the reporting date, therefore there are no post-acquisition earnings to include in the group amount.

By cross-casting the net assets of each company, and cancelling the investment in S against the share capital and reserves of S, we arrive at the consolidated statement of financial position given below.

P consolidated statement of financial position at 31 December 20X4

	$000
Non-current assets $(60,000 + 50,000)	110
Current assets $(40,000 + 40,000)	80
	190
Share capital ($1 ordinary shares)	100
Retained earnings	30
Current liabilities $(20,000 + 40,000)	60
	190

Note: Under no circumstances will any share capital of any subsidiary company ever be included in the figure of share capital in the consolidated statement of financial position.

The mechanics of consolidation

A standard group accounting question will provide the accounts of P and the accounts of S and will require the preparation of consolidated accounts.

The best approach is to use a set of standard workings.

(W1) Establish the group structure

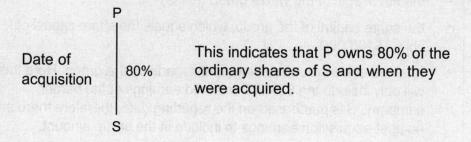

(W2) Net assets of subsidiary

	At date of acquisition $	At the reporting date $
Share capital	X	X
Reserves:		
Share premium	X	X
Retained earnings	X	X
	X	X

(W3) Goodwill

	$
Parent holding (investment) at fair value	X
NCI value at acquisition	X
	X
Less:	
Fair value of net assets at acquisition (W2)	(X)
Goodwill on acquisition	X

(W4) **Non controlling interest**

NCI value at acquisition (as in W3)	X
NCI share of post-acquisition reserves (W2)	X
	—
	X
	—

(W5) **Group retained earnings**

	$
P's retained earnings (100%)	X
P's % of sub's post-acquisition retained earnings	X
	—
	X
	—

Goodwill

Goodwill on acquisition

In example 1 the cost of the shares in S was $50,000. Equally the net assets of S were $50,000. This is not always the case.

The value of a company will normally exceed the value of its net assets. The difference is **goodwill**. This goodwill represents assets not shown in the statement of financial position of the acquired company such as the reputation of the business.

Goodwill on acquisition is calculated by comparing the value of the subsidiary acquired to its net assets.

Where 100% of the subsidiary is acquired, the calculation is therefore:

	$
Cost of investment (= value of the subsidiary)	X
Net assets of subsidiary	(X)
	—
Goodwill	X

Where less than 100% of the subsidiary is acquired, the value of the subsidiary comprises two elements:

* The value of the part acquired by the parent
* The value of the part not acquired by the parent, known as the non-controlling interest

There are 2 methods in which Goodwill may be calculated:

(i) Proportion of net assets method (as seen in consolidation workings). Not examinable

(ii) Fair value method (as seen in consolidation workings). Examinable

The proportion of net assets method calculates the portion of goodwill attributable to the parent only, while the fair value method calculates the goodwill attributable to the group as a whole. This is known as the gross goodwill i.e. goodwill is shown in full as this is the asset that the group controls.

Illustration 2 – Goodwill

Daniel acquired 80% of the ordinary share capital of Craig on 31 December 20X6 for $78,000. At this date the net assets of Craig were $85,000. NCI is valued using the fair value method and the fair value of the NCI on the acquisition date is $19,000

What goodwill arises on the acquisition?

Solution

	$
Parent holding (investment) at fair value	78,000
NCI value at acquisition	19,000
	97,000
Less:	
Fair value of net assets at acquisition	(85,000)
Goodwill on acquisition	12,000

IFRS 3 Business Combinations

IFRS 3 revised governs accounting for all business combinations other than joint ventures and a number of other unusual arrangements not included in this syllabus. The definition of goodwill is:

Goodwill is an asset representing the future economic benefits arising from other assets acquired in a business combination that are not individually identified and separately recognised.

Goodwill is calculated as the excess of the consideration transferred and amount of any non-controlling interest over the net of the acquisition date identifiable assets acquired and liabilities assumed.

Treatment of goodwill

Positive goodwill

- Capitalised as an intangible non-current asset.
- Tested annually for possible impairments.
- Amortisation of goodwill is not permitted by the standard.

Impairment of positive goodwill

If goodwill is considered to have been impaired during the post-acquisition period it must be reflected in the group financial statements. Accounting for the impairment differs according to the policy followed to value the non-controlling interests.

Proportion of net assets method:

Dr Group reserves (W5)
Cr Goodwill (W3)

Fair value method:

Dr Group reserves (% of impairment attributable to the parent – W5)
Dr NCI (% of impairment attributable to NCI – W4)
Cr Goodwill (W3)

Negative goodwill

- Arises where the cost of the investment is less than the value of net assets purchased.

- IFRS 3 does not refer to this as negative goodwill (instead it is referred to as a bargain purchase), however this is the commonly used term.

- Most likely reason for this to arise is a misstatement of the fair values of assets and liabilities and accordingly the standard requires that the calculation is reviewed.

- After such a review, any negative goodwill remaining is credited directly to the income statement.

Pre- and post-acquisition reserves

Pre and post-acquisition profits

Pre-acquisition profits are the reserves which exist in a subsidiary company at the date when it is acquired.

They are capitalised at the date of acquisition by including them in the goodwill calculation.

Post-acquisition profits are profits made and included in the retained earnings of the subsidiary company following acquisition.

They are included in group retained earnings.

Group reserves

When looking at the reserves of S at the year end, e.g. revaluation reserve, a distinction must be made between:

- those reserves of S which existed at the date of acquisition by P (pre-acquisition reserves) and

- the increase in the reserves of S which arose after acquisition by P (post-acquisition reserves).

As with retained earnings, only the group share of post-acquisition reserves of S is included in the group statement of financial position.

Illustration 3 – Pre- and post-acquisition reserves

The following statements of financial position were extracted from the books of two companies at 31 December 20X9.

	Derek $	Clive $
Non-current assets:		
Property, plant & equipment	75,000	11,000
Investments		
Shares in Clive	27,000	
	102,000	
Current assets	214,000	33,000
	316,000	44,000
Equity:		
Share capital	80,000	4,000
Share premium	20,000	6,000
Retained earnings	40,000	9,000
	140,000	19,000
Current liabilities	176,000	25,000
	316,000	44,000

Derek acquired all of the share capital of Clive one year ago. The retained earnings of Clive stood at $2,000 on the day of acquisition. Goodwill is calculated using the fair value method. There has been no impairment of goodwill since acquisition.

Required:

Prepare the consolidated statement of financial position of Derek as at 31 December 20X9.

Solution

Derek consolidated statement of financial position at 31 December 20X9

	$000
Non-current assets:	
Goodwill (W3)	15
PPE $(75,000 + 11,000)	86
Current assets $(214,000 + 33,000)	247
	348
Share capital (Derek only)	80
Share premium (Derek only)	20
Group retained earnings (W5)	47
	147
Current liabilities $(176,000 + 25,000)	201
	348

(W1) Establish the group structure

```
              Derek
                |
1 Jan 20X9    100%
                |
              Clive
```

(W2) Net assets of Clive

	At date of acquisition $	At the reporting date $
Share capital	4,000	4,000
Reserves:		
Share premium	6,000	6,000
Retained earnings	2,000	9,000
	12,000	19,000

(W3) Goodwill

	$
Parent holding (investment) at fair value	27,000
Less:	
Fair value of net assets at acquisition (W2)	(12,000)
Goodwill on acquisition	15,000

(W4) NCI

Not applicable to this example as Clive is 100% owned.

(W5) Group retained earnings

	$
Derek retained earnings (100%)	40,000
Clive – group share of post-acquisition retained earnings 100% × $(19,000 – 12,000 (W2))	7,000
	47,000

Non-controlling interests

What is a non-controlling interest?

In some situations a parent may not own all of the shares in the subsidiary, e.g. if P owns only 80% of the ordinary shares of S, there is a non-controlling interest of 20%.

Note, however, that P still controls S.

Accounting treatment of a non-controlling interest

As P controls S:

- in the consolidated statement of financial position, include all of the net assets of S (to show control).

- 'give back' the net assets of S which belong to the non-controlling interest within the equity section of the consolidated statement of financial position (calculated in W4).

Test your understanding 1

The following SFPs have been prepared at 31 December 20X8.

	D $	J $
Non-current assets:		
Property, plant & equipment	85,000	18,000
Investments:		
Shares in J	60,000	
	145,000	
Current assets	160,000	84,000
	305,000	102,000
Equity:		
Ordinary $1 shares	65,000	20,000
Share premium	35,000	10,000
Retained earnings	70,000	25,000
	170,000	55,000
Current liabilities	135,000	47,000
	305,000	102,000

D acquired its 80% holding in J on 1 January 20X8, when Js' retained earnings stood at $20,000.On this date, the fair value of the 20% non-controlling shareholding in J was $12,500.

The D Group uses the fair value method to value the non-controlling interest.

Prepare the consolidated statement of financial position of D as at 31 December 20X8.

2 Fair values

Fair value of consideration and net assets

To ensure that an accurate figure is calculated for goodwill:

- the consideration paid for a subsidiary must be accounted for at fair value

- the subsidiary's identifiable assets and liabilities acquired must be accounted for at their fair values.

The **fair value** of assets and liabilities is defined in IFRS 3 (and several other IFRSs) as 'the amount for which an asset could be exchanged or a liability settled between knowledgeable, willing parties in an arm's length transaction'.

Fair values

In order to account for an acquisition, the acquiring company must measure the cost of what it is accounting for, which will normally represent:

- the cost of the investment in its own statement of financial position

- the amount to be allocated between the identifiable net assets of the subsidiary, the non-controlling interest and goodwill in the consolidated financial statements.

The subsidiary's identifiable assets and liabilities are included in the consolidated accounts at their fair values for the following reasons.

- Consolidated accounts are prepared from the perspective of the group, rather than from the perspectives of the individual companies. The book values of the subsidiary's assets and liabilities are largely irrelevant, because the consolidated accounts must reflect their cost to the group (i.e. to the parent), not their original cost to the subsidiary. The cost to the group is their fair value at the date of acquisition.

- Purchased goodwill is the difference between the value of an acquired entity and the aggregate of the fair values of that entity's identifiable assets and liabilities. If fair values are not used, the value of goodwill will be meaningless.

Identifiable assets and liabilities recognised in the accounts are those of the acquired entity that existed at the date of acquisition.

Assets and liabilities are measured at fair values reflecting conditions at the date of acquisition.

The following do not affect fair values at the date of acquisition and are therefore dealt with as post-acquisition items.

- Changes resulting from the acquirer's intentions or future actions.
- Changes resulting from post-acquisition events.
- Provisions for future operating losses or reorganisation costs incurred as a result of the acquisition.

Fair value of net assets acquired

IFRS 3 revised requires that the subsidiary's assets and liabilities are recorded at their fair value for the purposes of the calculation of goodwill and production of consolidated accounts.

Adjustments will therefore be required where the subsidiary's accounts themselves do not reflect fair value.

How to include fair values in consolidation workings

(1) Adjust both columns of W2 to bring the net assets to fair value at acquisition and reporting date.

This will ensure that the fair value of net assets is carried through to the goodwill and non-controlling interest calculations.

	At acquisition $000	At reporting date $000
Ordinary share capital + reserves	X	X
Fair value adjustments	X	X
	X	X

(2) At the reporting date make the adjustment on the face of the SFP when adding across assets and liabilities.

Test your understanding 2

Hazelnut acquired 80% of the share capital of Peppermint two years ago, when the reserves of Peppermint stood at $125,000. Hazelnut paid initial cash consideration of $1 million.

Below are the statements of financial position of Hazelnut and Peppermint as at 31 December 20X4:

	Hazelnut $000	Peppermint $000
Investment in Peppermint at cost	1,000	
Property, plant & equipment	5,500	1,500
Current assets:		
Inventory	550	100
Receivables	400	200
Cash	200	50
	7,650	1,850
Share capital	2,000	500
Retained earnings	1,400	300
	3,400	800
Non-current liabilities	3,000	400
Current liabilities	1,250	650
	7,650	1,850

At acquisition the fair values of Peppermint's plant exceeded its book value by $200,000. The fair value of the 20% non-controlling interest was $380,000

Prepare the consolidated statement of financial position as at 31 December 20X4.

3 Intra-group trading

Types of intra-group trading

P and S may well trade with each other leading to the following potential problem areas:

- current accounts between P and S
- loans held by one company in the other
- dividends and loan interest.
- unrealised profits on sales of inventory
- unrealised profits on sales of non-current assets (not examinable)

Current accounts

If P and S trade with each other then this will probably be done on credit leading to:

- a receivables (current) account in one company's SFP
- a payables (current) account in the other company's SFP.

These are amounts owing within the group rather than outside the group and therefore they must not appear in the consolidated statement of financial position.

They are therefore cancelled (contra'd) against each other on consolidation.

Cash/goods in transit

At the year end, current accounts may not agree, owing to the existence of in-transit items such as goods or cash.

The usual rules are as follows:

- If the goods or cash are in transit between P and S, make the adjusting entry to the statement of financial position of the recipient:
  - cash in transit adjusting entry is:
    - Dr Cash in transit
    - Cr Receivables current account
  - goods in transit adjusting entry is:
    - Dr Inventory
    - Cr Payables current account

this adjustment is for the purpose of consolidation only.

- Once in agreement, the current accounts may be contra'd and cancelled as part of the process of cross casting the assets and liabilities.

- This means that reconciled current account balance amounts are removed from both receivables and payables in the consolidated statement of financial position.

Test your understanding 3

Fair value adjustments/intercompany balance

Statements of Financial Position of P and S as at 30 June 20X8 are given below:

	P $	S $
Non-current assets:		
Land	4,500	2,500
Plant & equipment	2,400	1,750
Investment	8,0000	
	14,900	4,250
Current assets		
Inventory	3,200	900
Receivables	1,400	650
Bank	600	150
	5,200	1,700
	20,100	5,9500
Ordinary share capital 50c	5,000	1,000
Retained earnings	8,300	3,150
	13,300	4,150
Current liabilities	6,800	1,800
	20,100	5,950

P acquired 75% of S on 1 July 20X5 when the balance on S's retained earnings was $1,150. P paid $3,500 for its investment in the share capital of S.

At the reporting date P recorded a payable to S of $400. This agreed to the corresponding amount in S's financial statements.

At the date of acquisition it was determined that S's land, carried at cost of $2,500 had a fair value of $3,750. S's plant was determined to have a fair value of $500 in excess of its carrying value. These values had not been recorded by S.

The P group uses the fair value method to value the non-controlling interest which was $1,100.

Required:

Prepare the consolidated statement of financial position of the P group as at 30 June 20X8.

4 Unrealised profit

Profits made by members of a group on transactions with other group members are:

- recognised in the accounts of the individual companies concerned, but
- in terms of the group as a whole, such profits are unrealised and must be eliminated from the consolidated accounts.

Unrealised profit may arise within a group scenario on:

- inventory where companies trade with each other
- non-current assets where one group company has transferred an asset to another. (not examinable)

Intra-group trading and unrealised profit in inventory

When one group company sells goods to another a number of adjustments may be needed.

- Current accounts must be cancelled (see earlier in this chapter).
- Where goods are still held by a group company, any unrealised profit must be cancelled.
- Inventory must be included at original cost to the group (i.e. cost to the company which then sold it).

PURP

Where goods have been sold by one group company to another at a profit and some of these goods are still in the purchaser's inventory at the year end, then the profit loading on these goods is **unrealised** from the viewpoint of the group as a whole.

This is because we are treating the group as if it is a single entity. No one can make a profit by trading with himself. Until the goods are sold to an outside party there is no **realised** profit from the group perspective.

For example, if Pineapple purchased goods for $400 and then sold these goods onto Satsuma during the year for $500, Pineapple would record a profit of $100 in their own individual financial statements. The statement of financial position of Satsuma will include closing inventory at the cost to Satsuma i.e. $500.

This situation results in two problems within the group:

(1) The profit made by Pineapple is unrealised. The profit will only become realised when sold on to a third party customer.

(2) The value in Satsuma's inventory ($500) is not the cost of the inventory to the group (cost to the group was the purchase price of the goods from the external third party supplier i.e. $400).

An adjustment will need to be made so that the single entity concept can be upheld i.e. The group should report external profits, external assets and external liabilities only.

Adjustments for unrealised profit in inventory

The process to adjust is:

(1) Determine the value of closing inventory included in an individual company's accounts which has been purchased from another company in the group.

(2) Use mark-up or margin to calculate how much of that value represents profit earned by the selling company.

(3) Make the adjustments. These will depend on who the seller is.

If the seller is the parent company, the profit element is included in the holding company's accounts and relates entirely to the group.

Adjustment required:

Dr Group retained earnings (deduct the profit in W5)

Cr Group inventory

If the seller is the subsidiary, the profit element is included in the subsidiary company's accounts and relates partly to the group, partly to non-controlling interests (if any).

Adjustment required:

Dr Subsidiary retained earnings (deduct the profit in W2 – at reporting date)

Cr Group inventory

Test your understanding 4

H bought 90% of the equity share capital of S, two years ago on 1 January 20X2 when the retained earnings of S stood at $5,000. Statements of financial position at the year end of 31 December 20X3 are as follows:

	H		S	
	$000	$000	$000	$000
Non-current assets:				
Property, plant & equipment		100		30
Investment in S at cost		34		
		——		——
		134		30
Current assets:				
Inventory	90		20	
Receivables	110		25	
Bank	10		5	
	——		——	
		210		50
		——		——
		344		80
		——		——
Equity:				
Share capital		15		5
Retained earnings		159		31
		——		——
		174		36
Non-current liabilities		120		28
Current liabilities		50		16
		——		——
		344		80
		——		——

S transferred goods to H at a transfer price of $18,000 at a mark-up of 50%. Two-thirds remained in inventory at the year end. The current account in H and S stood at $22,000 on that day.

The H group uses the fair value method to value the non-controlling interest. The fair value of the non-controlling interest at acquisition was $4,000

Prepare the consolidated statement of financial position at 31/12/X3.

5 Mid-year acquisitions

Calculation of reserves at date of acquisition

If a parent company acquires a subsidiary mid-year, the net assets at the date of acquisition must be calculated based on the net assets at the start of the subsidiary's financial year plus the profits of up to the date of acquisition.

To calculate this it is normally assumed that S's profit after tax accrues evenly over time.

Test your understanding 5

Consolidated Statement of Financial Position

On 1 May 2007 K bought 60% of S paying $76,000 cash. The summarised Statements of Financial Position for the two companies as at 30 November 2007 are:

	K $	S $
Non-current assets		
Property, plant & equipment	138,000	115,000
Investments	98,000	–
Current assets		
Inventory	15,000	17,000
Receivables	19,000	20,000
Cash	2,000	–
	272,000	152,000
Share capital	50,000	40,000
Retained earnings	189,000	69,000
	239,000	109,000
Current liabilities	33,000	43,000
	272,000	152,000

The following information is relevant:

(1) The inventory of S includes $8,000 of goods purchased from Kat cost plus 25%.

(2) The K Group values the non-controlling interest using the fair value method. At the date of acquisition the fair value of the 40% non-controlling interest was $50,000.

(3) S earned a profit of $9,000 in the year ended 30 November 2007.

Required:

Prepare the consolidated Statement of Financial Position as at 30 November 2007.

Chapter summary

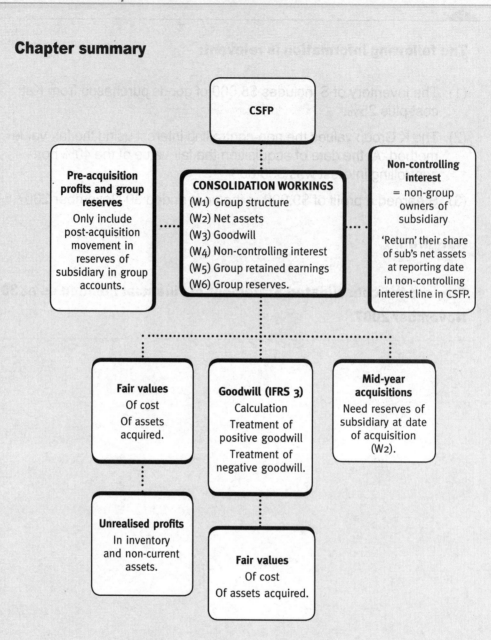

Test your understanding answers

Test your understanding 1

D consolidated statement of financial position as at 31 December 20X8

	$
Non-current assets	
Goodwill (W3)	22,500
PPE	
(85,000 + 18,000)	103,000
Current assets	
(160,000 + 84,000)	244,000
	———
	369,500
	———
Equity	
Share capital	65,000
Share premium	35,000
Group retained earnings (W5)	74,000
Non-controlling interest (W4)	13,500
	———
	187,500
Current liabilities	
(135,000 + 47,000)	182,000
	———
	369,500
	———

(W1) Group structure

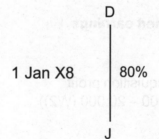

D

1 Jan X8   80%

J

(W2) **Net assets of J**

	At date of acquisition	At reporting date
Share capital	20,000	20,000
Share premium	10,000	10,000
Retained earnings	20,000	25,000
Net assets	50,000	55,000

(W3) **Goodwill**

Parent holding (investment) at fair value	60,000
NCI value at acquisition	12,500
	72,500
Less:	
Fair value of net assets at acquisition	(50,000)
Goodwill on acquisition	22,500

(W4) **Non-controlling interests**

NCI value at acquisition (as in W3)	12,500
NCI share of post-acquisition reserves (W2)	
	1,000
(20% × (25,000 – 20,000))	
	13,500

(W5) **Group retained earnings**

D	70,000
80% J post-acquisition profit	
(80% × $(25,000 – 20,000 (W2))	4,000
	74,000

Test your understanding 2

Hazelnut consolidated statement of financial position at 31 December 20X4

	$000
Goodwill (W3)	555
Property, plant & equipment (5,500 + 1,500 + 200)	7,200
Current assets:	
Inventory (550 + 100)	650
Receivables (400 + 200)	600
Cash (200 + 50)	250
	———
	9,255
	———
Share capital	2,000
Retained earnings (W5)	1,540
	———
	3,900
Non-controlling interest (W4)	415
	———
	4,315
	———
Non-current liabilities (3,000 + 400)	3,400
Current liabilities (1,250 + 650)	1,900
	———
	9,255
	———

Workings

(W1) **Group structure**

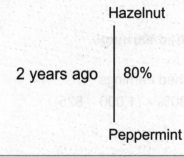

Hazelnut

2 years ago | 80%

Peppermint

(W2) Net assets of Peppermint

	At date of acquisition	At reporting date
Share capital	500	500
Retained earnings	125	300
Plant fair value adjustment	200	200
	825	1,000

(W3) Goodwill

Parent holding (investment) at fair value:	
Cash paid	1,000
NCI value at acquisition	380
	1,380
Less:	
Fair value of net assets at acquisition (W2)	(825)
Goodwill on acquisition	555

(W4) Non-controlling interest

NCI value at acquisition (as in W3)	380
NCI share of post acquisition reserves	35
(20% × (1,000 – 825) (W2))	
	415

(W5) Group retained earnings

Hazelnut retained earnings	1,400
Peppermint (80% × (1,000 – 825))	140
	1,540

Test your understanding 3

Consolidated statement of financial position as at 30 June 20X8

Non-current assets	$
Goodwill (W3)	700
Land (4,500 + 2,500 + 1,250)	8,250
Plant & equipment (2,400 + 1,750 + 500)	4,650
Investments (8,000 – 3,500)	4,500
	18,100
Current Assets	
Inventory (3,200 + 900)	4,100
Receivables (1,400 + 650 – 400 (inter-co))	1,650
Bank (600 + 150)	750
	6,500
	24,600
Equity	
Share capital	5,000
Retained earnings (W5)	9,800
Non-controlling Interest (W4)	1,600
	16,400
Non-current liabilities (4,000 + 500)	4,500
Current liabilities (2,800 + 1,300 – 400)	3,700
	24,600

Workings

(W1) Group structure

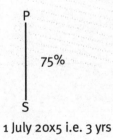

P

75%

S

1 July 20x5 i.e. 3 yrs

(W2) Net assets

	@Acq'n	@rep date
Share capital	1,000	1,000
Retained earnings	1,150	3,150
FV Adj Land (3,750 – 2,500)	1,250	1,250
FV Adj Plant	500	500
	3,900	5,900

(W3) Goodwill

Parent holding (investment) at fair value	3,500
NCI value at acquisition	1,100
	4,600
Less:	
Fair value of net assets at acquisition (W2)	(3,900)
Goodwill on acquisition	700

(W4) Non-controlling interest

NCI value at acquisition (as in W3)	1,100
NCI share of post acquisition reserves (W2)	500
(25% × (5,900 – 3,900))	
	1,600

(W5) Group retained earnings

100% P	8,300
75% of S post acq retained earnings	
(75% × (5,900 – 3,900))	1,500
	9,800

Test your understanding 4

Solution

Consolidated SFP for H as at 31/12/X3

Non-current assets		$000
Goodwill (W3)		28
Property, plant & equipment (100 + 30)		130
		158
Current Assets		
Inventory (90 + 20 – 4 (W6))	106	
Receivables (110 + 25 – 22 intra-co receivable)	113	
Bank (10 + 5)	15	
		234
		392
Equity		
Share capital		15.0
Group retained earnings (W5)		178.8
NCI (W4)		6.2
		200.0
Non-current liabilities (120 + 28)		148.0
Current liabilities (50 + 16 – 22 intra-co payable)		44.0
		392.0

Workings

(W1) **Group structure**

```
        H
        |   90%    01/01/X2
        |          2 years ago
        S
```

KAPLAN PUBLISHING

429

(W2) Net assets

	@ Acq	@ Rep date
Share capital	5	5
Retained earnings	5	31
PURP (W6)		(4)
	10	32

(W3) Goodwill

Parent holding (investment) at fair value	34
NCI value at acquisition	4
	38
Less:	
Fair value of net assets at acquisition (W2)	(10)
Goodwill on acquisition	28

(W4) Non-controlling interest

NCI value at acquisition (as in W3)	4
NCI share of post acquisition reserves (W2)	2.2
(10% × (32 – 10))	
	6.2

(W5) Group reserves

100% Health	159
90% safety Post-Acq	
(90% × ($32 – $10 (W2))	19.8
	178.8

(W6) PURP

Sales	$18	150%
COS		100%
Gross profit	$6	50%

×2/3
PURP = $4

Test your understanding 5

Consolidated Statement of Financial Position as at 30 November 2007

	$
Non-current assets	
Goodwill (W3)	22,250
PPE	
(138,000 + 115,000)	253,000
Investments	
(98,000 – 76,000)	22,000
Current Assets	
Inventory	
(15,000 + 17,000 – 1,600)	30,400
Receivables	
(19,000 + 20,000)	39,000
Cash	
	2,000
	368,650
Share capital	50,000
Group retained earnings (W5)	190,550
Non-controlling Interest (W4)	52,100
	292,650
Current liabilities	76,000
(33,000 + 43,000)	
	368,650

Workings

(W1) Group structure

K

| 60%

S

1 May 2007 i.e. 7 months

(W2) Net assets

	@ acq	@ rep date
Share capital	40,000	40,000
Retained earnings	63,750	69,000
	103,750	109,000
RE @ acq'n (balance) (ß)		63,750
Post acq profit (7/12 × 9,000)		5,250
RE @ reporting date		69,000

(W3) Goodwill

Parent holding (investment) at fair value	76,000
NCI value at acquisition	50,000
	126,000
Less:	
Fair value of net assets at acquisition (W2)	(103,750)
Goodwill on acquisition	22,250

(W4) Non-controlling interest

NCI value at acquisition (as in W3)	50,000
NCI share of post acquisition reserves (W2)	2,100
(40% × (109,000 – 103,750))	
	———
	52,100
	———

(W5) Group retained earnings

100% K	189,000
PURP	(1,600)
60% S post-acq profit	
(60% × (109,000 – 103,750 (W2)))	3,150
	———
	190,550
	———

(W6) PURP – Inventory

Profit in inventory (25/125 × 8,000)	1,600

19

Consolidated income statement

Chapter learning objectives

Upon completion of this chapter you will be able to

Describe the components of and prepare a consolidated statement of comprehensive income or extracts thereof including:

- Elimination of inter-company trading balances (excluding cash and goods in transit)
- Removal of unrealised profit arising on inter-company trading
- Acquisition of subsidiaries part way through the financial year

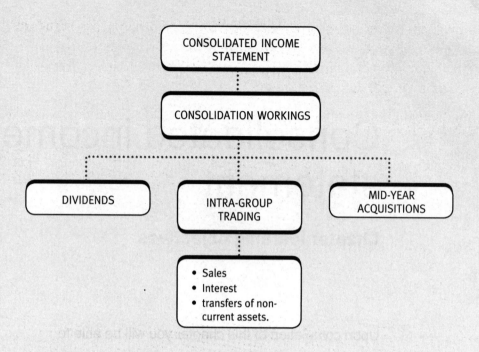

1 Introduction

The consolidated income statement shows the profit generated by all resources disclosed in the related consolidated statement of financial position, i.e. the net assets of the parent company (P) and its subsidiary (S).

2 The Basic Principles

The consolidated income statement follows these basic principles:

From revenue to profit for the year include all of P's income and expenses plus all of S's income and expenses (reflecting control of S), subject to adjustments (see below).

After profit for the year show split of profit between amounts attributable to the parent's shareholders and the non-controlling interest (to reflect ownership).

3 The mechanics of consolidation

As with the statement of financial position, it is common to use standard workings when producing a consolidated income statement

- group structure diagram
- net assets of subsidiary at acquisition (required for goodwill calculation if asked to calculate)
- goodwill calculation (if asked to calculate goodwill or if you are required to calculate an impairment that is to be charged to profits (see below)
- non-controlling interest (NCI) share of profit (see below)

Non-controlling interest

This is calculated as:

NCI % × subsidiary's profit after tax	X
Less:	
NCI % × fair value depreciation	(X)
NCI % × PURP (when the sub is the seller only)	(X)
NCI % × impairment (fair value method)	(X)
	X

Depreciation on fair value adjustments and impairment of goodwill is not examinable for this syllabus.

4 Intra-group trading

Sales and purchases

The effect of intra-group trading must be eliminated from the consolidated income statement. Such trading will be included in the sales revenue of one group company and the purchases of another.

- Consolidated sales revenue = P's revenue + S's revenue – intra-group sales.
- Consolidated cost of sales = P's COS + S's COS – intra-group sales.

5 Interest

If there is a loan outstanding between group companies the effect of any loan interest received and paid must be eliminated from the consolidated income statement.

The relevant amount of interest should be deducted from group investment income and group finance costs.

Dividends

Dividends

A payment of a dividend by S to P will need to be cancelled. The effect of this on the consolidated income statement is:

- only dividends paid by P to its own shareholders appear in the consolidated financial statements. These are shown within the consolidated statement of changes in equity which you will not be required to prepare for this examination.

- any dividend income shown in the consolidated income statement must arise from investments other than those in subsidiaries.

Illustration 1 – Simple CSI

The income statements for P and S for the year ended 31 August 20X4 are shown below. P acquired 75% of the ordinary share capital of S several years ago.

	P	S
	$000	$000
Revenue	1,200	400
Cost of sales and expenses	(1,080)	(360)
Gross profit	120	40
Investment income:		
Dividend received from S	7	
Profit before tax	127	40
Tax	(55)	(16)
Profit for the year	72	24

Prepare the consolidated income statement for the year.

Solution

P consolidate income statement for the year ended 31 August 20X4

	P $000
Revenue (1,200 + 400)	1,600
Cost of sales and expenses (1,080 + 360)	(1,440)
Profit before tax	160
Tax (55 + 16)	(71)
Profit for the year	89
Attributable to:	
Group (bal fig)	83
Non-controlling interest (W1)	6

(W1) Non-controlling interest

NCI share of subsidiary profit for the year

25% x $24 = 6

6 Provision for unrealised profits

Inventory

If any goods sold intra-group are included in closing inventory, their value must be adjusted to the lower of cost and net realisable value (NRV) to the group (as in the CSFP).

The adjustment for unrealised profit should be shown as an increase to cost of sales (return inventory back to true cost to group and eliminate unrealised profit).

Illustration 2 – PURP

On 1 January 20X9 P acquired 60% of the ordinary shares of S.

The following income statements have been produced by P and S for the year ended 31 December 20X9.

	P	S
	$000	$000
Revenue	630	260
Cost of sales and expenses	(210)	(105)
Gross profit	420	155
Distribution costs	(90)	(30)
Administration expenses	(60)	(45)
Profit from operations	270	80
Investment income from S	18	
Profit before taxation	288	80
Tax	(65)	(13)
Profit for the year	223	67

During the year ended 31 December 20X9 P had sold $42,000 worth of goods to S. These goods had cost P $28,000. On 31 December 20X9 S still had half of these goods in inventories at the year end.

Prepare the consolidated income statement to incorporate P and S for the year ended 31 December 20X9.

Solution

P consolidated income statement for the year ended 31 December 20X9

	P $000
Revenue (630 + 260 – 42)	848
Cost of sales and expenses (210 + 105 – 42 + 7 (W1))	(280)
Gross profit	568
Distribution costs (90 + 30)	(120)
Administration expenses (60 + 45)	(105)
Profit from operations	343
Tax (65 + 13)	(78)
Profit for the year	265
Amount attributable to:	
Equity holders of the parent (bal fig)	238.2
Non-controlling interest (W2)	26.8

(W1) Unrealised profit in inventory

	$000
Selling price	42
Cost of goods	(28)
Total profit	14
Provision for unrealised profit ½ × $14	7

(W2) Non-controlling interest

NCI share of subsidiary's profit after tax 40% × $67,000 = $26,800

Impairment of goodwill

Once any impairment has been identified during the year, the charge for the year will be passed through the consolidated income statement. This will usually be through operating expenses, however always follow instructions from the examiner.

If non-controlling interests have been valued at fair value, a portion of the impairment expense must be removed from the non-controlling interest's share of profit.

Fair values

If a depreciating non-current asset of the subsidiary has been revalued as part of a fair value exercise when calculating goodwill, this will result in an adjustment to the consolidated income statement.

The subsidiary's own income statement will include depreciation based on the value the asset is held at in the subsidiary's own SFP.

The consolidated income statement must include a depreciation charge based on the fair value of the asset, included in the consolidated SFP.

Extra depreciation must therefore be calculated and charged to an appropriate cost category (usually in line with examiner requirements).

7 Mid-year acquisitions

Mid-year acquisition procedure

If a subsidiary is acquired part way through the year, then the subsidiary's results should only be consolidated from the date of acquisition, i.e. the date on which control is obtained.

In practice this will require:

- Identification of the net assets of S at the date of acquisition in order to calculate goodwill.

- Time apportionment of the results of S in the year of acquisition. For this purpose, unless indicated otherwise, assume that revenue and expenses accrue evenly.

- After time apportioning S's results, deduction of post acquisition intra-group items as normal.

Illustration 3 – Mid-year acquistions

The following income statements have been produced by P and S for the year ended 31 March 20X9.

	P	S
	$000	$000
Revenue	151,800	108,850
Cost of sales and expenses	(71,900)	(51,100)
Gross profit	79,900	57,750
Operating expenses	(35,600)	(25,650)
Profit from operations	44,300	32,100
Investment income	1,400	600
Profit before taxation	45,700	32,700
Tax	(23,100)	(16,300)
Profit for the year	22,600	16,400

- On the 30 November 20X8 P acquired 75% of the issued ordinary share capital of S. No dividends were paid by either company during the year. The investment income is from quoted investments and has been correctly accounted for.

- The profits of both companies are deemed to accrue evenly over the year.

Prepare the consolidated income statement to incorporate P and S for the year ended 31 March 20X9.

Solution

P consolidated income statement for the year ended 31 December 20X9

	P $000
Revenue	188,083
(151,800 + (108,850 × 4/12)	
Cost of sales	(88,933)
(71,900 + (51,100 × 4/12)	
	————
Gross profit	99,150
Operating expenses	(44,150)
(35,600 + (25,650 × 4/12)	
	————
Profit from operations	55,000
Investment income	1,600
(1,400 + (600 × 4/12)	
	————
Profit before taxation	56,600
Tax	(28,533)
(23,100 + (16,300 × 4/12)	
	————
Profit for the year	28,067
Amount attributable to:	
Equity holders of the parent	26,700
Non-controlling interest	1,367
(25% × (16,400 × 4/12))	

Note

P acquired 75% of the issued ordinary share capital of S on 30 November 20X8. This is the date on which control passed and hence the date from which the results of S should be reflected in the consolidated income statement.

All reserves earned by S in the four months since that date are post acquisition reserves.

The remaining previous eight months' profit from 1 April 20X8 to 30 November 20X9 are all pre-acquisition.

8 IAS 28 Investments in associates

Definition of an associate

IAS 28 defines an **associate** as:

An entity over which the investor has significant influence and that is neither a subsidiary nor an interest in joint venture.

Significant influence is the power to participate in the financial and operating policy decisions of the investee but is not control or joint control over those policies.

Significant influence is assumed with a shareholding of 20% to 50%.

Principles of equity accounting and reasoning behind it

Equity accounting is a method of accounting whereby the investment is initially recorded at cost and adjusted thereafter for the post-acquisition change in the investor's share of net assets of the associate.

The effect of this is that the consolidated statement of financial position includes:

- 100% of the assets and liabilities of the parent and subsidiary company on a line by line basis

- an 'investments in associates' line within non-current assets which includes the group share of the assets and liabilities of any associate.

The consolidated income statement includes:

- 100% of the income and expenses of the parent and subsidiary company on a line by line basis

- one line 'share of profit of associates' which includes the group share of any associate's profit after tax.

Note: in order to equity account, the parent company must already be producing consolidated financial statements (i.e. it must already have at least one subsidiary).

Test your understanding 1

Set out below are the draft income statements of P and its subsidiary S for the year ended 31 December 20X7.

On the 1 January 20X6 P purchased 75% of the ordinary shares in S.

	P	S
	$000	$000
Revenue	300	150
Cost of sales and expenses	(180)	(70)
Gross profit	120	80
Operating expenses	(47)	(23)
Profit from operations	73	57
Finance costs		(2)
Profit before taxation	73	55
Tax	(25)	(16)
Profit for the year	48	39

- During the year S sold goods to P for $20,000, making a mark up of one third. Only 20% of these goods were sold before the end of the year, the rest were still in inventory.

- P values non-controlling interest using the fair value method.

Prepare the consolidated income statement for the year ended 31 December 20X7.

KAPLAN PUBLISHING

IAS 28 Investments in Associates

Accounting for associates according to IAS 28

The equity method of accounting is normally used to account for associates in the consolidated financial statements.

The equity method should not be used if:

- the investment is classified as held for sale in accordance with IFRS 5 or

- the parent is exempted from having to prepare consolidated accounts on the grounds that it is itself a wholly, or partially, owned subsidiary of another company (IAS 27).

9 Associates in the consolidated statement of financial position

Preparing the CSFP including an associate

The CSFP is prepared on a normal line-by-line basis following the acquisition method for the parent and subsidiary.

The associate is included as a non-current asset investment calculated as:

	$000
Cost of investment	X
Share of post acquisition profits	X
Less: impairment losses	(X)
Less: PURP (P = seller)	(X)
	X

The group share of the associate's post acquisition profits or losses and the impairment of goodwill will also be included in the group retained earnings calculation.

10 Associates in the consolidated income statement

Equity accounting

The equity method of accounting requires that the consolidated income statement:

- does not include dividends from the associate

- instead includes group share of the associate's profit after tax less any impairment of the associate in the year (included below group profit from operations).

Trading with the associate

Generally the associate is considered to be outside the group.

Therefore any sales or purchases between group companies and the associate are not normally eliminated and will remain part of the consolidated figures in the income statement.

It is normal practice to instead adjust for the unrealised profit in inventory.

Dividends from associates

Dividends from associates are excluded from the consolidated income statement; the group share of the associate's profit is included instead.

11 Chapter summary

```
        ┌─────────────────────────┐
        │  CONSOLIDATED INCOME    │
        │      STATEMENT          │
        └─────────────────────────┘
                    ┊
        ┌─────────────────────────┐
        │  Consolidation workings │
        │  • Consolidation schedule│
        │  • Group structure      │
        │  • Net assets of S      │
        │  • Goodwill             │
        │  • Non-controlling interest│
        └─────────────────────────┘
```

Dividends in CIS
Received: non-group
investments only.

**INTRA-GROUP
TRADING**

Mid-year acquisitions
Prorate S's results
in consolidation
schedule.

Sales
- Remove unrealised profit in seller's column.
- Deduct from sales and cost of sales in adjustments column.

Interest
- Deduct in adjustments column.

Sale of non-current assets
- Remove profit.
- Adjust depreciation in seller's column.

Test your understanding answers

Test your understanding 1

P consolidated income statement for the year ended 31 December 20X7

	P $000
Revenue (300 + 150 – 20)	430
Cost of sales and expenses (180 + 70 – 20 + 4 (W4))	(234)
Gross profit	196
Operating expenses (47 + 23)	(70)
Profit from operations	126
Finance costs	(2)
Profit before taxation	124
Tax (25 + 16)	(41)
Profit for the year	83
Amount attributable to:	
Equity holders of the parent	74.25
Non-controlling interest	8.75

(W1) Unrealised profit in inventory

	$000
Selling price	20
Cost (100/133% × $20)	(15)
Total profit	5
Provision for unrealised profit 80% × $5	4

(W2) Non-controlling interest

	$000
NCI share of subsidiary's profit after tax (25% × $39)	9.75
Less NCI share of PURP(25% × $4)	(1)
	8.75

Interpretation of financial statements

Chapter learning objectives

Upon completion of this chapter you will be able to:

- Understand the importance and purpose of analysis of financial statements
- Describe how the interpretation and analysis of financial statements is used in a business environment
- Explain the purpose of the interpretation of ratios
- Calculate key accounting ratios
  - Profitability
  - Liquidity
  - Efficiency
  - Position
- Explain the interrelationships between ratios

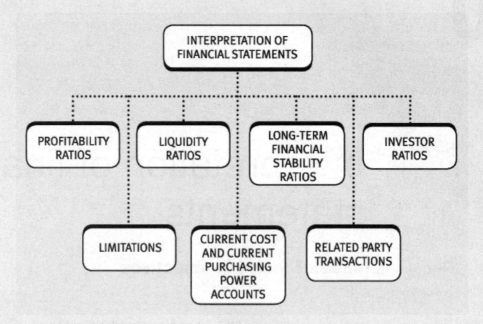

1 Interpreting financial information

Introduction

Financial statements on their own are of limited use. In this chapter we will consider how to interpret them and gain additional useful information from them.

Users of financial statements

When interpreting financial statements it is important to ascertain who are the users of accounts and what information they need:

- shareholders and potential investors – primarily concerned with receiving an adequate return on their investment, but it must at least provide security and liquidity

- suppliers and lenders – concerned with the security of their debt or loan

- management – concerned with the trend and level of profits, since this is the main measure of their success.

Other potential users include:

- bank managers

- financial institutions

- employees

- professional advisors to investors

- financial journalists and commentators.

Commenting on ratios

Ratios are of limited use on their own, thus, the following points should serve as a useful checklist if you need to analyse the data and comment on it:

- What does the ratio literally mean?
- What does a change in the ratio mean?
- What is the norm?
- What are the limitations of the ratio?

2 Profitability ratios

Gross profit margin

Gross profit margin or percentage is:

$$\frac{\text{Gross profit}}{\text{Sales revenue}} \times 100\%$$

This is the margin that the company makes on its sales, and would be expected to remain reasonably constant.

Since the ratio is affected by only a small number of variables, a change may be traced to a change in:

- selling prices – normally deliberate though sometimes unavoidable, e.g. because of increased competition
- sales mix – often deliberate
- purchase cost – including carriage or discounts
- production cost – materials, labour or production overheads
- inventory – errors in counting, valuing or cut-off, inventory shortages.

Gross profit margin

Comparing gross profit margin over time

If gross profit has not increased in line with sales revenue, you need to establish why not. Is the discrepancy due to:

- increased 'purchase' costs: if so, are the costs under the company's control (i.e. does the company manufacture the goods sold)?

- inventory write-offs (likely where the company operates in a volatile marketplace, such as fashion retail)? or

- other costs being allocated to cost of sales – for example, research and development (R&D) expenditure?

Inter-company comparison of gross profit margin

Inter-company comparison of margins can be very useful but it is especially important to look at businesses within the same sector. For example, food retailing is able to support low margins because of the high volume of sales. A manufacturing industry would usually need higher margins to offset lower sales volumes.

Low margins usually suggest poor performance but may be due to expansion costs (launching a new product) or trying to increase market share. Lower margins than usual suggest scope for improvement.

Above-average margins are usually a sign of good management although unusually high margins may make the competition keen to join in and enjoy the 'rich pickings'.

Operating profit margin (net profit)

The **operating profit margin** or net profit margin is calculated as:

$$\frac{\text{PBIT}}{\text{Sales revenue}} \times 100\%$$

Any changes in operating profit margin should be considered further:

- Are they in line with changes in gross profit margin?

- Are they in line with changes in sales revenue?

- As many costs are fixed they need not necessarily increase/decrease with a change in revenue.

- Look for individual cost categories that have increased/decreased significantly.

Operating profit margin

This is affected by more factors than the gross profit margin but it is equally useful and if the company does not disclose a cost of sales it may be used on its own in lieu of the gross profit percentage.

One of the many factors affecting the trading profit margin is depreciation, which is open to considerable subjective judgement. Inter-company comparisons should be made after suitable adjustments to align accounting policies.

By the time you have reached operating (net) profit, there are many more factors to consider. If you are provided with a breakdown of expenses you can use this for further line-by-line comparisons. Bear in mind that:

- some costs are fixed or semi-fixed (e.g. property costs) and therefore not expected to change in line with revenue

- other costs are variable (e.g. packing and distribution, and commission).

ROCE

$$\text{ROCE} = \frac{\text{Profit}}{\text{Capital employed}} \times 100\%$$

Profit is measured as:

- operating (trading) profit, or

- the PBIT, i.e. the profit before taking account of any returns paid to the providers of long-term finance.

Capital employed is measured as:

- equity, plus interest-bearing finance, i.e. the long-term finance supporting the business.

ROCE for the current year should be compared to:

- the prior year ROCE
- a target ROCE
- the cost of borrowing
- other companies' ROCE in the same industry.

ROCE

Once calculated, ROCE should be compared with:

- previous years' figures – provided there have been no changes in accounting policies, or suitable adjustments have been made to facilitate comparison (note, however that the effect of not replacing non-current assets is that their value will decrease and ROCE will increase)

- the company's target ROCE – where the company's management has determined a target return as part of its budget procedure, consistent failure by a part of the business to meet the target may make it a target for disposal

- the cost of borrowings – if the cost of borrowing is say 10% and ROCE 7%, then further borrowings will reduce EPS unless the extra money can be used in areas where the ROCE is higher than the cost of borrowings

- other companies in same industry – care is required in interpretation, because of the possibility, noted above, of different accounting policies, ages of plant, etc.

The ratio also shows how efficiently a business is using its resources. If the return is very low, the business may be better off realising its assets and investing the proceeds in a high interest bank account! (This may sound extreme, but should be considered particularly for a small, unprofitable business with valuable assets such as property.) Furthermore, a low return can easily become a loss if the business suffers a downturn.

Net asset turnover

The **net asset turnover** is:

$$\frac{\text{Sales revenue}}{\text{Capital employed (net assets)}} = \text{times pa}$$

It measures management's efficiency in generating revenue from the net assets at its disposal:

- the higher, the more efficient.

Note that this can be further subdivided into:

- non-current asset turnover (by making non-current assets the denominator) and
- working capital turnover (by making net current assets the denominator).

Relationship between ratios

ROCE can be subdivided into profit margin and asset turnover.

Profit margin	×	Asset turnover	=	ROCE
$\dfrac{\text{PBIT}}{\text{Sales revenue}}$	×	$\dfrac{\text{Sales revenue}}{\text{Capital employed}}$	=	$\dfrac{\text{PBIT}}{\text{Capital employed}}$

Profit margin is often seen as an indication of the quality of products or services supplied (top-of-range products usually have higher margins).

Asset turnover is often seen as a measure of how intensively the assets are worked.

A trade-off may exist between margin and asset turnover.

- Low-margin businesses (e.g. food retailers) usually have a high asset turnover.
- Capital-intensive manufacturing industries usually have relatively low asset turnover but higher margins (e.g. electrical equipment manufacturers).

Two completely different strategies can achieve the same ROCE.

- Sell goods at a high profit margin with sales volume remaining low (e.g. designer dress shop).
- Sell goods at a low profit margin with very high sales volume (e.g. discount clothes store).

3 Liquidity and Efficiency ratios
Working capital ratios

There are two ratios used to measure overall working capital:

- the current ratio
- the quick or acid test ratio.

Current ratio

Current or working capital ratio:

$$\frac{\text{Current assets}}{\text{Current liabilities}} : 1$$

The current ratio measures the adequacy of current assets to meet the liabilities as they fall due.

A high or increasing figure may appear safe but should be regarded with suspicion as it may be due to:

- high levels of inventory and receivables (check working capital management ratios)
- high cash levels which could be put to better use (e.g. by investing in non-current assets).

Current ratio

The current ratio measures the adequacy of current assets to meet the company's short-term liabilities. It reflects whether the company is in a position to meet its liabilities as they fall due.

Traditionally, a current ratio of 2:1 or higher was regarded as appropriate for most businesses to maintain creditworthiness. However, more recently a figure of 1.5:1 is regarded as the norm.

The current ratio should be looked at in the light of what is normal for the business. For example, supermarkets tend to have low current ratios because:

- there are few trade receivables
- there is a high level of trade payables
- there is usually very tight cash control, to fund investment in developing new sites and improving sites.

It is also worth considering:

- availability of further finance, e.g. is the overdraft at the limit? – very often this information is highly relevant but is not disclosed in the accounts
- seasonal nature of the business – one way of doing this is to compare the interest charges in the income statement with the overdraft and other loans in the statement of financial position; if the interest rate appears abnormally high, this is probably because the company has had higher levels of borrowings during the year
- long-term liabilities, when they fall due and how will they be financed
- nature of the inventory – where inventories are slow moving, the quick ratio probably provides a better indicator of short-term liquidity.

Quick ratio

Quick ratio (also known as the liquidity and acid test) ratio:

$$\text{Quick ratio} = \frac{\text{Current assets} - \text{Inventory}}{\text{Current liabilities}} : 1$$

The quick ratio is also known as the acid test ratio because by eliminating inventory from current assets it provides the acid test of whether the company has sufficient liquid resources (receivables and cash) to settle its liabilities.

Quick ratio

Normal levels for the quick ratio range from 1:1 to 0.7:1.

Like the current ratio it is relevant to consider the nature of the business (again supermarkets have very low quick ratios).

Sometimes the **quick ratio** is calculated on the basis of a six-week time-frame (i.e. the quick assets are those which will turn into cash in six weeks; quick liabilities are those which fall due for payment within six weeks). This basis would usually include the following in **quick assets:**

*   bank, cash and short-term investments
*   trade receivables.

thus excluding prepayments and inventory.

Quick liabilities would usually include:

*   bank overdraft which is repayable on demand
*   trade payables, tax and social security
*   dividends.

Income tax liabilities may be excluded.

When interpreting the quick ratio, care should be taken over the status of the **bank overdraft**. A company with a low quick ratio may actually have no problem in paying its amounts due if sufficient overall overdraft facilities are available.

Inventory turnover period

Inventory turnover period is defined as:

$$\frac{\text{Inventory}}{\text{COS}} \times 365 \text{ days}$$

Alternative
An alternative is to express the inventory turnover period as a number of times: $$\frac{\text{Cost of sales}}{\text{Inventory}} = \text{times pa}$$

An increasing number of days (or a diminishing multiple) implies that inventory is turning over less quickly which is regarded as a bad sign as it may indicate:

- lack of demand for the goods
- poor inventory control
- an increase in costs (storage, obsolescence, insurance, damage).

However, it may not necessarily be bad where management are:

- buying inventory in larger quantities to take advantage of trade discounts, or
- increasing inventory levels to avoid stockouts.

Inventory days

Year-end inventory is normally used in the calculation of inventory turnover. An average (based on the average of year-start and year-end inventories) may be used to have a smoothing effect, although this may dampen the effect of a major change in the period.

Inventory turnover ratios vary enormously with the nature of the business. For example, a fishmonger selling fresh fish would have an inventory turnover period of 1–2 days, whereas a building contractor may have an inventory turnover period of 200 days. Manufacturing companies may have an inventory turnover ratio of 60–100 days; this period is likely to increase as the goods made become larger and more complex.

For large and complex items (e.g. rolling stock or aircraft) there may be sharp fluctuations in inventory turnover according to whether delivery took place just before or just after the year end.

A manufacturer should take into consideration:

- reliability of suppliers: if the supplier is unreliable it is prudent to hold more raw materials
- demand: if demand is erratic it is prudent to hold more finished goods.

Receivables collection period

This is normally expressed as a number of days:

$$\frac{\text{Trade receivables}}{\text{Credit sales}} \times 365 \text{ days}$$

The collection period should be compared with:

- the stated credit policy
- previous period figures.

Increasing accounts receivables collection period is usually a bad sign suggesting lack of proper credit control which may lead to irrecoverable debts.

It may, however, be due to:

- a deliberate policy to attract more trade, or

- a major new customer being allowed different terms.

Falling receivables days is usually a good sign, though it could indicate that the company is suffering a cash shortage.

Receivables days

The trade receivables used may be a year-end figure or the average for the year. Where an average is used to calculate the number of days, the ratio is the average number of days' credit taken by customers.

For many businesses total sales revenue can safely be used, because cash sales will be insignificant. But cash-based businesses like supermarkets make the substantial majority of their sales for cash, so the receivables period should be calculated by reference to credit sales only.

The result should be compared with the stated **credit policy**. A period of 30 days or 'at the end of the month following delivery' are common credit terms.

The receivables days ratio can be distorted by:

- using year-end figures which do not represent average receivables

- factoring of accounts receivables which results in very low trade receivables

- sales on unusually long credit terms to some customers.

Payables payment period

This is usually expressed as:

$$\frac{\text{Trade payables}}{\text{Credit purchases}} \times 365 \text{ days}$$

This represents the credit period taken by the company from its suppliers.

The ratio is always compared to previous years:

- A long credit period may be good as it represents a source of free finance.

- A long credit period may indicate that the company is unable to pay more quickly because of liquidity problems.

If the credit period is long:

- the company may develop a poor reputation as a slow payer and may not be able to find new suppliers

- existing suppliers may decide to discontinue supplies

- the company may be losing out on worthwhile cash discounts.

In most sets of financial statements (in practice and in examinations) the figure for purchases will not be available therefore cost of sales is normally used as an approximation in the calculation of the accounts payable payment period.

4 Financial position

Introduction

The main points to consider when assessing the longer-term financial position are:

- gearing

- overtrading.

Gearing

Gearing ratios indicate:

- the degree of risk attached to the company and

- the sensitivity of earnings and dividends to changes in profitability and activity level.

Preference share capital is usually counted as part of debt rather than equity since it carries the right to a fixed rate of dividend which is payable before the ordinary shareholders have any right to a dividend.

High and low gearing

In highly geared businesses:

- a large proportion of fixed-return capital is used

- there is a greater risk of insolvency

- returns to shareholders will grow proportionately more if profits are growing.

Low-geared businesses:

- provide scope to increase borrowings when potentially profitable projects are available

- can usually borrow more easily.

Gearing

Not all companies are suitable for a highly-geared structure. A company must have two fundamental characteristics if it is to use gearing successfully.

Relatively stable profits

Loan stock interest must be paid whether or not profits are earned. A company with erratic profits may have insufficient funds in a bad year with which to pay the interest. This would result in the appointment of a receiver and possibly the liquidation of the company.

Suitable assets for security

Most issues of loan capital are secured on some or all of the company's assets which must be suitable for the purpose. A company with most of its capital invested in fast depreciating assets or inventory subject to rapid changes in demand and price would not be suitable for high gearing.

The classic examples of companies that are suited to high gearing are those in property investment and the hotel/leisure services industry. These companies generally enjoy relatively stable profits and have assets which are highly suitable for charging. Nonetheless, these are industries that could be described as cyclical.

Companies not suited to high gearing would include those in the extractive, and high-tech, industries where constant changes occur. These companies could experience erratic profits and would generally have inadequate assets to pledge as security.

Measuring gearing

There are two methods commonly used to express gearing as follows.

Debt/equity ratio:

$$\frac{\text{Loans} + \text{Preference share capital}}{\text{Ordinary share capital} + \text{Reserves} + \text{Non-controlling interest}}$$

Percentage of capital employed represented by borrowings:

$$\frac{\text{Loans} + \text{Preference share capital}}{\text{Ordinary share capital} + \text{Reserves} + \text{Non-controlling interest} + \text{Loans} + \text{Preference share capital}}$$

Interest cover

$$\text{Interest cover} = \frac{\text{PBIT}}{\text{Interest payable}}$$

Interest cover indicates the ability of a company to pay interest out of profits generated:

- low interest cover indicates to shareholders that their dividends are at risk (because most profits are eaten up by interest payments) and
- the company may have difficulty financing its debts if its profits fall
- interest cover of less than two is usually considered unsatisfactory.

Interest cover

A business must have a sufficient level of long-term capital to finance its long-term investment in non-current assets. Part of the investment in current assets would usually be financed by relatively permanent capital with the balance being provided by credit from suppliers and other short-term borrowings. Any expansion in activity will normally require a broadening of the long-term capital base, without which 'overtrading' may develop (see below).

Suitability of finance is also a key factor. A permanent expansion of a company's activities should not be financed by temporary, short-term borrowings. On the other hand, a short-term increase in activity such as the 'January sales' in a retail trading company could ideally be financed by overdraft.

A major addition to non-current assets such as the construction of a new factory would not normally be financed on a long-term basis by overdraft. It might be found, however, that the expenditure was temporarily financed by short-term loans until construction was completed, when the overdraft would be 'funded' by a long-term borrowing secured on the completed building.

Example 1 – Interpretation

Statements of financial position and income statements for Ocean Motors are set out below.

Statement of financial position for Ocean Motors

	20X2		20X1	
	$000	$000	$000	$000
Non-current assets:				
Land and buildings				
Cost	1,600		1,450	
Depreciation	(200)		(150)	
		1,400		1,300
Plant and machinery:				
Cost	600		400	
Depreciation	(120)		(100)	
		480		300
		1,880		1,600
Current assets:				
Inventory	300		100	
Receivables	400		100	
		700		200
Total assets		2,580		1,800
Equity:				
Share capital – $1 ordinary shares		1,200		1,200
Retained earnings		310		220
		1,510		1,420
Current liabilities:				
Bank overdraft	590		210	
Payables and accruals	370		70	
Taxation liability	110		100	
		1,070		380
		2,580		1,800

Income statements for Ocean Motors

	20X2 $000	20X1 $000
Sales revenue	1,500	1,000
Cost of sales	(700)	(300)
Gross profit	800	700
Administration and distribution expenses	(400)	(360)
Net profit before tax	400	340
Income tax expense	(200)	(170)
Net profit after tax	200	170

The dividend for 20X1 was $100,000 and for 20X2 was $110,000. Calculate the following ratios for Ocean Motors and briefly comment upon what they indicate:

Profitability ratios:

- gross profit margin
- operating profit margin
- ROCE
- net asset turnover.

Liquidity and working capital ratios:

- current ratio
- quick ratio
- inventory collection period
- accounts receivable collection period
- accounts payable payment period

Solution

Profitability ratios

	20X2	20X1
ROCE	400/1,510 = 26.4%	340/1,420 = 23.9%
Gross profit margin	800/1,500 = 53.3%	700/1,000 = 70.0%
Operating profit margin	400/1,500 = 26.7%	340/1,000 = 34.0%
Asset turnover	1,500/1,510 = 0.99	1,000/1,420 = 0.70
Check:	0.99 × 26.7 = 26.4%	0.70 × 34.0% = 23.8%

Comment

Key factors:

- revenue has increased by 50%

- gross profit margin significantly decreased maybe due to lowering of selling prices in order to increase market share and sales revenue

- operating profit margin has decreased in line with gross profit margin

- ROCE has increased due to the improvement in asset turnover.

Liquidity and working capital ratios

	20X2	20X1
Current ratio	700/1,070	200/380
	= 0.65 : 1	= 0.53 : 1
Quick ratio	400/1,070	100/380
	= 0.37 : 1	= 0.26 : 1
Inventory collection period	300/700 × 365	100/300 × 365
	156 days	122 days
	2.3 times	3.0 times
Accounts receivable collection period	400/1,500 × 365	100/1,000 × 365
	97 days	36.5 days
Accounts payable payment period	370/700 × 365	70/300 × 365
	193 days	85 days

Comment

Overall the liquidity of the company would appear to be in some doubt:

- Both the current ratio and quick ratio appear very low although they have improved since the previous year.

- We do not know anything about the type of business therefore it is difficult to comment on these absolute levels of liquidity.

- Inventory turnover indicates that inventory is held for a considerable time and that this time is increasing.

- Accounts receivable collection period has deteriorated rapidly although given the increase in revenue this may be due to a conscious policy of offering extended credit terms in order to attract new custom.

- Accounts payable payment period has also more than doubled and is even longer than the period of credit taken by customers.

- Clearly the business is heavily dependent upon its overdraft finance.

5 Investor ratios

EPS

Limitations of EPS

EPS is used primarily as a measure of profitability, so an increasing EPS is seen as a good sign. EPS is also used to calculate the price earnings ratio which is dealt with below.

The limitations of EPS may be listed as follows.

- In times of rising prices EPS will increase as profits increase. Thus any improvement in EPS should be viewed in the context of the effect of price level changes on the company's profits.

- Where there is a new share issue for cash, the shares are included for, say, half the year on the grounds that earnings will also increase for half of the year. However, in practice a new project funded by that cash does not begin generating normal returns immediately, so a new share issue is often accompanied by a decrease in EPS.

- EPS is dependent on an earnings figure which is subject to many judgements. Some elements of that earnings figure, such as movements on provisions, are particularly sensitive to different judgements.

- A single earnings figure should not be used as a key performance measure. This is to take a far too simplistic approach to the analysis of performance.

- EPS cannot be used as a basis of comparison between companies, as the number of shares in issue in any particular company is not related to the amount of capital employed. For example, two companies may have the same amount of capital employed but one company has 100,000 $1 shares in issue and reserves of $4,900,000. Another company may have 5 million 50c shares in issue and reserves of $2,500,000. If earnings are the same, EPS is different.

- EPS is an historical figure based on historical accounts. This is a disadvantage where it is used for a forward-looking figure such as the price earnings ratio.

- The diluted EPS (DEPS) is a theoretical measure of the effect of dilution on the basic EPS. DEPS should serve as a warning to equity shareholders that their future earnings will be affected by diluting factors. Thus, notes in the accounts relating to convertible loan stock, convertible preference shares and share options should all be analysed carefully.

P/E ratio

$$\text{P/E ratio} = \frac{\text{Current share price}}{\text{Latest EPS}}$$

- Represents the market's view of the future prospects of the share.
- High P/E suggests that high growth is expected.

P/E ratio

This is the most widely referred to stock market ratio, also commonly described as an earnings multiple. It is calculated as the 'purchase of a number of years' earnings', but it represents the market's consensus of the future prospects of that share. The higher the P/E ratio, the faster the growth the market is expecting in the company's future EPS. Correspondingly, the lower the P/E ratio, the lower the expected future growth.

Another aspect of interpreting it, is that a published EPS exists for a year and therefore the P/E ratio given in a newspaper is generally based on an increasingly out-of-date EPS. To give an extreme but simple example:

Company X

- For the year ended 31 December 20X6, EPS = 10c

- Overall market P/E ratio = 10.

- P/E ratio for X = 20 (because market expects above average growth).

- Market price at 30 April 20X7 (date of publication of previous year's accounts) = $2.

- During the year, X does even better than expected and by 29 April 20X8, the share price is up to $3, therefore giving a P/E ratio of 30 (based on EPS for year ended 31 December 20X6).

- Year ended 31 December 20X7, EPS = 15c, announced on 30 April 20X8. This is in line with expectations so share price is unchanged and P/E ratio drops again to 20 ($3/15c).

The earnings yield is the reciprocal of the P/E ratio, calculated as earnings as a percentage of market price. For Company X at 30 April 20X8 it is 5% (15c as a % of $3).

Dividend yield

$$\text{Dividend yield} = \frac{\text{Dividend per share}}{\text{Current share price}}$$

- can be compared to the yields available on other investment possibilities
- the lower the dividend yield, the more the market is expecting future growth in the dividend, and vice versa.

Dividend cover

$$\text{Dividend cover} = \frac{\text{Profit after tax}}{\text{Dividends}}$$

- This is the relationship between available profits and the dividends payable out of the profits.
- The higher the dividend cover, the more likely it is that the current dividend level can be sustained in the future.

Example 2 – Interpretation

Given below are the income statements for Pacific Motors for the last two years.

Income statements

	20X2	20X1
	$000	$000
Sales revenue	1,500	1,000
Cost of sales	(700)	(300)
Gross profit	800	700
Administration and distribution expenses	(400)	(360)
Net profit before tax	400	340
Income tax expense	(200)	(170)
Net profit after tax	200	170

In 20X1 dividends were $100,000 and in 20X2 they were $110,000.

The company is financed by 1,200,000 $1 ordinary shares and let us suppose that the market price of each share was $1.64 at 31 December 20X2 and $1.53 at 31 December 20X1.

For each year calculate the following ratios and comment on them briefly:

- EPS
- P/E ratio
- dividend yield
- dividend cover.

Solution

	20X2	20X1
EPS	200/1,200	170/1,200
	= 16.7 c	14.2 c
P/E ratio	164/16.7	153/14.2
	= 9.8	= 10.77
Dividend yield	(110/1,200)/164	(100/1,200)/153
	= 5.6%	= 5.5%
Dividend cover	200/110	170/100
	= 1.8 times	1.7 times

Comment

There has not been a significant amount of change in the investor ratios over the two years but the following specific comments could be made:

- both EPS and dividend per share have increased by a small amount over the two years which is a policy often designed to satisfy shareholders

- the P/E ratio has declined which indicates that the market does not think as highly of the shares this year as last year

- dividend cover is slightly higher which means that a slightly higher proportion of the profits for the year have been retained within the business.

Test your understanding 1

Interpretation of Financial Statements

Neville is a company that manufactures and retails office products. Their summarised financial statements for the years ended 30 June 20X4 and 20X5 are given below:

Income Statements for the year ended 30 June

	20X4 $000s	20X5 $000s
Revenue	1,159,850	1,391,820
Cost of Sales	(753,450)	(1,050,825)
Gross profit	406,400	340,995
Operating expenses	(170,950)	(161,450)
Profit from operations	235,450	179,545
Finance costs	(14,000)	(10,000)
Profits before tax	221,450	169,545
Tax	(66,300)	(50,800)
Net profit	155,150	118,745

Statements of Financial Position as at 30 June

	20X4 $000s	20X5 $000s
Non-current assets	341,400	509,590
Current Assets		
Inventory	88,760	109,400
Receivables	206,550	419,455
Bank	95,400	–
	732,110	1,038,445
Share capital	100,000	100,000
Share premium	20,000	20,000
Revaluation reserve	–	50,000
Retained earnings	287,420	376,165
	407,420	546,165
Non-current liabilities	83,100	61,600
Current liabilities		
Payables	179,590	345,480
Overdraft	–	30,200
Tax	62,000	55,000
	732,110	1,038,445

The directors concluded that their revenue for the year ended 30 June 20X4 fell below budget and introduced measures in the year end 30 June 20X5 to improve the situation. These included:

- Cutting prices;
- Extending credit facilities to customers;
- Leasing additional machinery in order to be able to manufacture more products.

The directors' are now reviewing the results for the year ended 30 June 20X5 and have asked for your advice as an external business consultant, as to whether or not the above strategies have been successful.

Required:

Prepare a report to the directors of Neville assessing the performance and position of the company in the year ended 30 June 20X5 compared to the previous year and advise them on whether or not you believe that their strategies have been successful.

Chapter summary

```
                    ┌─────────────────────────┐
                    │   INTERPRETATION OF     │
                    │  FINANCIAL STATEMENTS   │
                    └─────────────────────────┘
```

PROFITABILITY RATIOS

- Gross profit margin
- Net profit margin
- ROCE
- Net asset turnover.

LIQUIDITY RATIOS

- Current ratio
- Quick ratio
- Inventory turnover
- Receivables collection period
- Payables payment period.

LONG-TERM FINANCIAL STABILITY RATIOS

- Gearing
- Interest cover.

INVESTOR RATIOS

- EPS
- P/E ratio
- Dividend yield
- Dividend cover.

LIMITATIONS

- Difficulty of prediction when using historical cost accounts
- Problem of window dressing
- Effects of changes in accounting policies
- Limitations of ratio analysis
- Limited information available
- Many ratios not applicable to specialised not for profit organisations.

CURRENT COST AND CURRENT PURCHASING POWER ACCOUNTS

- Advantages over historical cost accounts
- Limitations.

RELATED PARTY TRANSACTIONS

May distort financial statements

Test your understanding answers

Test your understanding 1

Neville

Report

To: Directors of Neville

From: Business Consultant

Date: XX.XX.XX

Subject: Performance of Neville

Introduction

As requested I have analysed the financial statements of Neville for the year ended 30 June 20X5 compared to the previous year to assess the performance and position of the entity and to determine whether the strategies that you have implemented have been successful. The ratios that I have calculated are in an appendix to this report.

Performance

Profitability

The revenue of the entity has increased by 20% on last year. It would therefore appear that the strategy of cutting prices and extending credit facilities has attracted customers and generated an increase in revenue. Whether or not the revenue is now above budget, as was the directors' aim, is unknown.

Despite this increase however, the profitability of the company has worsened with both gross profit and operating profit being lower than the previous year. Similarly the operating profit margin has declined from 20.3% to 12.9%. There are likely to be several reasons behind this deterioration.

The reduction in prices of goods will have contributed to the worsening gross profit. To rectify this, Neville may consider approaching their suppliers for some bulk-buying discounts on the basis that since they are selling more items they will be purchasing more material from suppliers.

The move of leasing additional machinery may also have contributed to the lower profitability. Assuming that the leases are being treated as operating leases the lease payments will be being expensed to the income statement. Given that non-current liabilities have decreased this year it would appear that the leases are being treated as operating leases and not finance leases.

The return on capital employed has dropped significantly from 48% to 29.5%. This is mainly due to the lower operating profit margins and reasons discussed above, as opposed to a decline in the efficient use of assets since the asset utilisation has suffered only a slight fall.

The revaluation of non-current assets will also have contributed to the fall in the return on capital employed and would explain why the asset utilisation has fallen slightly.

The revaluation will have caused additional depreciation charges in the income statement and thus is another factor in the worsening profits.

The increase in non-current assets is not fully explained by the revaluation. Hence it can be concluded that Neville have probably purchased additional machinery (as well as leasing) to meet the increased production needs. These new machines may not have been fully operational in the current year and so would also explain the lower returns. The higher depreciation charges will also have contributed to lower profits.

Position

Liquidity

Again, the company's results are showing a worsening position in this area with the current ratio declining from 1.62 to 1.23.

The cause for this would seem to be the extension of credit facilities to customers.

Receivables days have increased from an appropriate level of 65 days to 110 days. Although the benefits of this strategy have been shown by the increase in revenue, it would seem that Neville have now allowed customers too much credit. It would be recommended that receivables days should be reduced to closer to 90 days.

As a result of the increase in the receivables collection period, Neville have been taking longer to pay their suppliers. Their payables days are now at an unacceptably high level of 120 days. This is likely to be causing dissatisfaction with suppliers and would reduce the ability of Neville being able to negotiate discounts as discussed above.

Inventory holding days have increased slightly from 38 days to 43 days. This does not give any immediate cause for concern and is probably due to increased production levels.

As a consequence of these factors, by the end of the year Neville are operating a significant overdraft.

Gearing

The gearing ratio has fallen from 16.9% to 10.1% as a result of the reduction in non-current liabilities. Assuming that these are loans, it would appear that Neville have further utilised their cash resources to repay these loans. This does not seem to have been a sensible move given their poor liquidity position.

The revaluation of non-current assets would also have contributed to the lowering of this ratio.

Further, the gearing ratio last year does not seem particularly high – comparison with an industry average would confirm this – and the company had a significant level of profits covering their finance costs.

Hence it would have seemed appropriate to have increased the longer term debt of the company to finance the growth rather than increasing their current liabilities.

If Neville had leased their additional machinery under finance leases, it is likely that less would be charged to their income statement and so would improve their profitability while the subsequent increase in the gearing ratio would not have caused significant concern.

Also, it was identified above that Neville may have purchased additional non-current assets. Given the gearing and liquidity positions, it would seem that these have been financed from short-term sources rather than more appropriate long-term sources.

Summary

Although the directors' initial aim of improving revenue has been achieved with the measures taken, the strategies do not appear to have been successful overall. The cutting of prices has caused lowering profit margins and combined with additional lease expenses and depreciation charges has resulted in a worsening profit situation overall.

The extension of credit periods has again been successful to the extent that it has helped increase revenue but has caused a poor liquidity position.

It would seem that Neville are showing signs of overtrading.

To rectify the situation it would seem appropriate to increase the long-term debt of the company as a matter of priority.

Appendix

	20X4	20X5
Revenue	1,159,850	1,391,820 +20%
Gross profit	406,400	340,995 – 16.1%
Operating profit	235,450	179,545 – 23.7%

OP% $\dfrac{235,450}{1,159,850}$ 20.3% $\dfrac{179,545}{1,391,765}$ 12.9%

ROCE $\dfrac{235,450}{490,520}$ 48.0% $\dfrac{179,545}{607,765}$ 29.5%

Asset turnover $\dfrac{1,159,850}{490,520}$ 2.36 $\dfrac{1,391,820}{607,765}$ 2.29

Inventory days $\dfrac{88,760 \times 365}{753,480}$ 43 days $\dfrac{109,400 \times 365}{1,050,825}$ 38 days

Receivables days $\dfrac{206,550 \times 365}{1,159,850}$ 65 days $\dfrac{419,455 \times 365}{1,391,820}$ 110 days

Payables days $\dfrac{179,590 \times 365}{753,450}$ 87 days $\dfrac{345,480 \times 365}{1,050,825}$ 120 days

Current ratio $\dfrac{390,710}{241,590}$ 1.62 $\dfrac{528,855}{430,680}$ 1.23

Gearing $\dfrac{83,100}{490,520}$ 16.9% $\dfrac{61,600}{607,765}$ 10.1%

The regulatory and conceptual framework

Chapter learning objectives

Upon completion of this chapter you will be able to:

- explain the regulatory system:
  - International Accounting Standards Committee (IASC) Foundation
  - International Accounting Standards Board (IASB),
  - the Standards Advisory Council (SAC) and
  - the International Financial Reporting Interpretations Committee (IFRIC)

- explain how International Financial Reporting Standards (IFRSs) affect the financial reporting process

- explain the meaning of the qualitative characteristics of financial reporting and define and apply each of the following:
  - relevance (including materiality)
  - reliability (including faithful representation, substance over form, neutrality, prudence and completeness)
  - comparability
  - understandability

- illustrate the problems of achieving a balance between the qualitative characteristics

- explain the meaning of accounting concepts and define and apply each of the following:
  - going concern
  - accruals
  - consistency
  - materiality
  - substance over form
  - prudence
- explain the advantages and disadvantages of historical cost accounting (HCA) in times of changing prices
- explain in principle the main alternatives to HCA:
  - replacement cost
  - net realisable value
  - economic value.

1 The regulatory framework

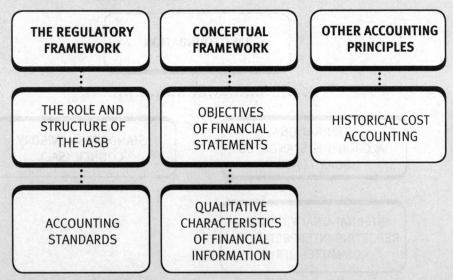

The need for regulation

- Regulation ensures that accounts are sufficiently reliable and useful, and prepared without unnecessary delay.

- Financial accounts are used as the starting point for calculating taxable profits.

- The annual report and accounts is the main document used for reporting to shareholders on the condition and performance of a company.

- The stock markets rely on the financial statements published by companies.

- International investors prefer information to be presented in a similar and comparable way, no matter where the company is based.

The role of international accounting standards

- International accounting standards are the rules that govern accounting for transactions.

- They don't have the force of law. They are effective only if adopted by the national regulatory bodies.

2 The role and structure of the IASB

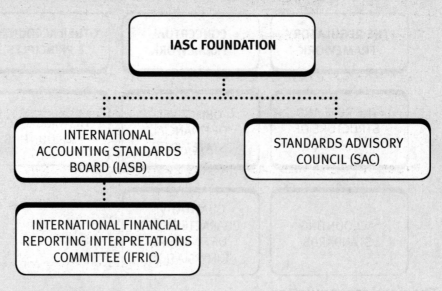

The **IASC Foundation** is the supervisory body. Its objective is to:

- develop, in the public interest, a single set of high-quality accounting standards
- promote the use and rigorous application of those standards
- bring about the convergence of national accounting standards and international accounting standards.

- The **IASB** is responsible for issuing new International Financial Reporting Standards (IFRSs).

- The **IFRIC** issue rapid guidance where there are differing interpretations of IASs/IFRSs.

- The **SAC** advises the IASB in developing new accounting standards.

The regulatory framework

The regulatory framework

The main source of regulations for the purpose of the ACCA's Preparing Financial Statements examination is the International Accounting Standards Board (IASB) which has issued a number of authoritative IASs and IFRSs.

Structure of the International Accounting Standards Board

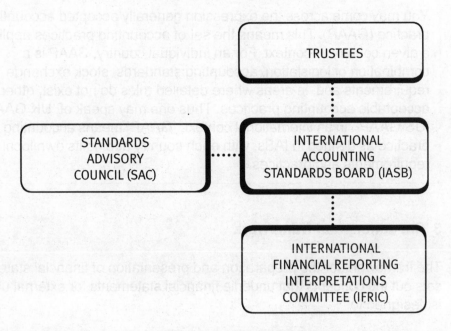

International Financial Reporting Interpretations Committee (IFRIC)

The IFRIC's main task is to interpret the application of IASs and IFRSs if difficulties arise. They may issue Draft Interpretations for public comment before finalising an Interpretation. They report to the IASB and must obtain Board approval for their Interpretations before issue.

Standards Advisory Council

The SAC exists to provide the IASB with advice on major standard-setting projects and other matters. It has about 50 members, including representatives of national standard setters and other interested parties.

Benchmark and allowed alternative treatments

An IAS sometimes contains more than one permitted accounting treatment for a transaction or event. One of them may be designated the benchmark treatment. The other treatments, if acceptable, are classified as allowed alternative treatments. The IASB tries to limit the number of alternative treatments allowed in an IAS, and thus tries to minimise the number of Standards containing allowed alternative treatments.

Generally accepted accounting practice (GAAP)

You may come across the expression generally accepted accounting practice (GAAP). This means the set of accounting practices applied in a given country or context. For an individual country, GAAP is a combination of legislation, accounting standards, stock exchange requirements and, in areas where detailed rules do not exist, other acceptable accounting practices. Thus one may speak of 'UK GAAP' or 'US GAAP'. In an international context, 'GAAP' means accounting practice as defined in IASs, with each country adding its own local requirements and practices.

3 The conceptual framework

The framework for the preparation and presentation of financial statements sets out the concepts that underlie financial statements for external users. It is designed to:

- assist the Board of the IASB in developing new standards and reviewing existing ones

- assist in harmonising accounting standards and procedures

- assist national standard-setting bodies in developing national standards

- assist preparers of financial statements in applying IASs/IFRSs and in dealing with topics not yet covered by IASs/IFRSs

- assist auditors in forming an opinion as to whether financial statements conform with IASs/IFRSs

- assist users of financial statements in interpreting financial statements

- provide those interested in the work of the IASB with information about its approach to the formulation of IFRSs.

The scope of the framework

The framework deals with:

- the objective of financial statements
- the qualitative characteristics that determine the usefulness of information in financial statements
- the definition, recognition and measurement of the elements from which financial statements are constructed (not examinable at this level).
- concepts of capital and capital maintenance (not examinable at this level).

Underlying assumptions of the framework

The framework identifies two underlying assumptions:

(1) the accruals basis of accounting

The accruals basis of accounting means that the effects of transactions and other events are recognised as they occur and not as cash or its equivalent is received or paid.

(2) the going concern basis.

The going concern basis assumes that the entity has neither the need nor the intention to liquidate or curtail materially the scale of its operations.

These also appear in IAS 1.

Faithful representation

There is no absolute definition of fair presentation (known as the true and fair view in the UK). It is felt that its meaning evolves over time and with changes in generally accepted accounting practice (GAAP).

When do financial statements show fair presentation?

Financial statements will generally show a fair presentation when:

- they conform with accounting standards
- they conform with the any relevant legal requirements
- they have applied the qualitative characteristics from the Framework.

True and fair override

IAS 1 states that an entity whose financial statements comply with IFRSs should disclose that fact.

However in extremely rare circumstances management may conclude that compliance with an IFRS or interpretation would be misleading.

In this case an entity should depart from the requirement of the standard provided the relevant regulatory framework permits such departure.

4 Objectives of financial statements

The objective of financial statements is to provide information about:

- the financial position of an entity (provided mainly in the statement of financial position)
- the financial performance (provided mainly in the statement of comprehensive income) and
- changes in the financial position of an entity (provided in the statement of changes in equity and statement of cash flows)

that is useful to a wide range of users in making economic decisions.

Interest parties

User groups

- equity investors (existing and potential)
- existing lenders and potential lenders
- employees
- stock market analysts and advisers
- business contacts including customers, suppliers and competitors
- the government, including the tax authorities
- the general public.

5 Qualitative characteristics of financial statements

The qualitative characteristics of financial statements are a set of attributes which together make the information in the financial statements useful to users.

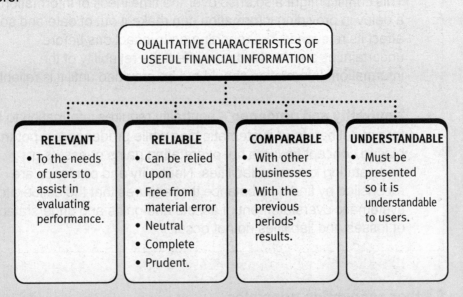

Qualitative characteristics

Problems of achieving a balance between the qualitative characteristics

At any given point in time it is unlikely that all of the qualitative characteristics can be satisfied, and therefore there will be conflicts between them. Examples are as follows:

- **Relevance and timeliness**

  If financial statements are to be tailored to the needs of each individual user, then they will take longer to prepare.

- **Understandability and completeness**

  If all aspects of the business are to be shown, this may make the financial statements less comprehensible.

- **Relevance and reliability** – sometimes the information that is most relevant is not the most reliable or vice versa. In such conflicts, the information that is most relevant of the information that is reliable should be used.

  This conflict might also arise over the timeliness of information, e.g. a delay in providing information can make it out of date and so affect its relevance, but reporting on transactions before uncertainties are resolved may affect the reliability of the information. Information should not be provided until it is reliable.

- **Neutrality and prudence** – neutrality requires information to be free of deliberate or systematic bias while prudence is a potentially biased concept towards not overstating gains or assets or understating losses or liabilities. Neutrality and prudence are reconciled by finding a balance that ensures that the deliberate and systematic overstatement of assets and gains and understatement of losses and liabilities do not occur.

6 Other accounting principles

These generally recognised principles underlie accounting and financial statements.

Going concern	The assumption that the business will continue in operation for the foreseeable future without significantly curtailing its activity.
Accruals/Matching	To calculate the profit for the period, one must include all the revenue and expenditure relating to the period, whether or not the cash has been received or paid. This concept also states that income and expenses should be matched against each other within an accounting period as far as possible.
Consistency	Items should be treated in the same way year on year. This will enable valid comparisons to be made. However, if circumstances change then a business is allowed to change policies to give a fairer representation of the financial statements.

Materiality	Materiality is a threshold quality that is demanded of all information given in the financial statements, i.e. information that is material should be given in the financial statements but information that is not material need not be given. Information is material if its omission or misstatement might reasonably be expected to influence the economic decisions of users. Whether or not information is material will depend on the size and nature of the item and the size of the business.
Substance over form	The economic substance of a transaction should be recorded rather than simply its legal form. E.g. A non-current asset acquired under a hire purchase agreement should be accounted for as an owned asset. This is the commercial substance of such a situation, even though it is not the case legally.
Prudence	Prudence is the inclusion of a degree of caution when making estimates under conditions of uncertainty. It ensures that assets and income are not overstated and liabilities or expenses are not understated.

Test your understanding 1

Which of the following statements are correct?

(1) Materiality means that only tangible items may be recognised as assets.

(2) Substance over form means that the commercial effect of a transaction must always be shown in the financial statements even if this differs from legal form.

(3) A business may only change an accounting policy to achieve a fairer representation.

A   2 and 3 only

B   All of them

C   1 and 2 only

D   1 and 3 only

7 Historical cost

The limitations of historical cost accounting

Under historical cost accounting, assets are recorded at the amount of cash or cash equivalents paid, or the fair value of the consideration given for them.

Liabilities are recorded at the amount of proceeds received in exchange for the obligation. This method of accounting has advantages, but it also has serious disadvantages.

Advantages and disadvantages of historical cost accounting

The limitations of historical cost accounting

Introduction

Virtually everything you have studied so far in this book has been based on historical cost accounting. Under historical cost accounting, assets are recorded at the amount of cash or cash equivalents paid, or the fair value of the consideration given for them.

Liabilities are recorded at the amount of proceeds received in exchange for the obligation. This method of accounting has advantages, but it also has serious disadvantages.

Advantages of historical cost accounting

(1) Records are based on objectively verifiable amounts (actual cost of assets, etc.).

(2) It is simple and cheap.

(3) The profit concept is well understood.

(4) Within limits, historical cost figures provide a basis for comparison with the results of other companies for the same period or similar periods, with the results of the same company for previous periods and with budgets.

(5) Lack of acceptable alternatives.

Disadvantages of historical cost accounting

(1) It overstates profits when prices are rising through inflation. Several factors contribute to this. For example, if assets are retained at their original cost, depreciation is based on that cost. As inflation pushes prices up, the true value to the enterprise of the use of the asset becomes progressively more than the depreciation charge.

   This disadvantage can be overcome by revaluing non-current assets. IAS 16 then requires depreciation to be based on the revalued amount.

(2) It maintains financial capital but does not maintain physical capital.

   If an enterprise makes a profit it must necessarily have more net assets. If the whole of that profit is distributed as dividend by a company, or withdrawn by a sole trader, the enterprise has the same capital at the end of the year as it had at the beginning. In other words, it has maintained its financial capital. However, it will not have maintained its physical capital if prices have risen through inflation during the year, because the financial capital will not buy the same inventory and other assets to enable the enterprise to continue operating at the same level.

(3) The statement of financial position does not show the value of the enterprise. A statement of financial position summarises the assets and liabilities of the enterprise, but there are several reasons why it does not represent the true value of the enterprise. One reason for this could be that the use of historical cost accounting means that assets are included at cost less depreciation based on that cost rather than at current value. (Another reason is, of course, that not all the assets are included in the statement of financial position– internally generated goodwill does not appear.)

(4) It provides a poor basis for assessing performance. The profit is overstated as explained in (1), while assets are understated as discussed in (3) above. The result is that return on capital employed is doubly distorted and exaggerated.

(5) It does not recognise the loss suffered through holding monetary assets while prices are rising. An enterprise holding cash or receivables through a period of inflation suffers a loss as their purchasing power declines.

The impact of changing prices

When prices are not changing, historical cost accounting (HCA) does accurately and fairly show profits made by the enterprise and the value of the assets less liabilities to the enterprise. When prices are changing, however, there are problems.

Depreciation

Under a system of HCA, the purpose of depreciation is simply to allocate the original cost (less estimated residual value) of a non-current asset over its estimated useful life. If depreciation is charged in the income statement, then by reducing the amount which can be paid out as a dividend, funds are retained within the company rather than paid to the shareholders. When the time comes to replace the asset, management must ensure that those funds are available in a sufficiently liquid form.

When inflation is taken into account, we can note that:

(1) The depreciation charge is based on the original cost of the asset measured in terms of historical $s, whereas the revenues against which depreciation is matched are measured in terms of current $s. The profit figure we calculate is not meaningful as it ignores price changes which have taken place since the asset was purchased.

(2) Although the concept of depreciation ensures that the capital of the enterprise is maintained intact in money terms, it does not ensure that the capital of the enterprise is maintained intact in real terms (see examples below).

The accumulated depreciation at the end of the asset's useful life will fall short of its replacement cost.

Example 1

An enterprise starts off with $1,000 cash and buys two machines at a cost of $500 each. All profits are distributed to the owners. At the end of ten years the company has no machines and $1,000 cash. Thus the capital of the enterprise has been maintained intact in money terms. Suppose at the end of ten years the current replacement cost of one machine is $1,000. Therefore the $1,000 cash at the end of the ten years will buy only one machine. In real terms, the capital at the end of the period is half that at the beginning of the period.

Profit has been over-distributed. If profit is a true surplus, the owners should be able to withdraw all the profit and be in exactly the same position as before in real terms.

Inventory and cost of sales

Assume a company values inventory on a historical cost basis using the FIFO method. During a period of inflation the effect of this method is to overstate the real profit of the enterprise, since sales (in current terms) are matched with cost of sales (in historical terms). If the company distributed the whole of its historical cost profit, it would not be maintaining the capital of the enterprise intact in real terms.

Example 2

An enterprise starts off on 1 January 20X7 with $1,000 cash (contributed by the proprietor). On the same day it purchases 500 motors at $2 each. These are sold on 31 March 20X7 for proceeds of $1,650. At this date the replacement cost of an identical motor is $2.20.

Under HCA the profit for the three months is $650 ($1,650 – $1,000). If the proprietor withdraws this profit, the closing statement of financial position at 31 March would show capital account $1,000 represented by cash of $1,000.

Although capital has been maintained intact in money terms (it was $1,000 at 1 January), it has not been maintained intact in real terms. At 31 March $1,000 cash will buy only 455 (approximately!) motors.

Comparability of data over time

Example 3

We saw earlier a need for users of accounts to be able to compare the results of the enterprise over a number of years so that trends could be identified. Thus, if sales were $100,000 four years ago and $130,000 in the current year, we could conclude that sales have increased by 30%. However, in real terms the increase may not be this amount, as price levels may have changed in the previous four years. If price levels have risen by 40% in the last four years, then the sales should be $140,000 in the current year in order to maintain the real value of sales. There has therefore been a real decline.

Alternatives to historical cost accounting

Alternatives to historical cost accounting

- Replacement cost involves recording assets at the cost of replacing them. An advantage is that the replacement cost is more up to date than the historical cost.

- Net realisable value assets and liabilities are carried at the amount which could currently be obtained by an orderly disposal. Assets are recorded at the amount after deducting the actual/expected disposal costs. Liabilities are recorded at their settlement values.

- Economic value involves recording assets at the value of keeping them in the business. i.e. not disposing of them. Assets recorded in this way are normally carried at the present value of the future discounted net cash flows. Liabilities are recorded at their discounted net present values.

Test your understanding 2

In a time of rising prices, what effect does the use of the historical cost concept have on an entity's profit and asset values?

A Both profit and asset values are understated

B Profit is understated and asset values overstated

C Profit is overstated and asset values understated

D Both profit and asset values are overstated

Chapter summary

```
            ┌─────────────────────────┐
            │  REGULATORY AND         │
            │  CONCEPTUAL FRAMEWORK   │
            └─────────────────────────┘
```

The regulatory framework
- IASB produce accounting standards.
- SAC and IFRIC assist in standard-setting process.

The conceptual framework
- The framework for the preparation and presentation of accounts.

Other accounting principles
- Going concern
- Accruals
- Consistency
- Materiality
- Substance over form
- Prudence.

Objective of financial statements
- Aim to provide information about financial position and performance of an entity.

Historical Cost Accounting
- Advantages
- Disadvantages
- Alternatives.

Qualitative characteristics
- Relevant
- Reliable
- Comparable
- Understandable.

Test your understanding answers

Test your understanding 1

The correct answer is A

Test your understanding 2

The correct answer is C

MULTIPLE CHOICE QUESTIONS

Chapter 2: Statement of financial position and income statement

(1) **Which of the following is the accounting equation**

A   Assets – Liabilities – Capital = Drawings + Profit

B   Assets = Liabilities – Capital + Profit – Drawings

C   Assets – Liabilities – Capital = Profit – Drawings

D   Assets + Liabilities = Capital + Profit – Drawings

(2 mark)

(2) **Which of the following statements is true?**

A   The income statement illustrates a business' financial position.

B   The income statement includes dividends paid

C   The income statement illustrates the business' financial performance

D   The income statement has to show the results for one year

(2 mark)

(3) **What is included in the statement of financial position of a business?**

A   Capital, drawings, assets and liabilities

B   Capital, dividends paid, sales and assets

C   Assets, liabilities, profit on disposals of non-current assets and introduced capital

D   Dividends paid, assets, discounts and liabilities

(2 mark)

(4) **Which of the following is incorrect?**

A   The statement of financial position and income statement form part of the financial statements of a business

B   The statement of financial position illustrates the accounting equation

C   The income statement illustrates the accounting equation

D   The statement of financial position and income statement illustrate the financial position and performance of the business

(2 mark)

(5) Which statement is not true?

A Inventory is shown on the income statement and in the statement of financial position

B Expenses should be included on the income statement

C Inventory should be included on the statement of financial position only

D Receivables are included in current assets on the statement of financial position

(2 mark)

Chapter 3: Double entry bookkeeping

(6) Which of the following is correct?

A A debit entry will increase non-current assets

A debit entry will increase drawings

A debit entry will increase profit

B A credit entry will increase a bank overdraft

A debit entry will increase payables

A credit entry will increase receivables

C A debit entry will increase profit

A debit entry will increase receivables

A debit entry will decrease payables

D A debit entry will increase receivables

A credit entry will decrease non-current assets

A credit entry will increase profit

(2 mark)

(7) A credit balance on a ledger account indicates:

A an asset or an expense

B a liability or an expense

C an amount owing to the organisation

D a liability or revenue

(2 mark)

(8) **The double entry system of bookkeeping normally results in which of the following balances on the ledger accounts?**

Debit balances	*Credit balances*
A Assets and revenues	Liabilities, capital and expenses
B Revenues, capital and liabilities	Assets and expenses
C Assets and expenses	Liabilities, capital and revenues
D Assets, expenses and capital	Liabilities and revenues

(2 mark)

(9) **The main aim of accounting is to:**

A   maintain ledger accounts for every asset and liability

B   provide financial information to users of such information

C   produce a trial balance

D   record every financial transaction individually

(2 mark)

(10) **A Debit entry could lead to:**

A   an increase in assets or a decrease in expenses

B   an increase in sales or an increase in liabilities

C   a decrease in sales or a decrease in assets

D   a decrease in liabilities or an increase in expenses

(2 mark)

(11) **A credit entry could lead to:**

A   an increase in assets or increase in liabilities

B   an increase in expense or an increase in share capital

C   an increase in liabilities or an increase in share capital

D   an increase in liabilities and a decrease in sales

(2 mark)

Chapter 4: Inventory

(12) Tracey's business sells three products – A, B and C. The following information was available at the year-end:

	A	B	C
	$	$	$
	per unit	per unit	per unit
Original cost	7	10	19
Estimated selling price	15	13	20
Selling and distribution costs	2	5	6
Units of inventory	20	25	15

The value of inventory at the year-end should be:

A $675

B $670

C $795

D $550

(2 marks)

(13) An inventory record card shows the following details:

January	1	50 units in inventory at a cost of $10 per unit
	4	90 units purchased at a cost of $15 per unit
	10	65 units sold
	20	30 units purchased at a cost of $20 per unit
	26	40 units sold

What is the value of inventory at 31 January using the FIFO method?

A $1,125

B $725

C $975

D $1,000

(2 marks)

(14) **What would be the effect on a business' profit, which has been calculated including inventory at cost, of discovering that one of its inventory items which cost $7,500 has a net realisable value of $8,500?**

A   an increase of $8,500

B   an increase of $1,000

C   no effect at all

D   a decrease of $1,000

(2 mark)

(15) **According to IAS 2 Inventories, which of the following costs should be included in valuing the inventories of a manufacturing company?**

(1) Carriage outwards

(2) Depreciation of factory plant

(3) Carriage inwards

(4) General administrative overheads

A   All four items

B   1, 3 and 4 only

C   1 and 2 only

D   2 and 3 only

(2 mark)

(16) The closing inventory of X amounted to $116,400 excluding the following two inventory lines:

– 400 items which had cost $4 each. All were sold after the statement of financial position date for $3 each, with selling expenses of $200 for the batch.

– 200 different items which had cost $30 each. These items were found to be defective at the statement of financial position date. Rectification work after the statement of financial position amounted to $1,200, after which they were sold for $35 each, with selling expenses totalling $300.

Which of the following total figures should appear in the statement of financial position of X for inventory?

A $122,300

B $121,900

C $122,900

D $123,300

(2 marks)

Chapter 5: Sales tax

(17) All the sales of Gail, a retailer, were made at a price inclusive of sales tax at the standard rate of 17.5% and all purchases and expenses bore sales tax at the standard rate. For the three months ended 31 March 2005 gross sales were $23,500, purchases were $12,000 (net) and expenses $800 (net).

How much is due to the tax authority for the quarter?

A $1,260

B $1,400

C $1,594

D $1,873

(2 marks)

(18) **The sales account is:**

A   credited with the total of sales made, including sales tax

B   credited with the total of sales made, excluding sales tax

C   debited with the total of sales made, including sales tax

D   debited with the total of sales made, excluding sales tax

(2 mark)

(19) **If sales (including sales tax) amounted to $27,612.50 and purchases (excluding sales tax) amounted to $18,000, the balance on the sales tax account, assuming all items are subject to sales tax at 17.5%, would be:**

A $962.50 debit

B $962.50 credit

C $1,682.10 debit

D $1,682.10 credit

(2 marks)

(20) A business commenced with capital in cash of $1,000. Inventory costing $800 net of sales tax at 17.5% is purchased on credit. Half of this inventory is then sold for $1,000 plus sales tax, the customer paying promptly in cash.

The accounting equation after these transactions would show:

A   assets $1,775 less liabilities $175 equals capital $1,600

B   assets $2,775 less liabilities $975 equals capital $1,200

C   assets $2,575 less liabilities $800 equals capital $1,775

D   assets $2,575 less liabilities $975 equals capital $1,600

(2 marks)

Chapter 6: Accruals and prepayments

(21) The electricity account for the year ended 30 April 2005 was as follows:

	$
Electricity accrued at 1 May 2004	250
Payments made during the year in relation to:	
Quarter ending 30 June 2004	400
Quarter ending 30 September 2004	350
Quarter ending 31 December 2004	425
Quarter ending 31 March 2005	450

Which of the following is the appropriate entry for electricity?

	Accrued at 30 April 2005	Charge to income statement for year ended 30 April 2005
A	$Nil	$1,375
B	$150	$1,525
C	$300	$1,675
D	$450	$1,825

(2 marks)

(22) The year end of Lansdown is 31 December. The company pays for its electricity by a standing order of $100 per month. On 1 January 2005 the statement from the electricity supplier showed that the company had overpaid by $25. Lansdown received electricity bills for the four quarters starting on 1 January 2005 and ending on 31 December 2005 for $350, $375, $275 and $300 respectively.

Which of the following is the correct entry for electricity in Lansdown's income statement and statement of financial position for the year ending 31 December 2005?

IS	*SFP*
A $1,300	$75 accrual
B $1,300	$75 prepayment
C $1,200	$125 accrual
D $1,200	$125 prepayment

(2 marks)

(23) At 1 January 2005, Michael had a prepayment of $200 in respect of rent. He paid $1,200 on 1 March 2005 in respect of the year ended 28 February 2006

What is the charge to the income statement in respect of rent for the year ended 31 December 2005?

A $1,400

B $1,200

C $1,100

D $1,300

(2 mark)

(24) At 31 December 2003, Tony had accrued $240 in respect of light and heat for the quarter ending 31 December 2003. In January 2004 he discovered that he had under-accrued by $10.

The bills for the next four quarters were as follows (q.e. = quarter ended):

Amount	Relating to	Data paid
$260	q.e. 31 March 2004	15 April 2004
$220	q.e. 30 June 2004	17 July 2004
$210	q.e. 30 September 2004	14 October 2004
$230	q.e. 31 December 2004	19 January 2005

Tony always accrues for expenses based on the last bill.

What is the charge to the income statement in respect of light and heat for the 15-month period ended 31 March 2005?

A $1,160

B $1,150

C $930

D $920

(2 marks)

(25) Stationery paid for during the year amounted to $1,350. At the beginning of the year there was an inventory of stationery on hand of $165 and an outstanding stationery invoice for $80. At the end of the year there was an inventory of stationery on hand of $140 and an outstanding stationery invoice for $70.

The stationery figure to be shown in the income statement for the year is:

A $1,195

B $1,335

C $1,365

D $1,505

(2 mark)

Chapter 7: Irrecoverable debts and allowances for receivables

(26) At 30 April 2005, Gareth has a receivables balance of $50,000 and an allowance for receivables of $800. Following a review of receivables, Gareth wishes to write off an irrecoverable debt of $1,000 and adjust his allowance to 5% of receivables.

What will be the adjusted balance of the allowance for receivables?

A $1,650

B $2,450

C $2,500

D $3,450

(2 mark)

(27) As at 31 March, Phil had receivables of $82,500. Following a review of receivables, Phil has decided to write off the following irrecoverable debts:

John	$1,000
Beatrice	$500
Peter	$3,250

Phil would like to provide against a specific debt of $250 and based on past experience, make a general allowance at 2% of receivables. The current balance on the allowance for receivables account is $2,000. Phil also received $300 from a debt that had been previously been written off.

What is the charge to the income statement in respect of irrecoverable debt expense and the entry on the statement of financial position for net receivables at 31 March?

	Income statement charge	Statement of financial position
A	$4,250	$75,950
B	$4,450	$77,750
C	$4,450	$75,950
D	$4,250	$77,750

(2 marks)

(28) At the start of the year Joe had an allowance of $700 against receivables. During the year $450 of this amount went bad and $150 was received; the balance remained unpaid at the year end. Another amount of $170 went bad. At the year-end it was decided to provide for a new debt of $240.

What was the total irrecoverable debt expense for the year?

A $170

B $260

C $410

D $710

(2 marks)

(29) Doris currently has a receivables balance of $47,800 and an allowance for receivables of $1,250. She has received $150 in respect of half of a debt that she had provided against. She now believes the other half of the debt to be bad and wishes to write it off. She also wishes to maintain her allowance at 2% receivables.

What is the total charge to the income statement in respect of these items?

A $150 debit

B $150 credit

C $300 debit

D $300 credit

(2 marks)

(30) At the year end, Harold has a receivables balance of $100,000 and an allowance for receivables of $5,000. He has not yet accounted for a receipt of $500 in respect of a debt which he had previously provided against or a receipt of $1,000 in respect of a debt which had been written off in the previous year. Harold wishes to maintain his allowance for receivables at 7% of receivables.

What balances will be shown in his statement of financial position at the year-end for receivables and the allowance for receivables?

	Receivables	Allowance
A	$98,500	$6,465
B	$99,500	$6,465
C	$98,500	$6,965
D	$99,500	$6,965

(2 marks)

(31) James has been advised that one of his customers has ceased trading and that it is almost certain that he will not recover the balance of $720 owed by this customer.

What entry should James make in his general ledger?

A	Dr	Receivables	$720
	Cr	Irrecoverable debts	$720

Being write off of irrecoverable debt

B	Dr	Irrecoverable debts	$720
	Cr	Receivables	$720

Being write off of irrecoverable debt

C	Dr	Receivables	$720
	Cr	Bank	$720

Being write off of irrecoverable debt

D	Dr	Bank	$720
	Cr	Receivables	$720

Being write off of irrecoverable debt.

(2 mark)

(32) Gordon's receivables owe a total of $80,000 at the year end. These include $900 of long-overdue debts that might still be recoverable, but for which Gordon has created an allowance for receivables. Gordon has also provided an allowance of $1,582, which is the equivalent of 2% of the other receivables' balances.

What best describes Gordon's allowance for receivables as at his year end?

A   a specific allowance of $900 and an additional allowance of $1,582 based on past history

B   a specific allowance of $1,582 and an additional allowance of $900 based on past history

C   a specific allowance of $2,482

D   a general allowance of $2,482

(2 mark)

Chapter 8: Non-current assets

(33) At 1 January 2005, Mary has motor vehicles which cost $15,000. On 31 August 2005 she sells a motor vehicle for $5,000 which had originally cost $8,000 and which had a NBV of $4,000 at the date of disposal. She purchased a new motor vehicle which cost $10,000 on 30 November 2005.

Her policy is to depreciate motor vehicles at a rate of 25% pa on the straight-line basis, based on the number of months' ownership.

What is the depreciation charge for the year ended 31 December 2005?

A $3,750

B $3,291

C $4,250

D $3,500

(2 marks)

(34) **Which of the following best explains what is meant by 'capital expenditure'?**

    A   expenditure on non-current assets, including repairs and maintenance

    B   expenditure on expensive assets

    C   expenditure relating to the issue of share capital

    D   expenditure relating to the acquisition or improvement of noncurrent assets

(2 mark)

(35) A non-current asset was purchased at the beginning of Year 1 for $2,400 and depreciated by 20% pa by the reducing-balance method. At the beginning of Year 4 it was sold for $1,200.

The result of this was:

    A   a loss on disposal of $240.00

    B   a loss on disposal of $28.80

    C   a profit on disposal of $28.80

    D   a profit on disposal of $240.00

(2 marks)

(36) Giles bought a new machine from abroad. The machine cost $100,000 and delivery and installation costs were $7,000. Testing it amounted to $5,000. Training employees on how to use the machine cost of $1,000.

What should be the cost of the machine in the company's statement of financial position?

    A $100,000

    B $107,000

    C $112,000

    D $113,000

(2 mark)

(37) Joseph's machinery cost account showed a balance of $5,000 at 1 January 2005. During the year he had the following transactions:

28 February   Disposed of machine costing $300

31 March   Acquired machine costing $1,000

1 November   Disposed of machine costing $600

Joseph depreciates machines at a rate of 10% pa on the straight-line basis based on the number of months' ownership.

What is the depreciation charge in respect of machinery for the year ended 31 December 2005?

A $545

B $540

C $510

D $630

(2 marks)

(38) B acquired a lorry on 1 May 20X0 at a cost of $30,000. The lorry has an estimated useful life of four years, and an estimated resale value at the end of that time of $6,000. B charges depreciation on the straight-line basis, with a proportionate charge in the period of acquisition.

What will the depreciation charge for the lorry be in B's ten-month accounting period to 30 September 20X0?

A $3,000

B $2,500

C $2,000

D $5,000

(2 mark)

Chapter 9: From trial balance to financial statements

The following is the extract of Jessie's trial balance as at 31 December 2005:

	Dr $	Cr $
Buildings	580,000	
Buildings accumulated depreciation		116,000
Plant and machinery	50,000	
Plant and machinery accumulated depreciation		12,500
Receivables	25,800	
Allowance for receivables		1,900
Rent	34,000	
Insurance	30,000	
Irrecoverable debts	1,800	

The following notes are provided:

(i) Buildings are depreciated at 2% pa on a straight-line basis.

(ii) Plant and machinery is depreciated at 25% pa on a reducing balance basis.

(iii) Additional irrecoverable debts of $3,200 were discovered at the year end. It has been decided to make an allowance for receivables of 5% on the adjusted receivables at the year end.

(iv) The monthly rental charge is $3,000.

(v) The insurance charge for the year is $24,000.

Using the above information attempt the following questions.

(39) **The depreciation charge for buildings for the year and the net book value (NBV) at the year-end will be:**

	Depreciation charge	NBV
	$	$
A	11,600	568,400
B	9,280	464,000
C	11,600	452,400
D	11,600	464,000

(2 marks)

(40) **The depreciation charge for plant and machinery for the year and the NBV at the year-end will be:**

	Depreciation charge	NBV
	$	$
A	9,375	37,500
B	12,500	25,000
C	9,375	40,625
D	9,375	28,125

(2 marks)

(41) **The total irrecoverable debt expense for the year and the closing net receivable balance will be:**

	Irrecoverable debt expense	Receivables
	$	$
A	4,230	21,470
B	5,000	21,470
C	5,770	21,830
D	2,430	19,670

(2 marks)

(42) **What is the charge for rent and insurance for the year and the closing accrual and prepayment?**

		Charge for the year		Closing accrual/prepayment
		$		$
A	Rent	30,000	Rent accrual	3,000
	Insurance	24,000	Insurance prepayment	6,000
B	Rent	36,000	Rent accrual	2,000
	Insurance	24,000	Insurance prepayment	6,000
C	Rent	36,000	Rent accrual	3,000
	Insurance	24,000	Insurance prepayment	6,000
D	Rent	30,000	Rent accrual	3,000
	Insurance	30,000	Insurance prepayment	6,000

(2 marks)

Chapter 10: Books of prime entry and control accounts

(43) **Which of the following is not the purpose of a receivables ledger control account?**

A   A receivables ledger control account provides a check on the arithmetic accuracy of the personal ledger

B   A receivables ledger control account helps to locate errors in the trial balance

C   A receivables ledger control account ensures that there are no errors in the personal ledger

D   Control accounts deter fraud

(2 mark)

(44) **Which one of the following is a book of prime entry and part of the double-entry system?**

A   the journal

B   the petty cash book

C   the sales day book

D   the purchase ledger

(2 mark)

(45) **On 1 January 2005 the balance of receivables was $22,000. Calculate the closing receivables after taking the following into consideration:**

	$
Sales	120,000
Bank receipts	115,000
Discount allowed	1,000
Discount received	3,000
Dishonoured cheque	9,000
Contra – Set off	5,000

A $30,000

B $23,000

C $12,000

D $28,000

(2 mark)

Chapter 11: Control account reconciliations

(46) A receivables ledger control account had a closing balance of $8,500. It contained a contra to the purchase ledger of $400, but this had been entered on the wrong side of the control account.

The correct balance on the control account should be:

A $7,700 debit

B $8,100 debit

C $8,400 debit

D $8,900 debit

(2 mark)

(47) The receivables ledger control account at 1 May had balances of $32,750 debit and $1,275 credit. During May sales of $125,000 were made on credit. Receipts from receivables amounted to $122,500 and cash discounts of $550 were allowed. Refunds of $1,300 were made to customers. The closing credit balance is $2,000.

The closing debit balances at 31 May should be:

A $35,175

B $35,675

C $36,725

D $34,725

(2 mark)

(48) A supplier sends you a statement showing a balance outstanding of $14,350. Your own records show a balance outstanding of $14,500.

The reason for this difference could be that:

A   The supplier sent an invoice for $150 which you have not yet received

B   The supplier has allowed you $150 cash discount which you had omitted to enter in your ledgers

C   You have paid the supplier $150 which he has not yet accounted for

D   You have returned goods worth $150 which the supplier has not yet accounted for

(2 mark)

(49) **A credit balance of $917 brought forward on Y's account in the books of X means that:**

A   X owes Y $917

B   Y owes X $917

C   X has paid Y $917

D   X is owed $917 by Y

(2 mark)

(50) **In a receivables ledger control account, which of the following lists is composed only of items which would appear on the credit side of the account?**

A   Cash received from customers, sales returns, irrecoverable debts written off, contras against amounts due to suppliers in the accounts payable ledger

B   Sales, cash refunds to customers, irrecoverable debts written off, discounts allowed

C   Cash received from customers, discounts allowed, interest charged on overdue accounts, irrecoverable debts written off

D   Sales, cash refunds to customers, interest charged on overdue accounts, contras against amounts due to suppliers in the accounts payable ledger

(2 mark)

Chapter 12: Bank reconciliations

(51) The following information relates to a bank reconciliation.

(i)   The bank balance in the cash book before taking the items below into account was $5,670 overdrawn.

(ii) Bank charges of $250 on the bank statement have not been entered in the cash book.

(iii) The bank has credited the account in error with $40 which belongs to another customer.

(iv) Cheque payments totalling $325 have been correctly entered in the cash book but have not been presented for payment.

(v)   Cheques totalling $545 have been correctly entered on the debit side of the cash book but have not been paid in at the bank.

What was the balance as shown by the bank statement before taking the items above into account?

A $5,670 overdrawn

B $5,600 overdrawn

C $5,740 overdrawn

D $6,100 overdrawn

(2 marks)

(52) At 31 August 2005 the balance on the company's cash book was $3,600 credit. Examination of the bank statements revealed the following:

- Standing orders amounting to $180 had not been recorded in the cash book.

- Cheques paid to suppliers of $1,420 did not appear on the bank statements.

What was the balance on the bank statement at 31 August 2005?

A $5,200 overdrawn

B $5,020 overdrawn

C $2,360 overdrawn

D $3,780 overdrawn

(2 mark)

(53) An organisation's cash book has an operating balance of $485 credit. The following transactions then took place:

- cash sales $1,450 including sales tax of $150

- receipts from customers of debts of $2,400

- payments to payables of debts of $1,800 less 5% cash discount

- dishonoured cheques from customers amounting to $250.

The resulting balance in the bank column of the cash book should be:

A $1,255 debit

B $1,405 debit

C $1,905 credit

D $2,375 credit

(2 marks)

(54) The cash book shows a bank balance of $5,675 overdrawn at 31 March 2005. It is subsequently discovered that a standing order for $125 has been entered twice and that a dishonoured cheque for $450 has been debited in the cash book instead of credited.

The correct bank balance should be:

A $5,100 overdrawn

B $6,000 overdrawn

C $6,250 overdrawn

D $6,450 overdrawn

(2 mark)

(55) **The attempt below at a bank reconciliation statement has been prepared by Q Limited. Assuming the bank statement balance of $38,600 to be correct, what should the cash book balance be?**

A $76,500 overdrawn, as stated

B $5,900 overdrawn

C $700 overdrawn

D $5,900 cash at bank

	$
Overdraft per bank statement	38,600
Add: deposits not credited	41,200
	79,800
Less: outstanding cheques	3,300
Overdraft per cash book	76,500

(2 mark)

(56) **After checking a business cash book against the bank statement, which of the following items could require an entry in the cash book?**

(1) Bank charges

(2) A cheque from a customer which was dishonoured

(3) Cheque not presented

(4) Deposits not credited

(5) Credit transfer entered in bank statement

(6) Standing order entered in bank statement.

A 1, 2, 5 and 6

B 3 and 4

C 1, 3, 4 and 6

D 3, 4, 5 and 6

(2 mark)

Chapter 13: Correction of errors and suspense accounts

(57) Faulty goods costing $210 were returned to a supplier but this was recorded as $120 in the ledger accounts.

What is the journal entry necessary to correct the error?

	Dr		Cr	
A	Suspense	90	Purchases returns	90
B	Purchases	90	Payables	90
C	Payables	90	Suspense	90
D	Payables	90	Purchases returns	90

(2 mark)

(58) A suspense account was opened when a trial balance failed to agree. The following errors were later discovered:

- a gas bill of $420 had been recorded in the gas account as $240

- discount of $50 given to a customer had been credited to discounts received

- interest received of $70 had been entered in the bank account only.

The original balance on the suspense account was:

A debit $210

B credit $210

C debit $160

D credit $160

(2 marks)

(59) Molly starts up in business as a florist on 1 April 2004. For the first six months, she has a draft profit of $12,355.

On investigation you discover the following:

- Rent paid for the 12 months ending 31 March 2005 of $800 has not been recorded in the accounts.

- Closing inventory in the accounts at a cost of $1,000 has a net realisable value of $800.

What is the adjusted profit for the period?

A $11,355

B $11,755

C $12,155

D $12,555

(2 mark)

(60) In an accounting system where individual receivables and payables ledger accounts are maintained as an integral part of the double entry, which of the following errors will not be identified by a trial balance?

A   overcasting of the sales day book

B   undercasting of the analysed cash book

C   failure to transfer a non-current asset to the disposal account when sold

D   transposition error in an individual receivables account

(2 mark)

(61) A trial balance has been extracted and a suspense account opened. One error relates to the misposting of an amount of $400, being discount received from suppliers, which was posted to the wrong side of the discount received account

What is the correcting journal entry?

		Dr	Cr
A	Discount received	$400	
	Suspense		$400
B	Suspense	$400	
	Discount received		$400
C	Discount received	$800	
	Suspense		$800
D	Suspense	$800	
	Discount received		$800

(2 mark)

(62) A company, Y, purchased some plant on 1 January 20X0 for $38,000. The payment for the plant was correctly entered in the cash book but was entered on the debit side of plant repairs account.

Y charges depreciation on the straight-line basis at 20% pa, with a proportionate charge in the year of acquisition and assuming no scrap value at the end of the life of the asset.

How will Y's profit for the year ended 31 March 20X0 be affected by the error?

A   Understated by $30,400

B   Understated by $36,100

C   Understated by $38,000

D   Overstated by $1,900

(2 marks)

(63) The trial balance of Z failed to agree, the totals being:

Debit $836,200

Credit $819,700

A suspense account was opened for the amount of the difference and the following errors were found and corrected:

(1)   The totals of the cash discount columns in the cash book had not been posted to the discount accounts. The figures were discount allowed $3,900 and discount received $5,100.

(2)   A cheque for $19,000 received from a customer was correctly entered in the cash book but was posted to the customer's account as $9,100.

What will the remaining balance on the suspense account be after the correction of these errors?

A $25,300 credit

B $7,700 credit

C $27,700 credit

D $5,400 credit

(2 marks)

(64) The trial balance of C did not agree, and a suspense account was opened for the difference. Checking in the bookkeeping system revealed a number of errors.

(1) $4,600 paid for motor van repairs was correctly treated in the cash book but was credited to motor vehicles asset account.

(2) $360 received from B, a customer, was credited in error to the account of BB.

(3) $9,500 paid for rent was debited to the rent account as $5,900.

(4) The total of the discount allowed column in the cash book had been debited in error to the discounts received account.

(5) No entries had been made to record a cash sale of $100.

Which of the errors above would require an entry to the suspense account as part of the process of correcting them?

A   3 and 4

B   1 and 3

C   2 and 5

D   2 and 3

(2 marks)

Chapter 14: Incomplete records

(65) Ashley started a business on 1 January 2005. He acquired the following assets:

Van	$2,000
Inventory	$1,000
Receivables	$500
Prepaid insurance for inventory	$100

He also opened a business bank account and paid in $4,000. At the end of the first year of trading, he had the following:

Van	$1,800
Fixtures	$500
Inventory	$840
Receivables	$600
Payables	$400
Cash	$3,400

He had drawn $1,000 in cash during the period.

What was Ashley's profit or loss for the year?

A $140 loss

B $140 profit

C $1,860 loss

D $1,860 profit

(2 marks)

(66) George started a business by investing $10,000 into a business bank account. At the end of his first year's trading he had earned a profit of $5,000 and had the following assets and liabilities:

Non-current assets	$20,000
Current assets	$15,000
Current liabilities	$8,000

During the year he had withdrawn $2,000 from the business.

How much further capital had he introduced in the year?

A $20,000

B $24,000

C $10,000

D $14,000

(2 mark)

(67) **If Harry's mark-up on cost of sales is 15%, what is his gross profit margin?**

A 12.5%

B 13.04%

C 15%

D 17.65%

(2 mark)

KAPLAN PUBLISHING

(68) A sole trader had opening capital of $10,000 and closing capital of $4,500. During the period the owner introduced capital of $4,000 and withdrew $8,000 for her own use.

Her profit or loss during the period was:

A $9,500 loss

B $1,500 loss

C $7,500 profit

D $17,500 profit

(2 mark)

(69) **From the following information, calculate the value of purchases:**

	$
Opening payables	142,600
Cash paid	542,300
Discounts received	13,200
Goods returned	27,500
Closing payables	137,800

A $302,600

B $506,400

C $523,200

D $578,200

(2 marks)

(70) Carol owns a shop. The only information available for the year ended 31 December 2005 is as follows:

Inventory at 1 January 2005	$3,500
Inventory at 31 December 2005	$1,350
Sales	$17,000
Gross profit margin	25%

What were the purchases of the shop for the year?

A $11,450

B $12,750

C $14,900

D $10,600

(2 mark)

(71) The following information is relevant to the calculation of the sales figure for Alpha, a sole trader who does not keep proper accounting records:

	$
Opening receivables	29,100
Cash received from credit customers and paid into the bank	381,600
Expenses paid out of cash received from credit customers before banking	6,800
Irrecoverable debts written off	7,200
Refunds to credit customers	2,100
Discounts allowed to credit customers	9,400
Cash sales	112,900
Closing receivables	38,600

The figure which should appear in Alpha's income statement for sales is:

A $525,300

B $511,700

C $529,500

D $510,900

(2 marks)

(72) A sole trader who does not keep full accounting records wishes to calculate her sales revenue for the year.

The information available is:

(1)	Opening inventory	$17,000
(2)	Closing inventory	$24,000
(3)	Purchases	$91,000
(4)	Standard gross profit percentage	40% on sales revenue

Which of the following is the sales revenue figure for the year calculated from these figures?

A $117,600

B $108,000

C $210,000

D $140,000

(2 mark)

(73) A business compiling its accounts for the year to 31 January each year pays rent quarterly in advance on 1 January, 1 April, 1 July and 1 October each year. After remaining unchanged for some years, the rent was increased from $24,000 per year to $30,000 per year as from 1 July 20X0.

Which of the following figures is the rent expense which should appear in the income statement for the year ended 31 January 20X1?

A $27,500

B $29,500

C $28,000

D $29,000

(2 mark)

(74) On 31 December 20X0 the inventory of V was completely destroyed by fire. The following information is available:

(1) Inventory at 1 December 20X0 at cost $28,400.

(2) Purchases for December 20X0 $49,600.

(3) Sales for December 20X0 $64,800.

(4) Standard gross profit percentage on sales revenue 30%.

Based on this information, which of the following is the amount of inventory destroyed?

A $45,360

B $32,640

C $40,971

D $19,440

(2 marks)

Chapter 15: Company accounts

(75) Geese's trial balance shows an overprovision in respect of income tax for the year ended 31 December 2004 of $5,000. Geese estimates that tax liability in respect of the year ended 31 December 2005 will be $23,000.

What is the tax charge in Geese's income statement and the statement of financial position entry for the year ended 31 December 2005?

	Income statement charge	Statement of financial position
A	$5,000	$18,000
B	$23,000	$18,000
C	$18,000	$23,000
D	$28,000	$23,000

(2 mark)

(76) **The correct journal entry to record the issue of 100,000 50c shares (fully paid) at an issue price of $2.50 a share is:**

			$	$
A	Dr	Bank	250,000	
	Cr	Share capital		100,000
	Cr	Share premium		150,000
B	Dr	Bank	250,000	
	Cr	Share capital		50,000
	Cr	Share premium		200,000
C	Dr	Bank	50,000	
	Cr	Share premium		50,000
D	Dr	Share capital	100,000	
	Dr	Share premium	150,000	
	Cr	Bank		250,000

(2 mark)

(77) A company has the following share capital:

	Authorised $000	Issued $000
25c ordinary shares	8,000	4,000
6% 50c preference shares	2,000	1,000

In addition to providing for the year's preference dividend, an ordinary dividend of 2c per share is to be paid.

What are total dividends for the year?

A $140,000

B $380,000

C $440,000

D $760,000

(2 mark)

(78) **Revenue reserves are:**

A   accumulated and undistributed profits of a company

B   amounts which cannot be distributed as dividends

C   amounts set aside out of profits to replace revenue items

D   amounts set aside out of profits for a specific purpose

(2 mark)

(79) On 1 April 2004 the balance on B's accumulated profit account was $50,000 credit. The balance on 31 March 2005 was $100,000 credit. On 10 March 2005 dividends of $50,000 were declared in respect of the year ended 31 March 2005, payable on 31 May 2005.

Based on this information, profit after tax (but before dividends) for the year ended 31 March 2005 was:

A   Nil

B $50,000

C $100,000

D $150,000

(2 mark)

Chapter 16: Accounting standards

(80) Jackson's year end is 31 December 2005. In February 2006 a major credit customer went into liquidation and the directors believe that they will not be able to recover the $450,000 owed to them.

How should this item be treated in the financial statements of Jackson for the year ended 31 December 2005?

A   The irrecoverable debt should be disclosed by note

B   The financial statements are not affected

C   The debt should be provided against

D   The financial statements should be adjusted to reflect the irrecoverable debt

(2 mark)

(81) A former employee is claiming compensation of $50,000 from Harriot, a limited liability company. The company's solicitors have stated that they believe that the claim is unlikely to succeed. The legal costs relating to the claim are likely to be in the region of $5,000 and will be incurred regardless of whether or not the claim is successful.

How should these items be treated in the financial statements of Harriot Ltd?

A   Provision should be made for $55,000

B   Provision should be made for $50,000 and the legal costs should be disclosed by note

C   Provision should be made for $5,000 and the compensation of $50,000 should be disclosed by note

D   No provisions should be made but both items should be disclosed by note

(2 mark)

(82) Cowper has spent $20,000 researching new cleaning chemicals in the year ended 31 December 2005. It has also spent $40,000 developing a new cleaning product which will not go into commercial production until next year. The development project meets the criteria laid down in IAS 38.

How should these costs be treated in the financial statements of Cowper for the year ended 31 December 2005?

A $60,000 should be capitalised as an intangible asset on the statement of financial position

B $40,000 should be capitalised as an intangible asset and should be amortised; $20,000 should be written off to the income statement

C $40,000 should be capitalised as an intangible asset and should not be amortised; $20,000 should be written off to the income statement

D $60,000 should be written off to the income statement

(2 mark)

(83) The directors of ABC estimated that inventory which had cost $50,000 had a net realisable value of $40,000 at 30 June 2005 and recorded it in the financial statements for the year ended 30 June 2005 at this lower value in accordance with IAS 2. They have since found out that the net realisable value of the inventory is only likely to be $30,000.

What adjustments, if any, should be made in the financial statements in respect of this inventory?

A   No adjustments required

B   Increase the value of inventory by $10,000

C   Decrease the value of inventory by $10,000

D   Decrease the value of inventory by $20,000

(2 mark)

(84) **Which of the following items are non-adjusting items per IAS 10?**

(a) the issue of new share or loan capital

(b) financial consequences of losses of non-current assets or inventory as a result of fires or floods

(c) information regarding the value of inventory sold at less than cost thus resulting in a reduction in the value of inventory

(d) mergers and acquisitions

(e) bankruptcy of a credit customer.

A   (a), (b) and (d)

B   (c) and (e)

C   (a), (d) and (e)

D   (b), (c) and (e)

(2 mark)

(85) **Which of the following correctly describes how research and development expenditure should be treated in accordance with IAS 38?**

A   Research and development expenditure must be written off to the income statement as incurred

B   Research and development expenditure should be capitalised as an intangible asset on the statement of financial position

C   Research expenditure should be written off to the income statement; development expenditure must be capitalised as an intangible asset provided that certain criteria are met

D   Research expenditure should be capitalised as an intangible asset provided that certain criteria are met; development expenditure should be written off to the income statement

(2 mark)

(86) **Who issues International Financial Reporting Standards?**

A   The Auditing Practices Board

B   The Stock Exchange

C   The International Accounting Standards Board

D   The government

(2 mark)

(87) **Which of the following statements concerning the accounting treatment of research and development expenditure are true, according to IAS 38 Intangible Assets?**

(1) If certain criteria are met, research expenditure may be recognised as an asset.

(2) Research expenditure, other than capital expenditure on research facilities, should be recognised as an expense as incurred.

(3) In deciding whether development expenditure qualifies to be recognised as an asset, it is necessary to consider whether there will be adequate finance available to complete the project.

(4) Development expenditure recognised as an asset must be amortised over a period not exceeding five years.

(5) The financial statements should disclose the total amount of research and development expenditure recognised as an expense during the period.

A 1, 4 and 5

B 2, 4 and 5

C 2, 3 and 4

D 2, 3 and 5

(2 marks)

(88) IAS10 Events after the reporting period regulates the extent to which events after the reporting period date should be reflected in financial statements.

Which of the following lists of such events consists only of items that, according to IAS10 should normally be classified as non-adjusting?

A Insolvency of a debtor whose account receivable was outstanding at the statement of financial position date, issue of shares or loan notes, a major merger with another company

B Issue of shares or loan notes, changes in foreign exchange rates, major purchases of non-current assets

C A major merger with another company, destruction of a major non-current asset by fire, discovery of fraud or error which shows that the financial statements were incorrect

D Sale of inventory giving evidence about its value at the statement of financial position date, issue of shares or loan notes, destruction of a major non-current asset by fire

(2 marks)

Chapter 17: Statement of cash flows

(89) In the year ended 31 December 2005, Lamb bought new vehicles from Warwick Motors with a list price of $100,000 for $70,000 cash and an allowance against old motor vehicles of $30,000. The value of the vehicles taken in part exchange was $27,000.

Lamb sold other vehicles with a net book value of $12,000 for $15,000 cash.

In Lamb's statement of cash flow for the year ended 31 December 2005, how would the above transactions be presented under the heading 'Investing activities'?

	Cash inflow	Cash outflow
A	–	$76,000
B	$45,000	$100,000
C	$15,000	$70,000
D	$15,000	$100,000

(2 marks)

(90) Baldrick has the following balances in its statement of financial position as at 30 June 2004 and 30 June 2005:

	30 June 2005 $	30 June 2004 $
Current liabilities		
Taxation payable	600	400
Dividends	3,300	2,500
(declared before the year-end)		
Non-current liabilities		
8% Loan notes	50,000	40,000
Capital and reserves		
Accumulated profits	65,500	45,500

In the year ended 30 June 2005 taxation of $550 was paid. The additional loan notes were issued on 30 June 2005.

What is the operating profit of Baldrick for the year ended 30 June 2005?

A $27,250

B $26,450

C $28,050

D $27,100

(2 marks)

(91) At 31 December 2004, Topaz had provided $50,000 in respect of income tax. At 31 December 2005, the company estimated that its income tax bill in respect of the year would be $57,000. The amount charged in the income statement for the year ended 31 December 2005 in respect of income tax was $60,000.

How much will appear in the statement of cash flows for the year ended 31 December 2005 in respect of income tax?

A $50,000

B $53,000

C $57,000

D $60,000

(2 mark)

(92) Evans had the following balances in its statement of financial positions as at 30 June 2004 and 2005:

	2004	2005
10% Loan notes	$150,000	$130,000
Share capital	$100,000	$120,000
Share premium	$35,000	$45,000

How much will appear in the cash flow statement for the year ended 30 June 2005 under the heading of 'Financing activities'?

A $nil

B $10,000 inflow

C $30,000 inflow

D $40,000 inflow

(2 mark)

The following information relates to Questions 93 and 94.

Scents had the following balances in its statement of financial positions as at 30 September 2004 and 2005:

	2004	2005
Loan interest accrual	$5,000	$3,000
Proposed ordinary dividends	$20,000	$25,000
10% Loan notes	$100,000	$100,000
Ordinary share capital	$150,000	$150,000
8% Preference share capital	$50,000	$50,000

(93) **How much will appear in the statement of cash flows for the year ended 30 September 2005 for the loan interest and preference dividend paid?**

A $10,000

B $12,000

C $16,000

D $32,000

(2 marks)

(94) **How much will appear in the statement of cash flows for the year ended 30 September 2005 for the ordinary dividend paid?**

A $20,000

B $24,000

C $25,000

D $29,000

(2 mark)

(95) IAS 7 Statement of cash flows requires the statement of cash flows prepared using the indirect method to include the calculation of net cash from operating activities.

Which of the following lists consists only of items which could appear in such a calculation?

A Depreciation, increase in receivables, decrease in payables, proceeds of sale of plant

B Increase in payables, decrease in inventories, profit on sale of plant, depreciation

C Increase in payables, depreciation, decrease in receivables, proceeds of sale of plant

D Depreciation, interest paid, equity dividends paid, purchase of plant

(2 mark)

Chapter 18: Consolidated statement of financial position

(96) At the 1 January 20X2 Y acquired 75% of the share capital of Z for $400,000. At that date the share capital of Z consisted of 600,000 ordinary shares of 50c each and its reserves were $50,000.

The fair value of NCI at the date of acquisition was $100,000.

In the consolidated statement of financial position of Y and its subsidiary Z at 31 December 20X6, what amount should appear for goodwill?

A $150,000

B $137,500

C $55,000

D $110,000

(2 marks)

(97) Skinny acquired 75% of the share capital Coltart for $35,000 on the 1 January 20X4. Details of the share capital and reserves of Skinny and Coltart at 31 December 20X6 are as follows:

	Skinny	Coltart
	$	$
Share capital	50,000	20,000
Reserves	40,000	15,000

At the date of acquisition Coltart had reserves of $10,000.

What figure should appear in the consolidated statement of financial position of Skinny and its subsidiary Coltart for reserves as at 31 December 20X6?

A $41,250

·B $42,750

C $43,250

D $43,750

(2 marks)

(98) Austen acquired 60% of the share capital of Dicken for $300,000 on 1 January 20X5. Details of the share capital and reserves of Austen and Dickens at 31 December 20X6 are as follows:

	Austen	Dickens
	$	$
Share capital	300,000	200,000
Reserves	200,000	75,000

At the date of acquisition Dickens had reserves of $60,000. The fair value of NCI at acquisition was $80,000.

What figure should appear in the consolidated statement of financial position of Austen and its subsidiary Dickens for reserves as at 31 December 20X6?

A $180,200

B $209,000

C $290,200

D $110,000

(2 mark)

(99) At the 1 January 20X5 Purves acquired 80% of the share capital of Trollope for $100,000. At that date the share capital of Trollope consisted of 50,000 $1 shares and reserves of $30,000. At the 31 December 20X6 the reserves of Purves and Trollope were as follows:

	Purves	Trollope
	$	$
Reserves	400,000	50,000

The fair value of NCI at acquisition was $75,000.

What figure should appear in the consolidated statement of financial position of Purves and its subsidiary Trollope, for non-controlling interest?

A $16,000

B $20,000

C $79,000

D $80,000

(2 marks)

(100) At the 1 January 20X3 Y acquired 80% of the share capital of Z for $750,000. At that date the share capital of Z consisted of 600,000 ordinary shares of $1 each and its reserves were $50,000.

The fair value of non-controlling interest was valued at $150,000.

In the consolidated statement of financial position of Y and its subsidiary Z at 31 December 20X6, what amount should appear for goodwill?

A $250,000

B $184,000

C $138,000

D $92,000

(2 marks)

Chapter 19: Consolidated income statement

(101) X owns 60% of the equity share capital of Y and 40% of the equity share capital of Z. The income statement of the three entities showed the following turnover for the year ended 31 August 20X7:

	$m
X	16
Y	8
Z	7

During the year X sold goods to Y and Z for $2 million and $1 million respectively. All goods were sold on to third parties by Y and Z by the end of the year.

How much will be included in the consolidated income statement of the X group for Turnover for the year ended 31 August 20X7?

A $24m

B $21m

C $22m

D $28m

(2 marks)

(102) Sat is the sole subsidiary of Shindo. The cost of sales figures for 20X1 for Sat and Shindo were $11 million and $10 million respectively. During 20X1 Shindo sold goods which had cost $2 million to Sat for $3 million. Sat has not yet sold any of these goods.

What is the consolidated cost of sales figure for 20X1?

A $16 million

B $18 million

C $19 million

D $20 million

(2 marks)

(103) Crunchy Co acquired 70% of the ordinary share capital of Nut Co six years ago. The following information relates to Nut Co for the year ended 30 June 20X3:

	$
Sales revenue	600,000
Cost of sales	338,000
Distribution costs	113,000
Taxation	38,000

What is the profit attributable to the non-controlling interest in the consolidated income statement?

A $33,300

B $78,750

C $45,000

D $77,700

(2 marks)

(104) K Co acquired 60% of the ordinary share capital of Special Co five years ago. The following information relates to Special Co for the year ended 30 September 20X3:

	$
Sales revenue	960,000
Cost of sales	540,000
Administration expenses	180,000
Taxation	60,000

What is the profit attributable tot the non-controlling interest in the consolidated income statement?

A $108,000

B $72,000

C $168,000

D $77,700

(2 marks)

(105) P Ltd acquired 60% of the ordinary shares of S Ltd several years ago when the reserves of S stood at $980. In the year ended 31 July 20X7 P sold goods to S costing $500 for $600.(20% mark up on cost). At the year end half of these goods still remained in inventory.

What will be the provision for unrealised profit adjustment for the year ended 31 July 20X7, for the P group?

A   Deduct $500 from the cost of sales

B   Deduct $50 from the cost of sales

C   Add $50 to the cost of sales

D   Add $100 to the cost of sales

(2 marks)

(106) **Which of the following statements regarding the method of consolidation is true?**

(1) Subsidiaries are equity accounted

(2) Associates are consolidated in full

A   Neither statement

B   Statement 1 only

C   Both statements

D   Statement 2 only

(2 marks)

(107)**Which of the following statements rare true?**

(1) An associated undertaking is when a parent has control over the associate

(2) Associates are equity accounted

(3) Subsidiaries are consolidated in full

(4) An associate is a non-controlling interest

A   all of the above

B   Statement 2 and 3 only

C   None of the above

D   Statement 1 only

(2 marks)

Chapter 20: Interpretation of financial statements

The following information relates to question 108 and 109.

	20X6 $m	20X5 $m
Income statement (extracts)		
Operating profit	550	360
Profit before tax	550	360
Statement of financial position (extracts)		
Capital and reserves	500	500
10% loan notes	2,000	1,500

(108)**What is the return on capital employed for the years 20X5 and 20X6?**

	20X6	20X5
A	22.0%	18%
B	20.8%	15.5%
C	20.8%	18%
D	22.0%	15.5%

(2 marks)

(109) **What is the total gearing for the years 20X5 and 20X6?**

	20X6	20X5
A	20%	33.3%
B	25%	25%
C	25%	33.3%
D	20%	25%

(2 marks)

(110) **From the following information regarding the year to 31 August 20X6, what is the payables payment period?**

	$
Sales	50,000
Cost of sales	40,000
Opening inventory	6,000
Closing inventory	3,800
Payables at 31 August 20X6	4,750

A   41 days

B   48 days

C   54 days

D   57 days

(2 marks)

(111) **From the following information regardinng the year to 31 March 20X6, what are the current and quick ratios?**

	$
Inventory	5,320
Receivables	10,420
Cash at bank	3,200
Payables	4,100
Overdraft	3,121

	Current ratio	Quick ratio
A	2.62	1.89
B	2.62	3.84
C	3.86	2.56
D	4.62	3.32

(2 marks)

(112)Sale are $260,000. Purchases are $150,000. Opening inventory is $22,000. Closing inventory is $26,000.

What is the inventory turnover?

A 6.1 times

B 10 times

C 7 times

D 10.8 times

(2 marks)

Chapter 21: The regulatory and conceptual framework

(113)When preparing financial statements under historic cost accounting in periods of inflation, directors:

A must reduce asset values

B must increase asset values

C must reduce dividends

D need make no adjustments

(2 mark)

(114)If the owner of a business takes goods from inventory for his own personal use, the accounting concept to be considered is the:

A relevance concept

B capitalisation concept

C money measurement concept

D separate entity concept

(2 mark)

(115)A 'true and fair view' is one which:

A   presents the accounts in such a way as to exclude errors which would affect the actions of those reading them

B   occurs when the accounts have been audited

C   shows the accounts of an organisation in an understandable format

D   shows the assets on the statement of financial position at their current market price

(2 mark)

(116)Which concept is followed when a business records the cost of a non-current asset even though it does not legally own it?

A   substance over form

B   prudence

C   accruals

D   going concern

(2 mark)

(117) The IASB Framework for the Preparation and Presentation of Financial Statements gives five characteristics that make financial information reliable.

These five characteristics are:

A   prudence, consistency, understandability, faithful representation, substance over form

B   accruals basis, going concern concept, consistency, prudence, true and fair view

C   faithful representation, neutrality, substance over form, completeness, consistency, faithful and free

D   free from material error, prudence, faithful representation, neutrality, completeness

(2 mark)

(118) **The accounting concept or convention which, in times of rising prices, tends to understate asset values and overstate profits, is the:**

A   going concern concept

B   prudence concept

C   realisation concept

D   historical cost concept

(2 mark)

MULTIPLE CHOICE ANSWERS

Chapter 2: Statement of financial position and income statement

(1) **C**

(2) **C**

(3) **A**

(4) **C**

(5) **C**

Chapter 3: Double entry bookkeeping

(6) **D**

(7) **D**

(8) **C**

(9) **B**

(10) **D**

(11) **C**

Chapter 4: Inventory

(12) **D**

	A	B	C	Total
	$	$	$	$
Cost	7	10	19	
NRV	13	8	14	
Lower of cost or NRV	7	8	14	
× Number of units	20	25	15	
Valuation	140	200	210	550

(13) **A**

$(35 \times \$15) + (30 \times \$20) = \$1,125$

(14) **C**

(15) **The correct answer is D**

(16) The correct answer is C

400 items		$
Cost	400 × $4	1,600
NRV	(400 × $3) – $200	1,000

Therefore use NRV.

200 items		$
Cost	200 × $30	6,000
NRV	(200 × $35) – $1,200 – $300	5,500

Therefore use NRV.

Total inventory figure = $116,400 + $1,000 + $5,500 = $122,900.

Chapter 5: Sales tax

(17) A

Sales tax

	$		$
Purchases	2,100	Sales	3,500
(17.5 % × 12,000)		23,500 × 17.5/117.5	
Expenses	140		
(17.5% × 800)			
Bal c/f	1,260		
	3,500		3,500
		Bal b/f	1,260

(18) B

(19) B

Sales tax

	$		$
Purchases	3,150.00	Sales	4,112.50
(17.5 % × 18,000)		27,612.50 × 17.5/117.5	
Bal c/f	962.50		
	4,112.50		4,112.50
		Bal b/f	962.50

(20) D

		$	$
Assets	Cash (1,000 + 1,175)		2,175
	Inventory		400
			————
			2,575
Liabilities	Payables (800 × 1.175)	940	
	Sales tax (175 – 140)	35	
		———	
			(975)
			————
			1,600
Capital	Capital		1,000
	Profit (1,000 – 400)		600
			————
			1,600
			————

Chapter 6: Accruals and prepayments

(21) B

Electricity			
	$		$
Bank	400	Bal b/f	250
Bank	350		
Bank	425	Income statement (balancing figure)	1,525
Bank	450		
Bal c/f (ß)	150		
	————		————
	1,775		1,775
	————		————

(22)**A**

Electricity

	$		$
Bal b/f	25		
Bank ('12 × 100)	1,200		
		Income statement	1,300
		(350 + 375 + 275 + 300)	
Bal c/f (ß)	75		
	———		———
	1,300		1,300
	———		———
		Bal b/f	75

(23)**B**

Rent

	$		$
Bal b/f	200		
Bank	1,200	Income statement (ß)	1,200
		Bal c/f	200
	———		———
	1,400		1,400
	———		———
Bal b/f (2/12 × 1,200)	200		

(24)**A**

Light and heat

	$		$
Bank (240 + 10)	250	Bal b/f	240
Bank	260		
Bank	220		
Bank ·	210	Income statement (ß)	1,160
Bank	230		
Bank c/f	230		
	———		———
	1,400		1,400
	———		———
		Bal b/f	230
		(last quarter's bill)	

(25) **C**

Stationery payable

	$		$
		Bal b/f	80
Bank	1,350	Purchases of stationery (ß)	1,340
Bal c/f	70		
	——		——
	1,420		1,420
	——		——
		Bal b/f	70

Opening inventory + Purchases – Closing inventory = $165 + $1,340 – $140
= $1,365

Chapter 7: Irrecoverable debts and allowances for receivables

(26) **B**

$$5\% \times (50,000 - 1,000) = \$2,450$$

(27) **A**

Receivables

	$		$
Bal b/f	82,500	Irrecoverable debts	4,750
		Bal c/f	77,750
	——		——
	82,500		82,500
	——		——
Bal b/f	77,750		

Irrecoverable debts

	$		$
Receivables	4,750	Decrease in allowance	200
(1000 + 500 + 3250)		Cash receipt from debt previously written off	300
		Income statement account	4,250
	——		——
	4,750		4,750
	——		——

Allowance at 31 March	$
Specific allowance	250
General allowance	1,550
(2% × (77,750 – 250))	1,800
	——
Current allowance balance	2,000
	——
Movement in allowance balance	200 decrease

Net receivables = $77,750 – $1,800 = $75,950

(28) **B**

Allowance for receivables

	$		$
		Bal b/f	700
Irrecoverable debts (ß)	360		
Bal c/f	340		
	——		——
	700		700
	——		——
		Bal b/f	340

Irrecoverable debts

	$		$
Receivables	450	Decrease in allowance	360
Receivables	170	Income statement account	260
	——		——
	620		620
	——		——

Allowance required at end of year = $700 – $450 – $150 + $240 = $340

(29) **B**

Receivables

	$		$
Bal b/f	47,800	Bank	150
		Irrecoverable debts	150
		Bal c/f	47,500
	47,800		47,800
Bal b/f	47,500		

Irrecoverable debt expense

	$		$
		Decrease in allowance	300
Receivables	150		
Income statement	150		
	300		300

(30) **D**

Receivables

	$		$
Bal b/f	100,000	Bank	500
		Bal c/f	99,500
	100,000		100,000
Bal b/f	99,500		

Allowance for receivables

	$		$
		Bal b/f	5,000
		Income statement (ß)	1,965
Bal c/f	6,965		
	─────		─────
	6,965		6,965
	─────		─────
		Bal b/f (7% × 99,500)	6,965

(31) B

This is an example of an irrecoverable debt being written off. Credit the receivables account in order to clear the debt and debit the irrecoverable debts account with the amount of the debt written off.

(32) A

There is a specific allowance for the debt of $900 which has still not been written off as irrecoverable, and an additional allowance equivalent to 2% of the remaining balance based on past history.

Chapter 8: Non-current assets

(33) B

	$
Assets held all year ($15,000 – 8,000) × 25%	1,750
Asset disposed of $8,000 × 25% × 8/12	1,333
Asset acquired $10,000 × 25% × 1/12	208
	─────
Total depreciation	3,291
	─────

(34) D

(35) B

	$
Proceeds of sale	1,200.00
NBV at disposal (2,400 – 480 – 384 – 307.20)	(1,228.80)
	─────
Loss on disposal	(28.80)
	─────

Depreciation to disposal

Yr 1: $2,400 × 20% = $480

Yr 2: $(2,400 − 480) × 20% = $384

Yr 3: $(2,400 − 480 − 384) × 20% = $307.20

(36) **C**

$100,000 + $7,000 + $5,000 = $112,000

(37) **B**

	$
Assets held all year (5,000 − 300 − 600) × 10%	410
Disposals	
$300 × 10% × 2/12	5
$600 × 10% × 10/12	50
Acquisition $1,000 × 10% × 9/12	75
	___
Total depreciation	540
	___

(38) **B**

$$\frac{\$30{,}000 - \$6{,}000}{4} \times \frac{5}{12} = \$2{,}500$$

Chapter 9: From trial balance to financial statements

(39) **C**

Depreciation charge = $11,600 (2% × $580,000)

NBV = $452,400 [$580,000 − ($116,000 + $11,600)]

(40) **D**

Depreciation charge = $9,375 [25% × $37,500 ($50,000 − $12,500)]

Net book value = $28,125 [$50,000 − ($12,500 + $9,375)]

(41) **A**

	$
Irrecoverable debts $1,800 + 3,200 =	5,000
Decrease in allowance for receivables	(770)
Total irrecoverable debt expense	**4,230**
Receivables ($25,800 – 3,200)	22,600
Less: Closing allowance for receivables	(1,130)
Net closing receivables	**21,470**

Closing allowance for receivables

	$
[5% × ($25,800 – 3,200)]	1,130
Opening allowance for receivables	1,900
Decrease in allowance for receivables	770

(42) **B**

	Charge for the year $			Closing $
Rent	**36,000**	**Rent accrual**		**2,000**
	(12 × $3,000)	Due	36,000	
		Paid	34,000	
		Accrual	2,000	
Insurance	**24,000**	**Insurance prepayment**		**6,000**
		Paid	30,000	
		Due	24,000	
		Prepayment	6,000	

Chapter 10: Books of prime entry and control accounts

(43) **C**

(44) **B**

(45) **A**

Receivables

	$		$
Bal b/f	22,000	Bank	115,000
Sales	120,000		
		Discounts allowed	1,000
Dishonoured cheque	9,000	Contra	5,000
		Bal c/f	30,000
	151,000		151,000
Bal b/f	30,000		

Chapter 11: Control account reconciliations

(46) **A**

$8,500 – ($400 × 2) = $7,700

(47) **C**

Receivables ledger control account

	$		$
Bal b/f	32,750	Bal b/f	1,275
Sales	125,000	Bank	122,500
Refunds	1,300	Discounts allowed	550
Bal c/f	2,000	Bal c/f	36,725
	161,050		161,050
Bal b/f	36,725	Bal b/f	2,000

(48) **B**

(49) **A**

(50) **A**

The other three lists all contain one item which should appear on the debit side of the account.

Chapter 12: Bank reconciliations

(51) **D**

Bank – cash book

	$		$
		Bal b/f (i)	5,670
		Bank charges (ii)	250
Bal c/f	5,920		
	5,920		5,920
		Bal b/f	5,920

	$
Balance per bank statement (ß)	(6,100)
Add: Error (iii)	(40)
Add: Outstanding cheques (iv)	(325)
Less: Outstanding lodgements(v)	545
Balance per cash book	(5,920)

(52) **C**

	$
Balance per bank statement (ß)	($2,360) old
Add: Outstanding cheques	($1,420)
Balance per cash book (3,600 + 180)	($3,780) old

(53) B

Bank – cash book

	$		$
Sales	1,450	Bal b/f	485
Receivables	2,400	Payables (0.95 × 1,800)	1,710
		Dishonoured cheques	250
		Bal c/f	1,405
	3,850		3,850
Bal b/f	1,405		

(54) D

Bank – cash book

	$		$
Standing order	125	Bal b/f	5,675
		Dishonoured cheque ($450 × 2)	900
Bal c/f	6,450		
	6,575		6,575
		Bal b/f	6,450

(55) C

The bank reconciliation should have been calculated as follows:

	$
Overdraft per bank statement	(38,600)
Add deposits not yet credited	41,200
Less outstanding cheques	2,600
	(3,300)
Overdraft per cash book	(700)

(56) A

Items 3 and 4 relate to timing differences only and would appear in the bank reconciliation.

Chapter 13: Correction of errors and suspense accounts

(57) D

(58) A

Suspense

	$		$
Bal b/f (ß)	210	Gas (420 – 240)	180
Interest receivable	70	Discounts (50 × 2)	100
	——		——
	280		280
	——		——

(59) B

Draft profit for the period	$12,355
Six months' rent 6/12 × 800	($400)
Closing Inventory adjustment (1,000 – 800)	($200)
	————
	$11,755
	————

(60) C

(61) D

(62) B

The profit will be understated by the following amount:

	$
Amount charged in error to the repairs account	38,000
Less depreciation chargeable on the plant (3/12 × 20% × $38,000)	(1,900)
	————
	$36,100
	————

(63) **D**

	$
Opening balance on suspense account ($836,200 – $819,700)	16,500 Cr
Difference remaining after postings to the discount accounts ($5,100 – $3,900)	(1,200)
Difference from cheque incorrectly posted ($19,000 – $9,100)	(9,900)
	$5,400 Cr

(64) **B**

Items 1 and 3 would result in an imbalance in the trial balance and therefore require an entry to the suspense account. Items 2, 4 and 5 do not affect the balancing of the accounts.

Chapter 14: Incomplete records

(65) **B**

Closing net assets – Opening net assets = Capital Introduced + Profit for year – Drawings

$6,740 – $7,600 = 0 + Profit for year – 1,000

Profit for year = $140

(66) **D**

Closing net assets – Opening net assets = Capital Introduced + Profit for year – Drawings in year

$27,000 – $10,000 =Capital Introduced + $5,000 – $2,000

Capital Introduced = $14,000

(67) **B**

	%
Sales	115
Cost of Sales	100
Gross profit	15

15/115 = 13.04%

(68) **B**

Closing net assets – Opening net assets = Capital Introduced + Profit for year – Drawings

$4,500 – $10,000 = $4,000 + Profit/(loss) – $8,000

Loss for year = $1,500

(69) **D**

Payables

	$		$
Bank	542,300	Bal b/f	142,600
Discounts received	13,200		
Returns outwards	27,500	Purchases (ß)	578,200
Bal c/f	137,800		
	720,800		720,800
		Bal b/f	137,800

(70) **D**

Cost of Sales = 75% × $17,000 = $12,750

Purchases = $12,750 + $1,350 – $3,500 = $10,600

(71) **A**

Credit sales can be calculated as a balancing figure on the Receivables ledger control account.

Receivables ledger control account

	$		$
Balance b/f	29,100	Bank takings	381,600
Bank – refunds	2,100	Expenses	6,800
Credit sales	412,400	Irrecoverable debts	7,200
(balance)		Discounts allowed	9,400
		Balance c/f	38,600
	443,600		443,600

Credit sales = $412,400, cash sales = $112,900,

Total sales = $525,300

(72) **D**

	$
Opening inventory	17,000
Purchases	91,000
Closing inventory	(24,000)
Cost of sales	84,000

Sales = $84,000 × 100/60 = $140,000

(73) **A**

The rent expense for the year should be:

(5/12 × $24,000) + (7/12 × $30,000) = $27,500

(74) **B**

Cost of sales = 70% × $64,800 =	$45,360

	$
Opening inventory	28,400
Purchases	49,600
Cost of sales	(45,360)
Loss of inventory	32,640

Chapter 15: Company accounts

(75) **C**

Income statement charge	$
2005 estimate	23,000
Overprovision 2004	(5,000)
	18,000
Tax liability	23,000

(76) **B**

(77) **B**

		$
Preference dividends (6% × 1,000,000)	=	60,000
Ordinary dividends (16,000,000 × 0.02)	=	320,000
Total dividend	=	380,000

(78) **A**

(79) **C**

	$
Profit after tax (balancing figure)	100,000
Dividends	(50,000)
Profit for year	50,000
Accumulated profit b/f	50,000
Accumulated profit c/f	100,000

Chapter 16: Accounting standards

(80) **D**

(81) **C**

(82) **C**

(83) **C**

(84) **A**

(85) **C**

(86) **C**

(87) **D**

Statements 2, 3 and 5 are correct

(88) **B**

The other lists contain adjusting items

Chapter 17: Statements of cash flow

(89) **C**

(90) **A**

	$
Retained profit for the year $(65,500 – 45,500)	20,000
Dividends	3,300
Taxation $(600 + 550 – 400)	750
Interest payable (8% × $40,000)	3,200
	———
Operating profit	27,250
	———

(91) **B**

Income tax

	$		$
		Bal b/f	50,000
Bank (ß)	53,000		
		Income statement	60,000
Bal c/f	57,000		
	———		———
	110,000		110,000
	———		———
		Bal b/f	57,000

(92) B

	$	
Issue of share capital $(20,000+10,000)	30,000	inflow
Repayment of loan notes	20,000	outflow
	10,000	inflow

(93) C

Loan interest payable

	$		$
		Bal b/f	5,000
Bank (ß)	12,000	Income statement	10,000
		(100,000 × 10%)	
Bal c/f	3,000		
	15,000		15,000
		Bal b/f	3,000

Preference dividends 8% × $50,000 = $4,000

Total payments = $12,000 + $4,000 = $16,000

(94) A

(95) B

All other lists contain one or more items that would not appear in the calculation of net cash from operating activities

Chapter 18: Consolidated statement of financial position

(96) A

	$
Cost of investment	400,000
Fv of NCI @ acquisition	100,000
Less NA @ acquisition	(350,000)
	150,000

(97) D

	$
Reserves 40,000 + (5,000 x 75%)	43,750
	43,750

(98) B

	$
Retained earnings (200,000 + (15,000 x 60%)	209,000
	209,000

(99) C

FV of NCI @acquisition	75,000
Share of post acquisition profits (20% x $20,000)	4,000
	79,000

(100) A

	$
Cost of investment	750,000
FV of NCI @ acquisition	150,000
Less NA @ acquisition	(650,000)
	250,000

Chapter 19: Consolidated income statement

(101) C

Turnover = X $16 + Y $8 - Intercompany transaction $2 = $22.

y is a subsidiary and Z is an associate. Therefore Z's turnover will not be included and the inter-company sales with z will not be eliminated.

(102) C

11 + 10 – 3 (intra group trading) + 1 (PURP) = 19

(103)**A**

Profit = (600 – 338 – 113 – 38) x 30% = 33,300

(104)**B**

Profit = (960 – 540 – 180 – 60) x 40% = 72,000

(105)**C**

Sales $600 – Cost $500 = Profit $100

Half of these goods are in inventory = PURP $100 × ½ = $50 which needs to be added back to cost of sales

(106)**A**

Subsidiaries are consolidated in full and associates are equity accounted.

(107)**B**

Chapter 20: Interpretation of financial statements

(108)**A**

20X6 550 / 2,500 = 22.0%

20X5 360 / 2,000 = 18%

(109)**D**

20X6 500 / 2,500 = 20%

20X5 500 / 2,000 = 25%

(110)**D**

Purchases = 3,800 + 32,500 – 6,000 = 30,300

4,750 / 30,300 = 57 days

(111)**A**

Current ratio

18,940 / 7,221 = 2.62

Quick ratio

5,320 + 10,420 + 3,200 = 13,620 / 7,221 = 1.89

(112)**A**

146,000 / 24,000 = 6.1 times

Chapter 21: The regulatory and conceptual

(113)**D**

(114)**D**

(115)**A**

(116)**A**

(117)**D**

The other three contain items which are not considered to contribute towards reliability.

(118)**D**

Index

Index

KAPLAN PUBLISHING

Index

Index